POLITICS & REMEMBRANCE

*

STUDIES IN MORAL, POLITICAL,
AND LEGAL PHILOSOPHY

* * *

General Editor: Marshall Cohen

POLITICS &
REMEMBRANCE

Republican Themes
in Machiavelli,
Burke, and Tocqueville

* * *

Bruce James Smith

PRINCETON UNIVERSITY PRESS
PRINCETON, NEW JERSEY

Copyright © 1985 by Princeton University Press
Published by Princeton University Press,
41 William Street,
Princeton, New Jersey 08540
In the United Kingdom:
Princeton University Press, Guildford, Surrey

All Rights Reserved

Library of Congress Cataloging in Publication Data
will be found on the last printed page of this book
ISBN 0-691-07681-2

Publication of this book has been aided by a grant from
The Andrew W. Mellon Foundation

This book has been composed in Linotron Palatino and Cartier

Clothbound editions of Princeton University Press books
are printed on acid-free paper, and binding materials
are chosen for strength and durability

Printed in the United States of America, by
Princeton University Press
Princeton, New Jersey

To the memory of my father,
LEWIS JAMES SMITH

*

CONTENTS

✳

PREFACE   ix

ONE. INTRODUCTION   3

TWO. MACHIAVELLI: REMEMBRANCE AND THE
    REPUBLIC   26
An Image of Rome   26
Machiavelli and History   29
Glory and Oblivion   38
Glory and the City   47
In the Beginning   54
Founding Knowledge   71
Virtue, Corruption, and Remembrance   84
The Theorist and the Pursuit of Glory   93

THREE. EDMUND BURKE: POLITICAL ORDER AND THE
    PAST   102
Remembrance and Rebellion   102
Custom and Oblivion   111
Action and Inheritance   122
The Political Imagery of the Sublime and the Beautiful   133
Ambition and Modernity   141

FOUR. ALEXIS DE TOCQUEVILLE: THE POLITICS OF
    AFFECTION   155
An Affair of the Heart   155
The Limits of Novelty   167
Aristocratic Pedagogy   181
The Theorist as Historian   200

✳ CONTENTS ✳

Ancient Vice   209

Forgotten Virtue   218

Democracy and the Future   238

FIVE. THINKING ABOUT THE REPUBLIC: A NOTE ON
    EQUALITY AND AUTHORITY   251

BIBLIOGRAPHY   273

INDEX   279

PREFACE

✳

This book grew out of an abiding interest in political action. Its purpose is political no less than intellectual. If it attempts to shed light on some of the labyrinthine mysteries of political action, it is also, less obviously, an effort to understand the acrimony and frustration with which many of my generation left the field of action a decade ago. About hope and despair, it explores a thread that connects deeds and imagination. That thread is memory. And memory, as Nietzsche knew, is "a means against resignation."

While I share the conclusion of many that there is in the processes of modernity much that is subversive of a vital public life, this book is concerned more often with the internal dynamics of political action. Political action has always been among the most precarious and uncertain of human endeavors, but contemporary political action has been peculiarly intermittent. Once familiar and defended by the attachments of familiarity, the appearance of public life has been in our time fleeting and episodic. Strangely enough, contemporary democratic theory has been inattentive to the implications of this change. Had it been listening, it might have heard older voices warning of the depletion of that most precious of public stocks—political experience.

I became convinced that this fugitive quality of public space was one of the distinctive features and fundamental problems of contemporary political practice. Too often in recent memory, movements and institutions, which at first seemed to hold out the promise of preserving a portion of the civic ideal, had proven inadequate to the task. While some of these had powerful enemies with which to contend, many seemed rather to have deserted the field of action than to have suffered defeat upon it. It was as if our growing political inexperience had caused us to forget certain essential aspects of the life of action.

I came to see these difficulties as coalescing around problems of political identity. The intermittent character of political action pointed to the decay of those shared and enduring self-conceptions that have always provided public liberty with its vantage point. Public life periodically and insistently reappears, but now it is often deprived of those histories of affection and traditions of action that give form and a measure of constancy to the public world. It seemed to me that an account of the place of recollection in political relations held some promise of shedding light on these matters.

Intertwined with these themes is another: republicanism. I say intertwined because republican theory has emphasized the importance of political identities, and the interplay of action and tradition in the creation and maintenance of such identities. The sensitivity of republican thought to problems of time and preservation in general, and to the importance of foundations in political life in particular, recommended it as a fertile place to take up an inquiry into the nature of political memory. Let me say something more about republicanism and my use of it here. At least since Rousseau, the accents of this tradition have struck us as often ironic and sometimes antique. Although in the last two decades there has been a renaissance of interest in republicanism, much of this recent work has about it a new and stronger air of anachronism. Republicanism has become, as it were, the object of history, a matter for historians. While this growing body of historical materials has deepened our understanding of the shape and character of republicanism as a tradition of discourse, it also has given that discourse something of the smell of Minerva's owl. I have tried to combat this sensibility by portraying the core of republicanism as a particular mode of consciousness indigenous to public spaces. An exploration of the reason, sentiments, and passions characteristic of such a consciousness has been among my aims. The republican tradition has been less a set of conclusions about the right form of government or type of regime than a way of thinking about political things. The strongest thread which runs through this tradition is the celebration of public life—the conviction that such a life is appropriate to and worthy of human dignity and that it nurtures greatness of spirit, but also a recognition that the preservation of public life is among the most difficult of human projects. This conviction often gives to republican discourse a certain texture which is related to its fascination with the active life. If republicanism is a tradition of discourse, it is in this peculiar fascination that the most important continuities are to be found.

The subjects of this study, Machiavelli, Burke, and Tocqueville, originally suggested themselves because of the place which remembering and forgetting occupies in their work. I have not attempted to give a full account of their political philosophies, or to construct a typology in which to fit them. Rather, I have tried to preserve the texture of their reflections in regard to the matter at hand—the nature of political memory. How well I have succeeded in this is, finally, for others to judge.

I have contracted many debts in the writing of this book. My first debts are to those old compatriots with whom I discovered the joys of public life and first learned the necessary relation of affection and action. They are surely too many to name here; in any case, they have wisely sought remembrance elsewhere than in the pages of books such as this.

Other debts, however, are too great to go unmentioned. My teachers, Benjamin Barber, Sebastian de Grazia, Wilson Carey McWilliams, and Gordon Schochet, have taught me, each in his own way, much about the character of deep political knowledge and the integrity it demands. To Professor Barber, I owe much more. He has been my critic, friend, and benefactor, as well as an unwavering ally during those times when I was set upon by fear and doubt.

I am especially indebted to Professors Norman Jacobson, Stephen Salkever, and Marshall Cohen for reading the final draft of the manuscript and offering their comments and criticisms. I have imposed upon their good will by making many of their ideas my own. Professors Laura Greyson and Robert Horwitz read earlier drafts of the manuscript, and their remarks were helpful in the development of several discussions.

Many thanks also are due my colleagues in the Department of Political Science at Vassar College. Their support and understanding, and generosity of spirit considerably eased the burden of completing this work. The always fruitful conversation of Sidney Plotkin and Peter Stillman helped me to clarify some of my conclusions. I also thank Sandy Thatcher of Princeton University Press for believing in my work and providing much guidance to an untutored author. Janet Stern brought wit and good sense to the task of copyediting, and did her best to save me from myself. Mildred Tubby typed the final copy with great care and diligence; bringing to her work an editor's eye that left its mark on many pages.

To Bob Bussel, my old and dearest friend, I owe an immeasurable debt. He has permitted me, time and again, to draw upon his many skills, and has performed signal services in the preparation of this manuscript. But far more important, through both his example and the encouragement and reproof that is the true office of a friend, he has kept me honest and working. Finally, I owe much to my wife, Sue, and my son, Jason, who have shown the wisdom that is patience, who took pleasure with me in the highlands and endured the valleys.

POLITICS & REMEMBRANCE

*

O N E

* * *

INTRODUCTION

Consider the herd grazing before you. These animals do
not know what yesterday and today are but leap about,
eat, rest, digest and leap again; . . . enthralled by the moment and for that reason neither melancholy nor bored.
It is hard for man to see this . . . because he wants nothing
other than to live like the animals, neither bored nor in
pain, yet wants it in vain because he does not want it like
the animal. . . . Man . . . wonder[s] about himself, that he
cannot learn to forget but always remains attached to the
past: however far and fast he runs, the chain runs with
him—Nietzsche[1]

Politics, thought Chesterton, is inescapably symbolic. In
public things, images are always in abundance. While these
are occasionally given solidity and substance in carved stone,
they live in the minds of men. Political action is rarely, if
ever, free from such imaginings. That tradition which links
action with heroes is a sound one. We've long suspected
that the heroic imagination originates in images of past
action. In the memorable deeds of predecessors, human
beings discover what they must become. The lover of action, like Melville's Starry Vere, finds his literature in his-

[1] Nietzsche, *On the Advantage and Disadvantage of History for Life*, p. 8.
Compare Nietzsche's grazing "herd" which "always immediately forget[s]" with Edmund Burke's "great cattle, reposed beneath the shadow
of the British oak, [who] chew the cud, and are silent," in *Reflections on
the Revolution in France*, p. 97.

3

tory. Reverence and piety are familiar sentiments to him, and he is often found at the temple of his ancestors.[2]

This religiosity, however, is not without a healthy admixture of what Michael Oakeshott has called "idolatry." The lover of action labors in the mines of the past with passion, for he seeks a home for himself; indeed, he seeks himself. In action, human beings look upon the past with the eyes of the present and upon the present with the eyes of the future, and they move easily from the contemplation of an ancient glory to a contemplation of their own. Caritas may enjoin humility; still, action and anonymity have never walked hand in hand any great distance. In all action there is this irreducible element, this image of the self-in-action. "I shall yield," says Benjamin Franklin in his *Autobiography*, "to the inclination, so natural to old men, of talking of themselves and their own actions." Revolutions are often made by religious men. They are never made by selfless ones. In political action, there is always to be found a dialectic of reverence and irreverence. Revolutionists, Hannah Arendt insists, are almost always secret traditionalists. Action, or that which makes the future, is, paradoxically, forever meditating on the past.[3]

To these observations may be added one other, and one for which the experience of modern men is ample testimony. Where the images of the past and the affections which attach to these (and around which action is organized) decay or are pulled apart, where human beings have forgotten or no longer agree on what Walter Lippmann called "the first and last things," there is opened up "a great vacuum in the public mind, yawning to be filled," and men rush in only to exhaust themselves.[4] At such times, society may continue to exist, or even prosper, but public life will have come to an end. I have called this

---

[2] Chesterton, "Place de la Bastille," pp. 65-71.

[3] Oakeshott, *Rationalism in Politics*, p. 35; Franklin, *Autobiography*, p. 2; Arendt, *On Revolution*, pp. 41-47.

[4] Lippmann, *The Public Philosophy*, p. 78.

relation between political action and the past *remembrance*. My reasons for doing so will be set forth in this introduction.

These considerations of the nature of action have a place, I believe, in the understanding of political action as a distinct mode of human activity, and in any discussion of the possibility of a truly revolutionary praxis. (In this regard, the relevant preliminary text is, of course, Karl Marx's *Eighteenth Brumaire*.)[5] Such questions, however, are not the concern of this inquiry. The essays which make up this volume address an earlier tradition of discourse which also took as its starting point problems associated with political practice and which is often called by the name *republican*. While this designation is not inappropriate, it raises two kinds of questions regarding the parameters of my subject matter.

---

[5] Followers of Marx usually have understood the problem of revolutionary praxis to be that of the subjective moment—the creation of a revolutionary consciousness. Less noticed, but more important, are Marx's reflections upon the character of revolutionary practice itself. At the center of these reflections are the relation of action and illusion and the difficulty such illusions pose for the success of such practice. Consider, for example, the following: "Men make their own history, but they do not make it just as they please; they do not make it under circumstances chosen by themselves, but under circumstances directly found, given and transmitted by the past. The tradition of all the dead generations weighs like a nightmare upon the brain of the living. And just when they seem engaged in revolutionizing themselves and things, in creating something entirely new, precisely in such epochs of revolutionary crisis they anxiously conjure up the spirits of the past to their service and borrow from them names, battle slogans and costumes in order to present the new scene of world-history in this time-honoured disguise and this borrowed language. Thus Luther donned the mask of the Apostle Paul, the Revolution of 1789 to 1814 draped itself alternately as the Roman Republic and the Roman Empire, and the Revolution of 1848 knew nothing better to do than to parody, in turn, 1789 and the revolutionary tradition of 1793 to 1795. In like manner the beginner who has learnt a new language always translates it back into his mother tongue, but he has assimilated the spirit of the new language and can produce freely in it only when he moves in it without remembering the old and forgets in it his ancestral tongue" (Marx, *The Eighteenth Brumaire of Louis Bonaparte*, in *The Marx-Engels Reader*, p. 437). See also Georg Lukács, *History and Class Consciousness*, pp. 164-68, 257-58.

The first is one of definition. What is the meaning of the term *republic*? That it has been put to torture more than once is well known.[6] Machiavelli's use of the word is comprehensive. "All the states, all the dominions that have had or now have authority over men have been and now are either republics or princedoms." Historically, the term has been applied most often to those states where the rule of a king has given way to that of a body of citizens. It was this practice in antiquity that Aristotle sought to capture in the idea of "ruling and being ruled." "Princedoms" are characterized by the action of one; republics by the action of many.[7]

The existence of a republic, however, is not simply a matter of numbers. Where citizens rule and are ruled in turn or, to speak more exactly, where men are citizens, something wholly different exists—res publica—"the public's thing." The proprietary character of Cicero's phrase is appropriate, but it also suggests the difficulty. A republic, it seems, presupposes the existence of a public. A republic is more than a thing. It is at once that which makes public life possible, a space within which public life takes place, and public life itself. The republic is a set of habits, customs, traditions, and institutions which buttress public life. But the republic is also the tissue of relations between citizens in space and time, and it is this which permits us, finally, to speak of *a public existence.*

---

[6] Consider, for example, *Federalist* 10 and 14.

[7] Machiavelli, *The Prince*, chapter 1, in *The Chief Works and Others*. Descriptions of the republic in terms of quantity are always risky. The generation that preceded us divided popular regimes into republics (rule of many) and democracies (rule of all). With the renaissance of interest in republican thought, such understandings have been found wholly wanting. The idea of res publica presupposes a sufficient number to constitute a public realm. That this is near tautology is a measure of the difficulty. The term republic describes aristocracies and democracies. But while a republic can be rule of the few, these cannot be too few. Hegel's work suggests the word "some" to which Arendt's "plurality" is comparable, but these are not terms of quantity at all, and they obscure rather than resolve the problem. For further consideration of this issue, see de Grazia, "Senses of Republic: Machiavelli and Bodin."

In these essays, I will consider the institutions and structure of republican government only to the extent that these throw light on the republican consciousness. It is a portion of the psychological geography of the republican regime that I seek. The republic is considered here as a mnemonic structure, a type of regime erected upon the injunction: remember. That this is not an outlandish proposition will be acknowledged, I think, if we reflect upon the status of the idea of the beginning in the tradition of political thought and upon the stature within that discourse of those who have founded political orders, such as Moses, Romulus, and Lycurgus. The conception of the republic as a vessel of remembrance would seem to hold out the possibility of talking about old topics in new ways. I have in mind particularly the problem of decay and its relation to forgetfulness. Part of my purpose, then, is to examine the republic as a form of government from the singular psychic vantage point of recollection.

The problem of boundaries and subject matter is not exhausted, however, by discussions of definition. The second question is the propriety of uniting the likes of Niccolò Machiavelli, Edmund Burke, and Alexis de Tocqueville into a single discourse and labeling that discourse "republican." Of the three, only Machiavelli may, with any confidence, be called a republican (Burke and Tocqueville both disclaiming allegiance to any *form* of government in particular). And even Machiavelli's republican sympathies often have been called into question. What is it, then, that places these thinkers in something that we are entitled to call a discourse?

Of some significance are the practical biases of all three. First, each has given us reason to believe that he preferred the active to the contemplative life, although each was possessed of great speculative powers. Machiavelli began writing in earnest only after the Medici's return to power made his active contribution to Florentine politics no longer welcome. And while Machiavelli's posture as an office seeker in the Dedication to *The Prince* is somewhat ironic, it also has its serious side. Burke, having once entered public life, never left it, and thereafter looked upon his writing and political speculations as a kind of theft from the pressing concerns of public business. Tocqueville, a celebrated thinker at an early age, had been first a man of practice who twice left public life, but did so in each case from principle rather than by preference. In a manner after Machiavelli, he spoke of study as consolation for his enforced leisure.[8]

Second, each entertained more or less radical attitudes toward the proper relations between philosophy and politics. Of the three, Machiavelli's position in this regard is the most difficult to make out. The status of metaphysics in Machiavelli's work remains controversial. However, this much can be said: Machiavelli's reticence in discussing metaphysical issues has led some commentators to find in his work the teaching that politics is "autonomous." Burke's fulminations against the application of abstract theory to political things are well known. Tocqueville, by his own admission, simply found metaphysics uninteresting, in large measure because of its apparent lack of relation to practical matters.[9]

Finally, and perhaps most important, each found in his *own* political practice a ground for his reflections on politics. To each the term *realist* might be applied. And in the work of each is to be found the belief that prudence is the proper foundation for the theory and practice of politics.[10]

[8] Compare, for example, the first and last paragraphs of Burke's *Reflections* with the first paragraph of Tocqueville's *Recollections* and with the Dedication to Machiavelli's *Prince*.

[9] See, for example, Tocqueville's critique of "metaphysics and all the purely theoretic sciences, which do not serve anything in the reality of life" (Letter to M. Charles, November 22, 1831), in Lively, *The Social and Political Thought of Alexis de Tocqueville*, p. 25.

[10] Burke's insistence on the relation of political knowledge and experience abounds in his many criticisms of the French experiment. Consider also Machiavelli's epistemological remarks regarding the teaching of *The Prince* (Dedication) and Tocqueville's delimiting his *Recollections* to those events which his "position" permitted him to "observe well" (*Recollections*, p. 2).

This prudential cast of mind rests, I believe, on the uncertain status of res publica in "the order of things," and
yet on the enduring conviction, founded on a personal
practice, of its intrinsic value. Dominion is as natural as
fatherhood, its model and original form. That dominion is
natural, or in nature, while *political* life is made—a human
artifact—is suggested by the inability to trace fatherhood
to its original unless one returns to the origin of the species
(a point Filmer was, for related reasons, at pains to demonstrate). In any case, the ur-father must necessarily go
unnamed. The unity of blood or the clan emerges from the
mists of prehistory intact. The same is not true of res publica. Political communities, or associations founded upon
civic rather than blood relations (and sometimes in opposition to kinship ties), are creatures of history, with a beginning and thus, presumably, an end. The suspicion that
political life or public liberty is an aberration in nature and
that only dominion has a natural existence, that political
life is artifice and thus subject to the vicissitudes of all
things human, left its mark early on the republican consciousness.

While republics have always had an acute sense of their
own temporality, customary societies generally see themselves as existing since time immemorial. Indeed, this is
the first meaning of custom. Kingship is older than history.
Hereditary monarchies often have seen themselves as modeled on a divine pattern and, in their more extravagant
forms, have found their origins in the beginning of time
itself. Yet political life, observes Aristotle, was "first con-
structed" in time. Republics generally have conceived of
themselves as having had a "beginning."[11]

Ancient political practice understood the problem of the
republic to be both spatial and temporal. To bring into
being a public "space," it was thought necessary to first
lay a foundation. The founder's art involved not only the

[11] Pocock, *The Machiavellian Moment*; Gunnell, *Political Philosophy and
Time*; Aristotle, *The Politics of Aristotle*, p. 7.

creation of a political order *in time,* but the projection of that order *through time.* Of the renowned Lacedaemonian foundation, Plutarch writes:

> Even so, Lycurgus, viewing with joy and satisfaction the greatness and beauty of his political structure, now fairly at work and in motion, conceived the thought to make it immortal too, and, as far as human forecast can teach, to deliver it down unchangeable to posterity.[12]

The radical "finitude" (the phrase is J. G. A. Pocock's) of public life in space and time finds terms of correspondence in republican discourse.[13] This discourse generally has used two words to denote participation in a public existence, *citizen* and *patriot.* While each of these terms carries a load of meaning that remains unexhausted by considering them as categories of space and time, these are the dimensions that I take to be fundamental. *Citizen* is a category of space. One is a citizen in relation to certain contemporaries who occupy the same space—one's fellow-citizens. Like *citizen, patriot* is a term of relation. But as the etymology of the word suggests, the patriot participates in a more peculiar relation, a relation through time. It is a relationship with predecessors—his "fathers"—that the patriot enjoys. The patriot commonly is thought of as the lover of a place ("land where my fathers died"), which also suggests the unity of the two concepts in any comprehensive understanding of res publica.

The foundation of a republic is that which unites a people in space *and* time. To the fellow-feeling which ties all citizens together into a single whole must be added that sentiment, often called reverence, which binds a generation to those who have preceded it. Only then can one truly speak of the existence of a people. To make the citizen also a patriot, this was the founder's art. Only then, Lycurgus

---

[12] Plutarch, "Lycurgus," p. 71.
[13] Pocock, *Machiavellian Moment,* p. viii.

knew, would it become possible to deliver res publica "down unchangeable to posterity."

Still, for the republic time remains the dimension of decadence. The vocabulary of republican thought is saturated with temporality. At the center of this vocabulary are the well-known polarities "virtue" and "corruption." While these terms often refer to a host of circumstances and practices, they essentially provide a language with which to discuss the process by which the integrity of public life is eroded. Moreover, the language of virtue and corruption is a temporal vocabulary of a particular kind. Decadence, the process which this vocabulary is meant to illuminate, is fundamentally psychological—the decay of a people's character over time. The well-being of the republic rests, finally, on the maintenance of a civic personality. As one contemporary theorist of the republic has put it, "a community which would preserve its ancient spirit must design the education of the latest generation to build a character identical to the first."[14]

It is the need for such a pedagogy that has led republics to sanctify their beginnings. Few things are more striking in the history of republican practice than such sanctification, and few things are more universal. The idea of a "beginning" has been, for republics, more than a historical fact; it has been a "principle" which, as Plato remarked, "is the savior of all things, if She receives the proper honor from each of those who make use of her." This felt need to preserve the beginning consecrated memory as the most public mode of consciousness. Yet the idea of remembrance and the problem of preservation implicit in it point to the dilemma of all such pedagogies.[15]

[14] McWilliams, *The Idea of Fraternity in America*, p. 218.
[15] Plato, *The Laws of Plato*, §775. The sanctification of beginnings is a phenomenon long observed but not well understood. Hegel suggested that remembrance and politics are coeval, and that the political order necessarily worships at "the temple of Mnemosyne." Before politics, the relations of men were but "wild arbitrariness." Only with the creation of

It is with this understanding of the republic's self-conscious temporality that we approach the text which is the true origin of the essays contained herein. In the concluding paragraph of chapter 5 of *The Prince*, a chapter whose avowed purpose is to teach new princes how to manage "those states . . . [which are] accustomed to living under their own laws and in liberty," Machiavelli writes: "In republics there is more life, more hate, greater longing for revenge; they are not permitted to rest—nor can they be—by the recollection of their ancient liberty." Chapter 5 follows three chapters which discuss ancestral practices, the last two of which discuss the difficulties these practices pose for new princes and what must be done about them. In chapters 2 through 4, Machiavelli speaks generally of "old conditions" and specifically of the "customs" of "fore-

---

political relations is there a "subject of serious remembrance." In the political anthropologies of Thucydides and Machiavelli, new "cities" and "republics" are often the creation of a people "driven out" by the "violence" of "some greater number." While we shall return to this point again in our consideration of Machiavelli, it does not seem inappropriate to speculate here on the implications of such "removals" for the republican psyche. In his *Reveries of the Solitary Walker*, Rousseau considered the consequences of chaos upon the human heart. "Everything is in continual flux on earth. Nothing on it retains a constant and static form, and our affections, which are attached to external things, necessarily pass away and change as they do. Always ahead of or behind us, they recall the past which is no longer or foretell the future which often is in no way to be: there is nothing solid there to which the heart might attach itself." Politics had imposed a measure of order on the "continual flux" and "wild arbitrariness" of man's natural condition, but, beyond the "walls" and the "space" of the city, chaos remained. The political order, res publica, was precarious. The heart's violent attachment to the first political things bespeaks a great fear. Such speculations suggest the profundity of that tradition of political "realism" which has placed gratitude and terror at the foundations of political societies. It is these, I suspect, which together made the "beginning" the first "object" of Mnemosyne. See Hegel, *The Philosophy of History*, pp. 60-62; Thucydides, *Hobbes' Thucydides*, Book I, chapter 1; Machiavelli, *Chief Works*, vol. 1; *The Discourses of Niccolò Machiavelli*, Book I, chapter 1 (hereafter, citations from book and chapter will be in this form: I-1); *The Art of War*, p. 623; *The History of Florence*, p. 1041; Rousseau, *The Reveries of the Solitary Walker*, p. 68. See also Gunnell, pp. 244-48. Regarding the anthropology of politics, consider the tale of Critias in Plato's *Timaeus*.

fathers." In chapter 2, which considers hereditary principalities (that is, where the rule of the prince is *customary*), remembrance is discussed only in connection with the forgetfulness or "oblivion" that is the foundation of such regimes. However, in chapter 5, which considers republics, Machiavelli describes the influence of the old way of life as a kind of "recollection."[16]

Machiavelli's curious observations about republics are made more so by this change in terminology. Other regimes, the preceding chapters tell us, have "customs." Republics have "recollections." It is these, Machiavelli seems to say, which are the source of an energy and activity that are peculiarly republican and which make conquering those accustomed to living "in liberty" always difficult and dangerous.

What is meant by "recollection"? What is the nature of its relation to political action? What are the implications of this relation for a theory of the republic? These and related issues provide the direction of the remainder of this introduction and the essays that follow. We turn first to those questions of meaning which the citation from Machiavelli has raised.

✳ ✳ ✳

"Societies," Pocock wrote "exist in time, and conserve images of themselves as continuously so existing. It follows that the consciousness of time acquired by the individual as a social animal is in large measure consciousness of his society's continuity and of the image of its continuity which that society possesses; and the understanding of time, and of human life as experienced in time, disseminated in a society, is an important part of that society's understanding

---

[16] Machiavelli, *The Prince*, chapters 2-5. To speak more exactly, Machiavelli describes "l'ordine de sua antenati" as "customi" in hereditary regimes. These regimes are associated with the loss of "le memorie." In chapter 5, however, when referring to the "ordini antiqui" of republics, Machiavelli uses the phrase "la memoria."

of itself—of its structure and what legitimates it, of the modes of action which are possible to it and in it."[17] In Machiavelli's use of the terms *custom* and *recollection* to distinguish between two types of states, it is possible to discern two distinct modes of historical self-conception which, Machiavelli also suggests, bear directly on the modes of action possible to each.

It is proper that we should begin with this distinction because the difficulties that present themselves also recur in one form or another in the work of Burke and Tocqueville and because this distinction raises immediately the relation of remembrance and action which is central to our inquiry. As the context suggests, the change of terminology aims especially at the illumination of a phenomenon peculiar to republics, one which Machiavelli thinks is significant. The introduction of customary societies earlier in *The Prince* becomes, as it were, a standard against which to compare republics. Following this method, I will make use of an idea of customary society in order to understand more completely the meaning of Machiavelli's aphorism regarding recollections. This idea of custom is stark and does not pretend to be a complete or sufficient account of prescriptive society. Rather, I have emphasized certain aspects of such societies and the people who inhabit them in an effort to bring into relief the character of recollection and its implications for the republic. This is not to suggest that customary societies and republics are, in some sense, opposites (although the idea of custom and that of recollection contain antithetical components). It is to suggest, however, that the meaning and place of that which is called "tradition" in political discourse stand in need of clarification. Machiavelli is the author of this suggestion.

We begin by observing that *custom* and *memory* are kindred terms. Both are concerned with the preservation of certain things through time. In politics, both are conjunctions of

---

[17] Pocock, *Politics, Language and Time,* p. 233.

a sort, emphasizing linkages between past and present. Indeed, were we not privy to Machiavelli's distinction, we might suppose the word *memory*, as applied to societies, to be only a figurative term for custom and tradition. To this kinship of meaning can be added a kinship in political usage. Theorists of the republic generally have praised habit, custom, and tradition as necessary bulwarks of "civic virtue." In practice, most healthy republics have abided by what Leo Strauss has called the equation of the ancient and the good, with the Roman republic only the most resolute in this regard.

As theorists of customary society from Burke to Oakeshott have pointed out, the secret of custom's power is its continuity. The affection it enjoys and the authority it commands are prescriptive. The behavior of the person of custom is, by and large, habitual. To the question "Why?" he is apt to respond simply, "This is the way it has always been done." All such questions are alien to the customary consciousness. A creature of habit, the person of custom does not reflect upon his condition. To the extent that a customary society "conceives" of its practice, it is likely to see it, says Pocock, as "an indefinite series of repetitions." If the customary society is, in reality, a fluid order always in the process of adaption, its continuity and incrementalism give rise to perceptions of changelessness and of the simple repetition of familiar motions. Such practice is rhythmic. It is characterized by a regularity that is often accommodated to the perennial aspect of nature. In such circumstances, "the habit of affection" has the sensibility and appearance of a natural attribute. Indeed, that custom operates as if it were "a second nature," thoroughly obscuring the distinction between nature and artifice, has always been among its chief recommendations to the traditionalist.[18]

[18] Pocock, *Politics, Language and Time,* p. 237; Oakeshott, p. 31; McWilliams, p. 39.

In customary societies, all knowledge is conceived as an inheritance, and practice is the only form of transmission. Customary knowledge and the practice founded upon it are essentially visual and tactile. The continuity upon which they depend is primarily a continuity of seeing and touching. The importance of ritual and reenactment in customary societies is in keeping with such radical empiricism, and it also suggests one paradox associated with the senses— their occasional discontinuity or even opposition. Customary society slights the ear. It is a way of life, says Oakeshott, that "cannot be explained." It is "not susceptible of speech." Thus, it is not surprising that the person of custom often finds it difficult to justify himself at the bar of principled criticism. (The conceptual articulation of the traditional mind that one finds in a Burke or an Oakeshott is the product of a man whose affection for custom is more than habitual, and thus more than customary.) Not a body of principles, custom, strictly speaking, cannot be "taught," but only "imparted." It is that complex of unreflective habits that one acquires "by living with people who always behave in a certain manner." Customary society and its practice require "continuous contact." Indeed, such knowledge is nothing but practice and vanishes with the disappearance of its practice. Custom is simply a habitual way of *doing* things. So understood, "repetition" and "ritual" are not simply characteristic of customary societies; they are the stuff of custom itself.[19]

---

[19] Pocock, *Politics, Language and Time*, pp. 239-40; Oakeshott, pp. 8-11, 35, 61-62, 178, 188. I have depended in large measure upon the work of Michael Oakeshott for this construction of the idea of customary society. It is immediately apparent, however, that my portrait is stark even by Oakeshottian standards. The most thoroughly customary societies are never wholly voiceless, as Eliade's work testifies, but speak, if only in the language of mythos. Still, political orders are distinguishable from customary societies on the bases of both the quality and quantity of speech. Incantation and recitation are different from public speech, although customary societies of sufficient complexity can develop a kind of public language. One way to understand the common law of England is as a language uniquely suited to its customary structure. Yet, if the crises of

In one sense, memory is the vehicle of custom, for it is through the medium of personal recollection that the continuity of ancestral practice is sustained. Yet the very relation of remembrance and custom points to significant differences between them. Custom is at once both more and less inclusive than remembrance. It includes things that are remembered and things that are forgotten. It is almost a definition of custom that its beginnings (or when that which is now custom was uncustomary) are lost. Custom is ordinary, ritualistic, often repeated ("as is our custom"). On the other hand, remembrance, which preserves the customary, is not exclusively preoccupied with the ordinary. Although it is true, as every disgruntled schoolchild knows, that repetition implants much in memory, as often, and perhaps more naturally, the substance of memory is the extraordinary—the phenomenal event, the memorable action. Custom obscures the distinctive; memory strains to preserve it.

Such considerations throw light on the more complex mnemonic structure of the republic. Political memory is more than custom. Custom is atmospheric. It simply is. The person of custom is unselfconscious, ignorant of the medium within which he moves. Like the fish who discovers the existence of water only in its absence, the person of custom discovers his way of life only in its loss. While custom has shape and form, its images lack specificity and content. It is through ritual that customary societies convey their images, and it is the quality of ritual to submerge distinctiveness in the repetition of motions which are a kind of silhouette. The mnemonic consciousness of the republic, on the other hand, is highly specific. While it is susceptible

---

the legal history of England are excepted, the common law generally has been conceived as a language which asks not "What are we to do?" but "What have we always done?" Finally (and in spite of his spirited defense of inarticulate custom), Oakeshott's insistence that tradition is to be understood in terms of its "intimations" and that men must converse about these only demonstrates the deeply political character of his thought.

to ritualization, it preserves more than ritual motion and bare outline. It preserves *actions* and *happenings* in all their specificity and significance. Glancing backward in time, the person of custom sees only a silhouette in motion; the citizen of a republic sees excellence in action. More exactly, the recollections of public life preserve personas—the characters of individuals. The republic is always filled with apparitions. In its streets and public forums, forever the abode of spirits, the images of deeds and the resonance of words long ancient are yet to be seen and heard.[20]

When we distinguish between custom and recollection, this dimension of audibility deserves a prominent place. As Burke knew, customary societies are deeply quiet. Reverence and trembling reduce voices to whispers. More often, the person of custom (a person of wholly concrete and habitual practice) has little to say. On the other hand, public life always has been associated with vociferous speech. Republics generally have been noisy places, home to oration and dialogue, catcall and epithet. Wherever public life has emerged, the din of res publica has always been heard: clamoring voices, sometimes reduced to jabbering, rarely in unison (although sometimes in harmony), the howl and prophecy of disorder to the inexperienced ear. So much has this been the case that some have suggested that public liberty might be measured by decibel alone. In short, the republic has been characterized by the presence of voices.

The republic also has been characterized by the ability to project voices, as well as discreet images, through time. The highly specific images of recollection undoubtedly owe much to an audible dimension. It is only sometimes true that a picture is worth a thousand words. In republics, words are more powerful than deeds; the tongue and the ear more potent than the eye. The optimum size of a polis, says Aristotle, is one whose limit is that of a single voice. To be sure, the familiarity and affection so essential to res

---

[20] Gunnell, p. 286; Pocock, *Politics, Language and Time*, p. 244; Lippmann, p. 32. It was precisely of such spirits that Marx complained so bitterly in *The Eighteenth Brumaire*.

publica are not without roots in seeing and touching. Aristotle's suggestion, however, is that in public life hearing becomes the dominant sense. This is, of course, only a corollary of the view that speech is the most characteristic political activity. Public speech most often depends upon deeds for its subject matter, but the deed (the unique action) depends upon speech for its power. Nothing is more fleeting than the deed. Only through speech can the deed remain entire and intact, distinguishable from and undissolved by the multitude of its consequences. Without speech to memorialize, says Arendt, there can be no remembrance.[21]

Hearing, of all the senses, seems to enjoy the most direct access to the mnemonic imagination. Perhaps nothing is better suited to conjure affective images than an old melody, which helps explain the prominent place song has often enjoyed in public life. It would be but a small exaggeration to suggest that the secret of the republic has been the principle of the echo. It is certainly no secret, for example, that Solon delivered his laws in verse, or that Lycurgus' constitution owed much to his aphoristic genius. Both were masters of the "shaped word." Verse enhances memorability while placing a minimum of strain on the structure of recollection. The ancient relationship of politics and poetics is well established, and Havelock has rightly suggested that this relation is rooted in the mnemonic consciousness of public life.[22]

The truth of res publica is always uttered. This is the chief cause of the influence that rhetoricians often have wielded in republics. In customary societies, where truth is wholly contained within practice, the word carries less force (an exasperating discovery made as often by revolutionaries as by agricultural or medical experts when they confront a people of custom).

Most human beings love "the old way of life," that which

[21] Arendt, *The Human Condition*, p. 204.
[22] Havelock, *Preface to Plato*, pp. 125-37.

19

is their own. In familiarity, in that which is close, we are inclined to place all value. Thus, Machiavelli warns his prince against disturbing ancestral practices. But with republics such prudence is not enough, for in states accustomed to living under their own laws, the "name" of liberty is never forgotten.

And even if their fathers have not recalled it, the public buildings, the offices of the magistrates, the insignia of the free organizations recall it. Of a certainty the citizens will perceive the meaning of these things with the utmost longing.[23]

At the center of the republican consciousness is the process of giving a name to a way of life—the *articulation* of the familiar.

To "name" is to make more tenacious. In investing the past with words and deeds, speech strengthens and transforms the attachments of human beings to that which is their own. Recollections add richness and texture to a way of life, creating *objects* to which the affections attach themselves. As Machiavelli suggests, such recollections are not dependent upon continuous practice, for in republics the public buildings, the names of streets, the insignias of civic life—objects of joy and sadness—seem almost to speak that which has not recently been seen. In Edwin O'Connor's *The Last Hurrah*, the young Adam has little attachment to his native city despite his familiarity with its appearance. It is only after Skeffington fills the space of the city with anecdotes, with that knowledge that only lives through words, that it comes to have "meaning" for his nephew. In politics, observes Skeffington, "everybody remembers everything."[24]

---

[23] Machiavelli, *The Prince*, chapter 5; *History of Florence*, p. 1123; Oakeshott, p. 4.

[24] O'Connor, *The Last Hurrah*, p. 61; see also chapter 10. Skeffington's observation is, of course, overstatement, but it is given force by his subsequent defeat at the hands of an alliance between those who remembered too well and those who remembered not at all.

In republics, traditions are rarely customary in the Oake-shottian sense. While it has become our custom to celebrate Thanksgiving, for example, this is not an immemorial practice, but, in a sense, the opposite. It is a memorial, a commemoration. And while ritualistic dimensions attach to its celebration ("We always roast a turkey on Thanksgiving"), its full meaning can be conveyed only through speech. When we no longer speak of, but simply practice, the Thanksgiving feast, only then will it have become a custom. In republics, however, access to the heart is to be had through the ear no less than through the eye.

The relation of the republic and the word suggests more. Words are the stuff of reflection, and the citizen's relation to this discourse is a self-conscious one. The citizen inherits more than a concrete form of behavior; he inherits a "testament." He inherits more than what his forebears have done; he inherits also what they have said about what they have done. This testimony, says Arendt, "selects and names." An articulate and coherent self-understanding, the "recollections" of the republic are properly called paideia. They embody a self-conscious way of life. Through these recollections, citizens learn where they "belong" and what they are "living for." In the accents of praise and blame are to be found a people's hierarchy of value—the location of its "treasures" and a measure of their "worth."[25]

A republic's self-conception is mediated through tales and stories—the remembrance of words and deeds. In these tales and stories is preserved a special kind of knowledge, the knowledge of "a free people." Political memory is the concrete conceptualization of the experience of a people. Such implications have led many students of the republic to call attention to the relationship between a people's maintenance of its liberty and its experience with public affairs. Only by sifting, distilling, rediscovering its tradi-

---

[25] Arendt, *Between Past and Future*, p. 5; Havelock, p. 175; Karl Jaspers, as quoted in Lippmann, p. 105.

tions can res publica preserve itself. Political memory is the reduction of action to a great story and herein lies its genius. As Lippmann once observed, *in practice* most men are "positivists." To common sense,

> only seeing is believing. Nothing is real enough to be taken *seriously*, nothing can matter of *deep concern*, which cannot, or at least might not, somewhere and sometime, be seen, heard, tasted, smelled, or touched.[26] (italics mine)

It is from sensuous knowledge that a free people draws its confidence—that peculiar union of passion and sobriety. The recollections of a republic find their proper form in narrative—concrete, yet capable of conceptualization, rooted, yet "unfinished." Such a tradition is susceptible to rearrangement (reinterpretation, recreation, recovery) because it is the object of "incessant talk." The republic is both the beneficiary and the victim of the inexactness of language. In the ambiguity of words we find one spring of republican vitality. The narrative which is political memory is at once the parent of both tumult and civility. Under the regime of remembrance, the struggle over the meanings of words is circumscribed by the limits of a public language drawn from common mnemonic images. The source of great conceptual energy, remembrance also contains what Lippmann called a "fabric of understandings" capable of directing and conserving such energy.[27]

Pocock has correctly (if somewhat unsympathetically) seen in such articulate traditions an attempt to erect "a linguistic universe in which [the citizen] can see himself to exist." But this must be so, for the inheritance of res publica cannot

---

[26] Lippmann, p. 125.

[27] Arendt, *On Revolution*, p. 320; Pocock, *Politics, Language and Time*, pp. 254-56, 288. See also Lippmann, p. 129. Custom and memory have their counterparts in rival historiographies. Briefly, history can be viewed as a process through which one thing becomes another or as a process in which something becomes nothing. One's preference depends in part on whether one is writing a history of behavior or a history of action.

be *received* (as custom is), but must be *made* one's own. It may not be "enjoyed" simply, for it is neither possessed nor retained with ease. It would bestow less a habit of behavior than a spirit, as its ritualization has often foretold its flight. Neither habits nor principles can provide a home for this spirit, for only memory can preserve excellence in action; only words and deeds can deliver it into one's hands.[28]

For Lippmann, who understood public life better than most, the phenomenon of res publica remained, finally, mysterious.

> Traditions are more than the culture of the arts and sciences. They are the public world to which our private worlds are joined. This continuum of public and private memories transcends all persons in their immediate and natural lives and it ties them all together. In it there is performed the mystery by which individuals are adopted and initiated into membership into the community.

> The body which carries this mystery is the history of the community, and its central theme is the great deeds and high purposes of the great predecessors. From them the new men descend and prove themselves by becoming participants in the unfinished story.[29]

The relation of the individual to the community of which Lippmann speaks is worthy of the designation "mystery." It is not to be confused with the placid and encompassing membership of customary society nor with the narrow and impoverished instrumentalism of modern liberalism. It involves the joining of "public" and "private worlds." Membership in res publica is bound up with "high purposes," and those who would truly belong must "prove themselves" in action. It is within this mystery that an expla-

[28] Pocock, *Politics, Language and Time*, p. 288; Pocock, *Machiavellian Moment*, p. 99; Oakeshott, pp. 35, 62, 173.

[29] Lippmann, p. 105. Compare to Havelock, p. 44.

nation of both the republic's "grandeur" and the republic's "idolatry" is to be found. The origin of its virtues and its vices, the republic's true religion generally has been the worship of human greatness. If some founders were "friends" of God, this relationship always accrued to the founder's honor and the glory and prosperity of his creation.[30]

It is appropriate to describe the republic as temporal in two senses. It is both worldly and, as I suggested earlier, profoundly concerned with its own finitude. The two meanings are distinguishable, but not easily separated. The republican tradition has always known that the pathos of political action could be plumbed only if greatness (or the truly memorable) was considered against the backdrop of the republic's temporality (or the likelihood of oblivion).

The republic has never shared the optimism of customary society, that ritual and repetition were enough. When the person of custom contemplates his past, he imagines he sees a chain of transmission stretching beyond memory and attaching him securely to the practical wisdom of his ancestors. It is on this process of transmission that he affixes all his attention and places all his hopes. The citizen of the republic, on the other hand, is fascinated with the boundaries of remembrance. His eyes are always on the horizon. His past is dominated by a vision of founding

[30] The relation of republics and worldly greatness has often been observed, and frequent examples are to be found throughout the work of Machiavelli and Thucydides, to name two students of the phenomenon. The term "grandeur" is employed most notably by Montesquieu in his extraordinary history of Rome. The political quality of Montesquieu's vocabulary ("grandeur" and "decadence") can be compared to the historian's preference for the terminology of process, such as "rise" and "fall." As we saw earlier, it is in Oakeshott that we find lovers of action labeled idolatrous (p. 35), by which I understand him to mean their attempts to objectify themselves in the world through their deeds. To the extent that republics are mnemonic structures whose purpose is to preserve words and deeds, they are truly houses of idols. This criticism of the republic, however, is almost as old as public life itself, and it can be found in one form or another in almost all critiques of the life of action. A reference to God's "friendship" can be found in chapter 26 of *The Prince*.

order whose creative power has sustained all that has come after. And while this beginning looms large on the limit of memory, it is always receding in time, suggesting to the patriot the possibility of its loss. In Rome, says de Grazia, "devotion to the republic was so strong that whenever the constitution seemed threatened orators spoke of its possible demise as a catastrophe tantamount to anarchy, to the disappearance of the state rather than a shift in it from one form to another." The republican tradition's fascination with the institution of censorship has not been idle mimesis of Rome or Sparta, but reflects a deep understanding of the status of res publica. The office of the censor arose less from a fear of the novel (which was, in any case, unavoidable) than from a fear of losing the beginning. Thus, it is significant that Cato is reputed to have been the first to write down the history of Rome, a book whose title, the *Origines*, announces the Censor's fear. To guard against dread possibility, free peoples have sought the "boon of Mnemosyne."[31]

[31] de Grazia.

T W O

* * *

MACHIAVELLI:
REMEMBRANCE AND
THE REPUBLIC

An Image of Rome

When Augustine insisted that "the seat of the mind is in memory," he was only giving voice to what had lain at the very center of the Roman political experience since the founding of that city. Among ancient peoples, it was the Romans whose gaze was drawn ineluctably to the past. For the Romans, the primitive equation of the good with the ancestral remained intact. The source of all authority, political and religious, lay in their recollection of their origin as a people. The sacredness of the foundation was the principle around which the entire political experience of the Roman people was organized; indeed, the sacred beginning was at once the source of political virtue and religious piety. (*Re-ligare* meant literally to be tied back.) Two of Rome's earliest and highest dieties had been Janus, the god of beginnings, and Minerva, the goddess of remembrance.

For the Romans, to remember was to remember the ways of the fathers. It had been paternity that had invested the founding with an aspect of the divine, and it remained paternity that tied every Roman back to the sacred origin. (The maternal principle could only raise the spectre of the Sabine with all its disintegrative implications.) Fathered by Mars, Romulus fathered a people. The Pallatine, site of Romulus' boyhood, made sacrosanct by twelve vultures, consecrated in a brother's blood, became the site of his city. Thus, from the beginning the Roman was a creature of place. Tied to the soil, it was the Roman who developed the notion of *patria*—the fatherland.

The uniqueness of the Roman perspective is not always appreciated. The Greeks, R. G. Collingwood observed, would never have contemplated raising the problem of the origin of the Hellenic race. The Romans were obsessed with their own. To be sure, the Greeks did not ignore the importance of foundations. The notion of a lawgiver had always been a staple of the practice and the theory of Greek politics. Theseus, Lycurgus, and Solon all had gained "their due mead of glory" by laying the foundations of their states. In *The Republic*, Socrates seduces his young listeners into joining his search for the ideal regime with the grand temptation of founding a state, if only in speech. But in the Greek mind, the act of foundation appeared, in Arendt's words, as "an almost commonplace experience." The practice of sending out a portion of the citizen-body to start a new city was a standard remedy for the problem of overpopulation.

What, for the Greeks, was an oft-repeated and thus repeatable act was for the Romans a unique event which left its indelible mark on a people and to which all subsequent political acts were tied. To be a citizen, to act politically, meant quite literally to preserve that which was laid in the beginning. Every act was thus bound back to this sacred origin and was in turn transformed into an example. The deeds of their ancestors became, as it were, the yardstick with which the Romans measured their conduct, and the recounting of these deeds nothing less than civic education. As Hannah Arendt has observed:

> The [Roman] past was sanctified through tradition. Tradition preserved the past by handing down from one generation to the next the testimony of the ancestors, who first had witnessed and created the sacred founding and then augmented it by their authority throughout the centuries. . . . To act without authority and tradition, without accepted time-honored standards and models, without the help of the wisdom of the founding fathers, was inconceivable.[1]

Intellectual historians have often called our attention to what they consider the remarkable absence of philosophical inquiry among an otherwise gifted people. But this is nothing to be wondered at. A people whose unity rests upon equating the good with the ancestral dares not abide a spirit which seeks to know the true origins of things human and divine.[2] It is history, not philosophy, which nurtures such a people. While such a history seeks to preserve the deeds of men from that oblivion which is forgetting, it is not the history of a Herodotus, which would preserve the deeds of Greek and barbarian alike. Still less is it a universal history, which would seek to tell the saga of all human action. Rather, it is what Collingwood has called "a national history where the hero is the spirit of a people." Roman historiography was a public history which sought to be a training ground for political life. This notion of a history—one that is public, that is committed to acting men, and that would harness the past to the present—is

[1] Arendt, *Between Past and Future*, p. 124 (see also pp. 120-26); Collingwood, *The Idea of History*, pp. 34-36.

[2] In this regard, the expulsion of Carneades, Diogenes, and Critolaus by Cato reveals the Censor to have been not only a great patriot but one with a profound understanding of the nature of the Roman polity. It is significant that Cato could both banish philosophy and compose the *Origines*, the earliest written history of Rome. For a discussion of Herodotus' "objectivity," see Arendt, *Between Past and Future*, p. 51.

perhaps nowhere described more succinctly than by its greatest practitioner, Titus Livy.

> This it is which is particularly salutary and profitable in the study of history, that you behold instances of every variety of conduct displayed on a conspicuous monument; that thence you may select for yourself and for your country that which you may imitate; thence note what is shameful in the undertaking, and shameful in the result, which you may avoid.[3]

For Livy, history was political theory. As such, Roman historians were engaged in the act of remembrance. But they never succeeded in articulating a theory of political memory. If, in the twilight of the empire, Augustine did succeed in conceptualizing that experience, it was only to destroy it first and then to supplant it. Not until Machiavelli were the theoretical implications of Roman political practice revealed. Therefore, it is to him that we must turn.

Machiavelli and History

Roman historiography was called upon to educate a citizenry through examples of political virtue and political vice. And yet historians such as Livy did not see such public utility as compromising the integrity of the science. In the same breath, Livy could reveal the public quality of history and defend the historical integrity of his enterprise.

> But either a fond partiality for the task I have undertaken deceives me, or there never was any either greater or more moral, or richer in good examples, nor one into which luxury and avarice made their entrance so late, and where poverty and frugality were so much and so long honored; so that the less wealth there was, the less desire was there. Of late riches have introduced avarice, and excessive pleasures a longing for

[3] Collingwood, p. 34; Livius, *Roman History*, p. xiv.

them, amid luxury and a passion for ruining ourselves and destroying everything else. But let complaints, which will not be agreeable even then, when perhaps they will also be necessary, be kept aloof from at least the first stage of beginning so great a work. We should rather, if it was usual with us [historians] as it is with poets, begin with good omens, vows and prayers to the gods and goddesses to vouchsafe good success to our efforts in so arduous an undertaking.[4]

For Livy, history was at once useful and true. If the gods were invoked "in so arduous an undertaking," it was to aid the historian in bringing a dead past to life, not in creating monsters which had never been. History, thought Livy, taught political truth unambiguously.

Niccolò Machiavelli is often thought to share this perspective. His *Discourses* on Livy's *History* take the form of commentaries upon history from which political maxims may be extracted. One can read almost any of Machiavelli's political works and discover an injunction to imitate the ancients; his instruction to princes in chapter 6 of *The Prince* to keep to "well-beaten paths" is perhaps the best known. In the *Discourses*, Machiavelli comes perilously close to saying explicitly that history teaches the truth unambiguously. Such passages have led scholars to echo De Sanctis in proclaiming Machiavelli the founder of the science of history because, they say, he studied facts to determine cause and effect, or to find in Machiavelli, with Pollock, "the pure passionless curiosity of the man of science," or, with Parel, the uniformity and comparative analysis of a "Galileo of politics."[5]

---

[4] Livius, p. xiv.

[5] Machiavelli, *The Prince*, chapter 6. See also *Art of War*, p. 567; I-39, II-19; Whitfield, *Machiavelli*, p. 58; Parel, *The Political Calculus*, p. 7. Excepting Machiavelli's *Discourses*, all citations from Machiavelli's works, unless otherwise noted, are taken from *The Chief Works and Others*. Hereafter in this chapter, I will cite only the titles and page number(s) of these particular works. For convenience, *The Prince* will be cited by chapter and the *Discourses* by book and chapter.

Less extravagant, but rooted in similar perceptions, are those who see Machiavelli as humanist and Renaissance man, admiring the past and seeking its recreation through imitation. These commentators often combine this interpretation with a criticism of Machiavelli's use of historical data which, they say, originates in an eagerness to learn a lesson from history. Such a view of his method was held by none other than Guicciardini, Machiavelli's friend, correspondent, and sometimes benefactor, who saw in Machiavelli an impractical and anachronistic infatuation with the past. "The Romans," remarked Guicciardini, "ought not to be always on our lips." Machiavelli's own wistful account of his afternoon "conversations" with the ancients in the now famous letter to Francesco Vettori lends credence to Guicciardini's assessment.[6]

But there is another Machiavelli—the brash innovator—who boasts about his decision "to enter upon a new way, as yet untrodden by anyone else." Machiavelli's claim to novelty does not mix easily with his apparent reverence for antiquity. Perhaps even more startling is Machiavelli's discussion of the character of history in the Preface to Book II of his *Discourses*. Here, Machiavelli calls history itself into question, tainting, as it were, the very source of political knowledge.

> The whole truth about olden times is not grasped, since what redounds to their discredit is often passed over in silence, whereas what is likely to make them appear glorious is pompously recounted in all its details.

But if "obsequious historians" make accounts of the past untrustworthy, how can imitation of the ancients be sane political counsel? This paradox has led some theorists to see in Machiavelli a deep contempt for all traditions or even to ascribe to him the most sinister of intentions. Merleau-

[6] Neal Wood, "Machiavelli's Humanism in Action," in Parel, p. 37; Whitfield, pp. 13-14, 110, 121-22, 131.

Ponty's warning is well taken. Machiavelli is, indeed, a "difficult writer."[7]

Like most caricatures, there is some truth in both of these rather severe portraits of the Florentine. To get to the heart of the matter, we will begin by returning to the aforementioned letter to Vettori. There are sound reasons for beginning here, but perhaps most important is that the letter is private correspondence in which rhetorical and political considerations, as well as Machiavelli's self-confessed propensity to deceive and dissimulate, are less likely to be in evidence. Machiavelli removes the clothes of the day, soiled with the petty corruptions of contemporary existence. He must prepare himself to receive (or to be received by) the ancients. We are struck by the ritual and reverence of Machiavelli's posture. In the "presence" of the ancients, confronted with their authority and antiquity, Machiavelli gives himself over to them. Thus, the first lesson Machiavelli learns from the ancients, and particularly from the Roman historians, is the reverence for things old. He sees it in himself and suspects the same is true for others. Reverence for ancient things appears to him an almost natural human sentiment. And if this is generally true in most human communities, it is particulary true in Italy which "seems born to raise up dead things." Machiavelli derives great pleasure from his afternoon conversations with the men of antiquity, and thereby learns a valuable rhetorical teaching. Henceforth, his own work would make use of the "delight" men experience in hearing of "noble acts" and "ancient deeds." Machiavelli would appeal to the prejudice in favor of ancient things.[8]

Nonetheless, there is something peculiar about contemporary politics. Machiavelli observes that "neither prince nor republic . . . repairs to antiquity for examples."

---

[7] *Discourses*, I-Preface, II-Preface; Arendt, *Between Past and Future*, p. 137; Strauss, *Thoughts on Machiavelli*, p. 37; Merleau-Ponty, *Signs*, p. 211.

[8] Letter to Francesco Vettori, December 10, 1513, p. 929; *Art of War*, pp. 567, 726; *The Life of Castruccio Castracani of Lucca*, p. 534. For Machiavelli's propensity to deceive, see his letter to Guicciardini, May 17, 1521, p. 973.

When I consider in what honor antiquity is held, and how—to cite but one instance—a bit of old statue has fetched a high price that someone may have it by him to give honor to his house and that it may be possible for it to be copied by those who are keen on this art; and how the latter then with great industry take pains to reproduce it in all their works; and when, on the other hand, I notice that what history has to say about highly virtuous actions performed by ancient kingdoms and republics by their kings, their generals, their citizens, their legislators, and by others who have gone to the trouble of serving their country, is rather admired than imitated; nay is so shunned by everybody in each little thing they do, that of the virtue of bygone days there remains no trace, it cannot but fill me at once with astonishment and grief.

Machiavelli's "astonishment" reveals the almost unnatural character of this situation, while his "grief" impels him to discover a cause and a remedy.

This is due in my opinion . . . to the lack of a proper appreciation of history, owing to people failing to realize the significance of what they read, and to their having no taste for the delicacies it comprises. Hence it comes about that the great bulk of those who read it take pleasure of hearing of the various incidents which are contained in it, but never think of imitating them, since they hold them to be not merely difficult but impossible of imitation, as if the heaven, the sun, the elements and man had in their motion, their order, and their potency, become different from what they used to be.[9]

[9] *Discourses*, I-Preface. An interesting variation on this theme is found at the beginning of *The Art of War*, where Fabrizio observes that his contemporaries imitate the ancients in things "delicate and soft" that are done "in the shade" but not "in things strong and rough . . . that are done in the sun" (p. 570).

Men continue to admire the past, but cannot imagine acting in similar ways. The problem is rooted in their perceptions—perceptions of modern things and ancient things. Modern politics appears so different from ancient politics that imitation is judged impossible. Machiavelli attempts to combat this perception with what amounts to an ontological argument. The cosmos remains the same, hence imitation is possible. But Machiavelli knows better than anyone the sophistry of his argument. Political things are intimately connected with perceptions. If perceptions are different, the human world has in fact undergone a change.

In one sense, history itself was at fault. While history conceived as a process would await the eighteenth century and the German school, its principles lay dormant in the Christian conception of the life of Christ. The life and death of Jesus of Nazareth had inalterably transformed the human condition. Such had been standard historical doctrine at least since Augustine. While Machiavelli seemingly absolves Christianity of responsibility for the contemporary state of historical criticism, his insistence on an unchanging cosmos is a preliminary to a reintroduction of pagan historiography: "Since I want to get men out of this wrong way of thinking, I have thought fit to write a commentary on all those books of Titus Livy which have not by the malignity of time had their continuity broken." But history is no longer unambiguous. History alone will not suffice but stands in need of commentary. Thus:

> It will comprise what I have arrived at by comparing ancient and modern events, and think necessary for the better understanding of them, so that those who read what I have to say may the more easily draw those practical lessons which one should seek to obtain from the study of history.[10]

History is comprised of "delicacies" and stands in need of a peculiar appreciation. For history to teach, something

[10] *Discourses*, II-Preface.

more than Livian narrative is necessary. Machiavelli appears to have put himself in the service of history, performing those tasks essential to historical criticism—clarification and explanation. Machiavelli has insisted only that the facts do not speak for themselves. The maiden, History, has remained inviolate, and Machiavelli ends his preface with the guarded confidence of the historian—that the past may yet yield up its treasures. Thus, we are properly astonished to learn in the Preface to Book II that history suffers from more severe difficulties than we had been led to suppose. Delicacies have become exaggerations, particularly in those "things appertaining to human life and human customs," in that which concerns the deeds of men. Because human deeds, unlike "the arts," must be recounted if they are to be known, "obsequious writers" have made historical accuracy unrecoverable.

Surprisingly, Machiavelli appears unperturbed by this revelation; rather, he seems intent upon exploring two new implications of the relation of past and present. The first insight is contained in a sentence. "Since it is either through fear or envy that men come to hate things, in the case of the past the two most powerful incentives for hating are lacking, since the past cannot hurt you nor give you cause for envy." The past is free from fear and envy and thus is free from hate; that is, it is free from danger and is unopposed. We are reminded of the reception Machiavelli tells us lies in store for new things.

> Although owing to the envy inherent in man's nature it has always been no less dangerous to discover new ways and methods than to set off in search of new seas and unknown lands because most men are much more ready to belittle than to praise another's actions.

While the full implications of Machiavelli's insight must await their proper place, it should be noted here that Machiavelli would now become History's master as he earlier feigned to be her servant. The suggestion is unmistakable.

New things are always opposed and are thus in danger. Old things are unopposed and enjoy safety. If the new could be made to appear old, its existence would be much less precarious. History would be the ideal vehicle for such an illusion. At the moment that history is discredited as political knowledge, she is reformed and made the hand-maiden of political rhetoric. The historian's problem becomes the theorist's opportunity.[11]

While this first teaching remains, as it were, hidden by an intervening book, the second teaching of the second preface is less so. Machiavelli observes that "men always praise bygone days and criticize the present, and so partial are they to the past that they not only admire past ages the knowledge of which has come down to them in written records, but also, when they grow old, what they remember having seen in their youth." Machiavelli concludes that this is because "the human mind is perpetually discontented . . . [which] makes it find fault with the present, praise the past, and long for the future, though for its doing so no rational cause can be assigned." The praising of the past and the condemning of the present seems to Machiavelli an almost universal phenomenon, transcending the particularities of individuals and cultures. Moreover, these are not idle complaints, but are associated with that discontentedness which longs for, and in effect creates, the future. Finally, this human propensity to look to the past appears to have no rational cause, but presumably is rooted in some pre-rational or non-rational sentiment. Taken together, the two teachings of the second preface can be reduced to this: he who would make the future must master the past.[12]

Livian historiography always had contained a strong element of public utility. As such, it had sought to teach by example. Machiavelli elevated the "practical lesson" to the

[11] *Discourses*, I-Preface, II-Preface.
[12] *Discourses*, II-Preface.

status of a first principle in the study of the past. A century later, another philosopher would condemn and yet, at the same time, capture the essence of Machiavellian history.

> To live with men of an earlier age is like travelling in foreign lands . . . But those who travel too long end by being strangers in their own homes, and those who study too curiously the actions of antiquity are ignorant of what is done among ourselves today. Moreover, these narratives tell of things that cannot have happened as if they had really taken place, and thus invite us to attempt what is really beyond our powers or to hope for what is beyond our fate. And even histories, true though they be, and neither exaggerating nor altering the value of things, omit circumstances of a meaner and less dignified kind in order to become more worthy of a reader's attention; hence the things which they describe never happened exactly as they describe them, and men who try to model their own acts upon them are prone to the madness of romantic paladins and mediate hyperbolical deeds.[13]

If Machiavellian history had a single purpose, it was to cultivate the deed; if by the seventeenth century such deeds appeared to Descartes "hyperbolical," this was due, Machiavelli would have replied, to that century's dearth of acting men. And yet, students of Machiavelli's antiquity would indeed be "strangers in their own homes, and . . . ignorant of what is done . . . today." But that had always been Machiavelli's intention. Machiavelli desired his readers to lose themselves in antiquity (and to lose sight of modernity), much as he would lose himself in those afternoon conversations with the ancients. To so lose oneself was to see that men could act in the world—a world where "the heaven, the sun, the elements and [even] man" had not changed. To forget modernity was to overcome the dismay

---

[13] Descartes, quoted in Collingwood, p. 59.

and terror that made modern man impotent. 'Let no one despair, then, of being able to effect that which has been effected by others; for men are born and live and die in an order which remains ever the same.'[14]

In teaching what men had done, Machiavellian history sought to teach men what they might do. This history was less a science of correct action than the origin of action itself. Machiavelli dared to make "the deed" the first principle of history because he believed he had discovered the primordial principles which tied men to the past.

Glory and Oblivion

Many writers have called our attention to the centrality of fear in Machiavelli's work. Machiavelli himself speaks almost endlessly of fear. Princes are counseled to place fear before love. It was fear of the Tarquins, we are told, that kept the Roman nobility in check. Numa, it seems, deserves more praise than Romulus because it was Numa who instilled fear in the Roman populace. The attempt to draw political lessons from the extreme situation also is a testimony to the place fear occupies in Machiavelli's thought. In the extreme situation, human fear is unmasked. Only then can the place of fear in human motivation be gauged accurately. Leo Strauss has argued that Machiavelli's *Discourses* deal with the hidden causes of horrors or with the terrors inherent in first and last things. In one sense, all of Machiavelli's work may be seen as an investigation into the relation of politics and terror. If Machiavelli lacked Hobbes's facility for systematic investigation, it was Machiavelli who first elevated fear to the status of a first principle in the science of human motivation, and who first saw its political implications. This is the insight which is at the root

[14] *Discourses*, I-11. Consider also this statement in *The Art of War*: "By Italy's condition I do not wish you to be dismayed or terrified, because this land seems born to raise up dead things, as she has in poetry, in painting, and in sculpture" (p. 726). See also Strauss, p. 91.

of Machiavelli's praise of ancient practice. Contemporary men had not so much forgotten the ancient fears as they had forgotten the relation of those fears to politics. Hence, Machiavelli's "new way" was a return to ancient practice, but a return which rested upon a higher theoretical understanding of the nature of human terror first made explicit by Machiavelli and, thus, truly a new way.[15]

Strauss's observation is suggestive—that Machiavelli writes about first and last terrors and that these are hidden. If these terrors are hidden, they also have always been known. The first terror, first in psychic as well as anthropological time, is the fear of unprotectedness. As Machiavelli rightly saw, it is this fear which lies in the beginning of states no less than in the beginning of individuals, for in the beginning of political things there is pestilence, famine, and war. The first terrors are deeply hidden in the darkest recesses of memory. Of this, neither Machiavelli nor Freud had any doubt. But in keeping with our method, that that which is most hidden should be brought to light last, we will leave off our discussion of first terrors, returning to them in a more appropriate setting, the discussion of beginnings.[16]

Unlike the first terrors, which are hidden early in the subconscious, human beings are made ever more aware of the last terror. This last terror is primordial also in that it has always been with the race, but it is not coeval with the first terror. In psychic time, the first terror predates the last terror. The first terror originates in our initial encounter with nature which gives rise to a sense of helplessness in the face of nature's awful power. The last terror is made known through a more extensive intercourse with nature.

[15] Strauss, p. 90. The truth about ancient practice had never been made explicit, but was contained in the actions, nay, in the very character of men such as Hannibal and Manlius Torquatus. It is the centrality of fear in Machiavelli's work that earns him his status as a modern and upon which his comradery with Hobbes is founded.

[16] *Discourses*, I-1.

It requires first an acquaintance with death, the knowledge that life is not forever. But it also requires an act of imagination, the imagining of a world without one's being. This last terror has its origin in the knowledge of our own mortality, but it is not simply a fear of death. Rather, it is a fear of the loss of being, of the abyss, of having left without a trace, of annihilation. This terror has a name—oblivion. The ancients knew it well. They understood the deep need "not to lie in the end with no name." Its name is most appropriate. Webster's New World Dictionary defines oblivion as "a forgetting or having forgotten" or "the condition or fact of being forgotten." To be lodged in the memory, then, is to be preserved.[17]

The fear of oblivion is perhaps rooted in the desire "to be" forever (that is, to be a god), but it is colored by a recognition, even an acceptance, of one's own mortality. Oblivion is thus not an unconquerable fear, as it can be tamed through remembrance. In confronting oblivion, the human spirit asks not "to be forever" but only "to make it known that it has been." It calls out, not to God, but to men, "remember me and that will be enough."[18]

It was this knowledge that led the ancients to found their practice on the pursuit of glory. Human life was radically impermanent. Humans were mortals. Almost paradoxically, this awful knowledge became the spring of human action. Through remembrance, the deed could acquire a permanence denied to the doer. Thus, the act was lifted out of nature, which was the same as out of time. It became

[17] Rousseau, *Emile*, pp. 222-23; Rousseau, "Discourse on the Origin and Foundations of Inequality Among Men," in *The First and Second Discourses*, p. 116.

[18] That this wish remains tied to man's secret aspiration to divinity can be seen in the doctrine of apotheosis, the investing of heroes and founders, and, later, emperors with immortality. But even this doctrine insists that men earn immortality through their deeds. To live beyond time, the more exalted promise of Christianity, is beyond the power of men: hence the doctrine of divine Grace, the free gift of a beneficent God. In direct contrast to the pagan understanding, the Christian conception of redemption emphasizes not man's power but his impotence.

a protest against morality. Nietzsche also knew this: "One thing will live, the monogram of their most authentic essence, a work, a deed, a rare inspiration, a creation."[19]

While the desire for glory is rooted in a private terror, glory itself is inescapably public. By definition, glory requires the recognition of the deed by others. The deed demands and must receive remembrance. To the ancients, it seemed that the *political* deed was best suited to gain a niche in the memory of men. "In no other realm," wrote Cicero, "does human excellence approach so closely the paths of the gods as it does in the founding of new and in the preservation of already founded communities." To approach the paths of the gods was to approximate their immortality, and this was best accomplished through political action. To a Roman like Cicero, the political community was the highest vessel of memory. Humans approach the divine "so closely" through the political deed because the political community is well suited to preserve the memory of past acts and because it remembers its own heroes above all others. He who would be remembered must be a political actor. Such was the teaching of Rome.[20]

In his *History of Florence*, Machiavelli echoes this teaching.

> There lived in those times a certain Stephano Porcari, a Roman citizen noble by blood and learning, but much more so through the excellence of his mind. He wished, according to the nature of men who long for glory, to do or to attempt at least, something worth remem-

---

[19] Nietzsche, p. 16. It might be said that this amounts to standing Arendt on her head. Arendt argues that action points to natality rather than mortality in that each new birth ushers into the world a "unique stranger" who brings with him the capability of pure innovation—a new beginning. Such a view leaves the new personality intact while the source of action remains hidden and, as it were, fully developed upon entering the world. While there is psychological warrant for this, Arendt's own emphasis on glory and remembrance points to a kind of knowledge gained in the world as the source of anything that would be recognizable as action. See Arendt, *The Human Condition*, especially chapter 1.

[20] Arendt, *Between Past and Future*, p. 121.

bering. And he judged he could attempt nothing other than the delivery of his native city from the hands of the prelates and her restoration to her ancient government. He hoped through such a deed, if he succeeded, to be called the new founder and second father to that city.

Porcari stood in need of the preservation that comes from memory. To Machiavelli, this seemed an elemental quality. Machiavelli also treated the backward glance of humankind with equal mystery, finding no "rational" origin for it. To remember is soon followed by a desire to be remembered. Glory became a good for men only after one man had tasted it. The first man to find himself a memory for another was at once startled and pleased. Stephano Porcari would have been the second father of his city because he remembered her first. To remember ancient men and deeds is to testify to the truth of immortality, and it is thereby an encouragement to those who come after. What one has achieved others may attempt. Hence, remembrance becomes a secret comfort to men who otherwise would be wretched and without hope. And so Machiavelli could say of the condemned Bernardo Nardi that "he wished his death should at least be accompanied by some action worth remembering."[21]

For Machiavelli, the problem remained one of creating the conditions under which the political deed could become possible. In the memory of a past lay a spring that would enable men to act for a future. Such remembrance made the contemplation of one's own glory possible. Without

---

[21] *History of Florence*, p. 1322. In Machiavelli's Florence, as in Cicero's Rome, such a teaching had an unmistakably republican tenor. In *The History of Florence*, a book commissioned by and later dedicated to a Medici pope, Machiavelli saw fit to conceal his teaching about the nature of glory through the literary ruse of incongruity. Hence the tale of Stephano Porcari is placed with little historical warrant in the middle of the narrative on the Tuscan wars. Favored by Machiavelli, these apparently incongruous asides contain those teachings which of necessity had to remain concealed, as we shall have occasion to see again. For Machiavelli's account of Bernardo Nardi, see *History of Florence*, pp. 1368-72.

the glorious deed and its foundation in political memory, men would no longer attempt the "rare and . . . unparalleled thing." Such a prospect threatened the very end of human history and the ushering in of the unbridled rein of fortune.[22]

In the Preface to Book I of his *Discourses*, Machiavelli had laid the blame for the problems of modern practice "not so much to . . . the religion of today" as to the state of historical education, which didn't prepare people to understand "the significance" of what they read and which kept them from "a proper appreciation" of the past. But the absolution of Christianity is short-lived.

> If one asks oneself how it comes about that the peoples of old were more fond of liberty than they are today, I think that the answer is that it is due to the same cause that makes men today less bold than they used to be; and this is due I think, to the difference of our education and that of bygone times, which is based on the difference between our religion and the religion of those days. For our religion, having taught us the truth and the true way of life, leads us to ascribe less esteem to worldly honor.

In other words, the problem of the republic in the modern world (for how are we to understand a fondness for liberty if not as republicanism?) is rooted in the problem of action (boldness), which in turn is rooted in the decay of esteem for "worldly honor." The truth and the true way of life banish glory from the world. The end of Christian education is embodied in the monastic orders whose members renounce the world of men and the vanity of the flesh. Christianity is thus a radical assault on the world of appearances upon which glory rests. To be unseen assures that one will also be unsung.[23]

[22] *Discourses*, III-6.
[23] *Discourses*, II-2. Arendt argues that Christianity imposed the requisite of forgetting upon works deemed good; that their otherworldliness necessitated a forgetting which literally took them out of the world. The

But the appeal of Christianity lay in its being founded upon the very fear that had driven the ancients to the glorious deed—the knowledge of human morality. Christianity began by infecting the idea of permanence through memory with the germ of futility and then offered, in its stead, the promise of redemption from death. Remembrance could only appear tawdry when compared to a life everlasting. It was this replacement of immortality in time with an immortality beyond time which underlay the "providential" coup of Christianity over the ancient world. But this expropriation of human fear did not exhaust Christianity's assault on the culture of glory. If Christian eschatology taught the futility of an immortality founded on human things, the Christian God seemed by his very omnipotence and omniscience (qualities which pagan deities lacked) to sap and degrade human power and effort. Henceforth, the actions of men "who know not what they do" could appear at best only rash and, more often, simply impotent. From this insight sprang Machiavelli's complaint that Christianity honors "humble and contemplative men, rather than men of action."[24]

It was the political consequences of the changes wrought by Christianity which concerned Machiavelli. If both pagan

---

victory of Christian humility over worldly honor was the central fact of European history in Machiavelli's view, and it represented the revenge of the East upon the West.

[24] An additional word on the relation between the fear of death and the fear of oblivion is in order. The fear of oblivion appears to contain the mature knowledge of the inevitability of biological death and, thus, a recognition of natural necessity and the substitution of a kind of immortality for the desired but impossible life forever. The apparently derivative character of this intellectual solution may seem to rob the notion of remembrance of its primeval status. However, Sigmund Freud's anthropological speculations suggest otherwise. According to Freud, it is to be supposed that primitive man first encountered the notion of life after death in the memory of those who were no longer with him. Memory, itself, gave rise to a sense of permanence and immortality. Thus, at one and the same time, primitive man submitted "to the supremacy of death with the same gesture with which he seemed to be denying it" (Freud, *Totem and Taboo*, p. 93).

glory and Christian salvation ministered to human fear, Christianity had cut the tie which bound such fearful men to the political community and which had been the spring of political action. Consequently,

> this pattern of life appears to have made the world weak, and to have handed it over as prey to the wicked, who run it successfully and securely since they are well aware that the generality of men, with paradise for their goal, consider how best to bear, rather than how best to avenge, their injuries.[25]

The mark of the Christian man has always been humility and forgiveness. Jesus had taught men to pray "forgive us our trespasses as we forgive those who trespass against us." It is a sound maxim which has always linked forgiving and forgetting. Jesus had sought to confine to oblivion that which separated man from his neighbor, for, as both Jesus and Machiavelli knew, the memory of past injury was at the root of much of man's enmity toward his fellow man. But Machiavelli understood that, unlike private evil, which is often diminished when forgotten, public evil only increases if it is not avenged, and political vengeance requires a long memory. Although Christianity never forbade the loving of one's country, the Christian's pursuit of other-worldly felicity, thought Machiavelli, made him forget injuries to the republic. Consequently, the fatherland went unloved, unhonored, and undefended. If Rome and not Christianity was responsible for wiping out "all republics and all their civic institutions," it was Christianity which made the soil of Machiavelli's Italy so inhospitable to the rebirth of republicanism.

The Christian conception of immortality, with all its transpolitical implications, had cut the civic tie and thereby denied the republic its citizens. The fatherland and "the memory of her ancient institutions" suffered the Christian

---

[25] *Discourses*, II-2.

"contempt for mundane things." In Machiavelli's shocking claim to love his country more than his soul is embedded a radical protest against the anti-political implications of redemption. It is a proud boast: "I would receive honor before Grace. I would be hero before saint. I would be remembered before I would be saved." In this, Machiavelli had donned the mantle of paganism.

The power of Christianity lay in its promise of mastery over death. Like ancient practice, this power was rooted in man's last terror. But unlike ancient practice, which sought to transform the fear of death and direct it to politically salutary ends, Christianity sought felicity through its conquest and replacement with the law of love. The failure of the Savonarolan experiment convinced Machiavelli of the weakness of the Christian teaching as a fundamental principle of political action. That armed prophets succeed where the unarmed fail because, when the people "no longer believe," a prophet must be ready to "make them believe by force" has always seemed a mysterious and paradoxical teaching. As the early history of Christianity had amply demonstrated, it is precisely *belief* that defies the compulsion of mere force. But this is not Machiavelli's meaning. Armed prophets succeed because they are armed with the knowledge of human terror and, like Moses, can make that terror manifest. Terror, unlike the simple threat of torture or death, gains access to the darkest corners of the mind. "And the Lord saith unto Moses, 'whosoever hath sinned against me; him will I blot out of my book.' "[26]

---

[26] *The Prince*, chapter 6; Exod. 32:33. This was the God of Israel's teaching regarding oblivion. Moses made that teaching accessible to men through the spectacle of terror: "Thus saith the Lord God of Israel, Put every man his sword by his side, and go in and out from gate to gate throughout the camp, and slay every man his brother, and every man his companion, and every man his neighbor./"And the children of Levi did according to the word of Moses: and there fell of the people that day about three thousand men./"For Moses had said, Consecrate yourselves today to the Lord, even every man upon his son, and upon his brother; that he may bestow upon you a blessing this day" (Exod. 32:26-30). The Mosaic terror left no one untouched. Of the remnant, each had tasted of the dread.

Glory and the City

"All the states, all the dominions that have had or now have authority over men have been and now are either republics or princedoms." So begins *The Prince*. Of all Machiavelli's dichotomies, this is the most famous. Time has erased much of the startling quality of this assertion, but Machiavelli's contemporaries could not have failed to notice the starkness of these two categories when compared to the traditional enumeration of the forms of government. However, Machiavelli's arresting claim was not intended to supplant the richness of the traditional distinctions. (The political history of his own city revealed an equally rich variety of political forms.) Machiavelli sought an altogether different distinction, one which he thought more important than those based upon enfranchisement or institutional structure. The distinction was whether the political order rested upon the actions of one man or many. The expansive horizon that glory enjoyed in the republic made room for human virtue and lay behind Machiavelli's republican preference. And while Machiavelli looked with great admiration on the Roman Republic, it was not without irony, for, as he knew, it was Roman virtue that had laid low the ancient republics of Tuscany. Usually hidden behind his more vocal praise of Italy's greatest republic, this side of Machiavelli momentarily reveals itself in *The Art of War*.

> Hence it follows where political powers are many, many able men appear; where such powers are few, few. . . . In Europe, excellent men are without number and we could list also many more if the malice of time had not destroyed their names. And even though in comparison with the Romans few others are named, that

---

The nation was consecrated and belief vouchsafed in the blood of brothers and sons. Compare to the consecration of Rome in the fratricide of Romulus and Brutus' execution of his own sons.

47

results from the malice of historians who follow fortune; usually they are satisfied to honor conquerors.[27]

Nothing could reveal more clearly the ambivalence of a politics founded upon the pursuit of glory (and what is true of the pursuit of glory among states is no less so within them). If Machiavelli preferred the republic because it expanded the avenues open to men who sought to be remembered, he was under few illusions regarding the nature of glory-seeking. If the republic maximized remembrance, glory remained a scarce good. Moreover, just as Rome's glory depended in part upon the eclipsing of other ancient republics, no less in memory than in fact, the greatness of one citizen stood in relation to the deeds of his fellow-citizens. Stability in the republic, even the integrity of the republic itself, depended upon keeping avenues open for the attainment of glory while containing its destructive potential. Part of Rome's genius lay in her ability to maximize opportunities for glory while balancing the glorious, one against another.

> For in time of war it availed itself of everybody in the city, whether they were nobles or not nobles, and in consequence there was always to be found in Rome at any given epoch so many virtuous men with various victories to their name that the people had no cause to be dubious in regard to any of them, since there were so many that one looked after the other.[28]

Getting modern man, be he prince or citizen, to seek true glory was a unique problem associated with the Christian creed of human impotence. The ancient problem had been something of the reverse: how to channel and contain the power and centrifugal force of a community of glory-seekers. Machiavelli saw both sides of the modern dilemma,

[27] *The Prince*, chapter 1; *Art of War*, p. 622.
[28] *Discourses*, I-30. In times of peace, republics often pass over outstanding men as a consequence of envy. Because Rome was always prepared for war, she kept her best men loyal by making "room for men of virtue."

the problems of both action and inaction. Modern proponents of action such as Arendt, in their effort to save action from an inhospitable modernity, ignore the problems that would immediately arise should they succeed. Arendt's choice of Periclean Athens as a model is instructive, for, as Plato knew too well, a city of Achilleses quickly destroys itself. For all of Machiavelli's augmenting of action, he remained a Socratic in his equal concern for the disintegrative character of the Periclean model. The choice of Rome as an alternative is important here.

Roman prudence comprehended the duality of the problem of action. A wise city provided avenues where glory might be pursued. This was especially necessary for a city that would make use of everyone. The thirst of a city's youth for a place in the sun must have its object if its youth is not to be turned against its parent. In his *Discourses*, Machiavelli directs the eyes of republican youth beyond the walls of the city, for a republic that shuns empire has less glory to distribute and thus must contend with the presence of noble but dangerously idle youth while depriving itself of the strength of the many. In this it approximates a principality which can only endure the glory of one. Hence, as Machiavelli begins to address "the young men who read what I have written," he leaves off his discussion of internal affairs and begins to speak of "the measures the Roman people took to increase their empire."[29]

The example of the founder is a perennial danger to the integrity of the republic. Cicero had reserved the highest glory for founders and preservers, but, as Machiavelli knew, that glory which shines brightest belongs to the founder alone. Men of *monumental* political ambition secretly wish not only to emulate but also to become "the father." Such men, if sometimes the saviors of their country, also pose a grave threat to the fatherland. The fratricidal example of Romulus is too well known.

[29] *Discourses*, II-Preface.

In the *Discourses*, a book whose aim is the integrity of republican government, Machiavelli is reticent about discussing the Roman founder. In the first chapter of Book I, Machiavelli promises to discuss the origin of Rome; however, by the end of that chapter we have been told only that Rome was founded in freedom and that, because of her origin, "great virtue was maintained for . . . many centuries." A more complete discussion is promised in I-9 in which Machiavelli confesses the unusual character of his method: "To some it will appear strange that I have got so far in my discussion of Roman history without having made any mention of the founders of that republic or of either its religious or military institutions." Machiavelli's reluctance is rooted in his fear of the Romulan example, fear which is now made explicit but put in the third person.

> Hence, that I may not keep the minds of those that are anxious to hear about such things any longer in suspense, let me say that many perchance will think it a bad precedent that the founder of a civic state, such as Romulus, should first have killed his brother, and then acquiesced in the death of Titus Tatius, the Sabine, whom he had chosen as his colleague in the kingdom. They will urge that, if such actions be justifiable, ambitious citizens, who are eager to govern, will follow the example of their prince.[30]

The remainder of the chapter seeks to "excuse" Romulus, but Machiavelli knows that this is insufficient. Men who seek glory above all things (those who are most "anxious" to hear of Romulus) care not for excuses. Thus, the very next chapter attempts to short-circuit the Romulan example through an indictment of tyrants, those who would imitate "their prince." Machiavelli's indictment is unusual in that it approaches the problem of tyranny through memory—whether actions will be praised or blamed; that is, it

[30] *Discourses*, I-9.

goes to the root of the problem of glory. The chapter begins with a distinction between those most deserving of praise, the founders of religions and states, and those most deserving of blame, the "infamous" and the "detestable" who "extirpate religion [and] subvert kingdoms and republics." This distinction, Machiavelli insists, is universally observed, for all men, be they "foolish or wise, wicked or good," will, if called upon, "praise the one that calls for praise, and blame the one that calls for blame." But no sooner has Machiavelli resolved the problem of glory than it emerges again in more stubborn guise: "And yet, notwithstanding this, almost all men, deceived by the false semblance of good and the false semblance of renown, allow themselves either wilfully or ignorantly to slip into the ranks of those who deserve blame rather than praise." Still, Machiavelli warns those who may be prone to such self-deception that the judgment of the future will affix praise and blame in just proportions; for it is not "possible for anyone . . . to read history and to make use of the records of ancient deeds, without preferring . . . to conduct himself in his fatherland rather as Scipio did than as Caesar did." History will remedy this false semblance of renown. It shows us unequivocally the fame of Scipio and the infamy of Caesar! But what kind of history is this? Machiavelli knows the weakness of his argument: "Nor should anyone be deceived by Caesar's renown" for "if anyone desires to know what writers would have said, had they been free, he has but to look at what they say of Cataline." But such writers are the chief architects of public memory, be they preservers of the deeds of patriots or apologists for tyrants. If both Caesar and Cataline are blame*worthy*, it remains true that Caesar enjoys almost universal renown while Cataline is universally despised. Despite Machiavelli's best rhetorical efforts, those who deserve praise are not easily distinguished by the judgment of the future from those who deserve blame. Thus, we are justly surprised when Machiavelli asserts "that every human being will [now] be afraid to imitate the bad times, and will be imbued with an ardent desire to emulate the good."[31]

The course of Machiavelli's argument has been tortured at best, more sophistic than real. But Machiavelli hopes he has left his readers "astonished and stunned" by these gymnastics. Only now does he dare to link the names of Romulus and Caesar, the one a founder and the other a destroyer of republics. In the course of the chapter, Machiavelli had sought to hide their similarities, and he has succeeded only by shifting the vantage point of his readers. Only from the perspective of the fatherland can Romulus be praised and Caesar blamed. By comparing bad times and good times, Machiavelli attempts to place his readers back within the city. He asks his readers to consider "in which he would rather be born." History, unaided, is unable to affix praise or blame. This is the city's prerogative. If the glory-seeker can be made to conceive of the city as the vessel of memory, he may moderate his pursuit within civic bounds. Chapter 10 ends with a warning, but a warning that only the city can make good.

> Let those to whom the heavens grant such opportunities reflect that two courses are open to them: either so to behave that in life they rest secure and in death become renowned, or so to behave that in life they are in continual straits, and in death leave behind an imperishable record of their infamy.[32]

History had proved at best ineffective (and at worst positively dangerous) in protecting the republic from citizens

[31] *Discourses*, I-10.

[32] *Discourses*, I-10. For an argument similar to that of *Discourses* I-10, see *The Art of War* (another book about republics), p. 575. In response to a question of Cosimo's regarding the fame of Caesar, Pompey, and Scipio, Fabrizio distinguishes between the glory of the "brave" and that of the "brave and good." Caesar's quest for glory was insatiable and thus not "good," while Scipio was content to be "famous enough." But it remains a dubious proposition that either men or states ever achieve "enough" glory.

who sought remembrance, for to the fratricidal example of Romulus was added that of Caesar. But another kind of history, one that would place the reader inside the city, might yet succeed. Bounded by the horizon of the city, human actions are judged by civic standards. Here, fame and infamy do indeed become imperishable. Machiavelli sketches the outlines of such a history in his *History of Florence*. In this regard, S. M. Shumer is correct in suggesting that the Florentine histories are, at least in part, an effort to limit and structure political action. Machiavelli tells us in the preface to his narrative that he will look primarily at things that have happened "inside" the city. The earlier historians of Florence had written almost exclusively of foreign affairs, that is, of events outside the city, and thus had not told a truly republican history.

> These historians did not remember that many who have not had opportunity to gain fame with praiseworthy deeds have striven to gain it with blameworthy actions, nor did they consider that conspicuous actions such as those of government and state, however they are carried on or whatever outcome they have, are always looked upon as bringing their doers honor rather than censure . . . [for] if the experiences of any republic are moving, those of a man's own city, when he reads about them, are much more moving and useful.

Republican histories place the citizen within the walls of his "own city" and bind him as a son is bound within the house of his father. Inside his father's house, the darkest truths about glory (that glory ultimately rests with success, that is, with conquerors, and that the highest glory is often founded upon a great irreverence) are more easily hidden from the eyes of the citizen.[33]

[33] Shumer, "Machiavelli—Republican Politics and Its Corruption," p. 19; *History of Florence*, pp. 1030-33. In fact, the intent of *The History of Florence* is open to question. These histories are addressed to two separate audiences—"the citizens" and those "free spirits" who might yet reform

Machiavelli would hedge round this strongest of human passions, not with the judgment of the future, but with the judgment of the past. Yet the burden of one's father's house remains a mysterious thing emerging out of the beginning but unexplained. The problem of glory is resolved, but only to reveal a mystery whose secret lies in the first things.

In the Beginning

Machiavelli's teaching in regard to republics resolves itself into a teaching of beginnings. But like that truth of which Machiavelli speaks in the Guicciardini letter, it is well concealed and "hard to find out." As we have seen, Machiavelli put off the discussion of the founding of Rome, but promised in I-9 to satisfy those who were in "suspense." However, a brief mention of the fratricide is followed only by the obfuscation of I-10 (fame and infamy). In I-11, Machiavelli resumes his discussion of early Rome, but with Numa, second king and founder of Rome's religion. Again he has failed to discuss the reign of Romulus. This is all the more surprising in that Livy, for whom Machiavelli pretends to be a commentator, shows great interest in and devotes much space to just this period. While Machiavelli is understandably reluctant to call attention to the fratricidal implications of the Roman founding, the fratricide is the only fact he chooses to reveal at all. Machiavelli is quite

---

Florence thoroughly. It might not be far from the truth to say that in his history are both sides of the Machiavellian personality, the patriot and the theorist, the loyal and the disobedient son. The author seeks to make known the "praiseworthy deeds" and "blameworthy actions" of Florence's citizens, but he also hints at a more radical reformation of the ancient flaws in the Florentine foundation. Later we shall have occasion to discuss this more "exalted" teaching. For our present purposes, the Florentine histories will be taken for what Machiavelli intended them to be for the majority of his readers, a history of a republic written for its citizens.

vocal in proclaiming the importance of beginnings and yet would tell us very little about such things.[34]

As in *The Prince*, Machiavelli begins the *Discourses* with a typology. This classification of cities is based upon their beginnings. Cities are built by either natives or foreigners, and these founders are either dependent or independent. Machiavelli quickly lays aside the first distinction in favor of the second, which seems a more fruitful tool of analysis. Rome was founded either by Aeneas, a foreigner, or by Romulus, a native, "but whichever be the case . . . it began as a free city, dependent upon no one." And those cities which are without freedom in the beginning rarely amount to much. A free beginning, Machiavelli insists, is critical but we are not told why. In a different context, however, Machiavelli discusses why a people accustomed to servitude can preserve their freedom only with difficulty. Machiavelli writes:

> That there should be such a difficulty is reasonable; for such a people differs in no wise from a wild animal which, though by nature fierce and accustomed to the woods, has been brought up in captivity and servitude and is thus loosed to rove the countryside at will, where, being unaccustomed to seeking its own food and discovering no place in which it can find refuge, it becomes the prey of the first comer who seeks to chain it up again.

Like Machiavelli's wild animal, a people raised in servitude are without a kind of knowledge through which they might preserve their freedom. If a free beginning contains such knowledge and preserves it for those who come after, Machiavelli has given us only its metaphoric content: that it is a kind of "food" and "refuge" for a people.[35]

Some commentators have seen the *Discourses* themselves

---

[34] Letter to Guicciardini, 17 May, 1521, p. 973; *Discourses*, I-1, I-2, II-1.
[35] *Discourses*, I-1, I-16.

as a kind of civic education, intended to give "the right knowledge." But if we pursue the conventional idea of political knowledge in the *Discourses*, the conclusions are startling. The Aristotelian teaching regarding popular wisdom was that the people could know things in general, but often erred in particular cases or in the application of general knowledge to particulars. Machiavelli seems to invert this teaching, suggesting that the people are wise in making particular choices, but err when generalizing from particulars. He then demonstrates the validity of this observation with an example from antiquity. The example pretends to show that while the populace of Capua hated the nobility in general and would have killed the entire Senate, they could not bring themselves to name particular plebians to replace individual senators. The ostensible conclusion is that while the people could not judge of the virtue of their own class and that of the nobility in general, they were quick to see virtue or the lack of it in particular men. But if we look more carefully at Machiavelli's example, we find that even the people's "knowledge" of particulars was the result of a ruse practiced upon them by Pacuvius Calavius. As if to call attention to the true meaning of this example, the very next chapter emphasizes the credulity and political naivete of the Roman people, and suggests that they were often and easily fooled. If the people seemed capable of recognizing individual virtue, they were often deceived in political things.[36]

In fact, Machiavelli has given us cause to doubt that knowledge plays any role in the activities of citizenship. Aristotle had sought, in the Socratic tradition, to base participation in ruling upon knowledge, and he justified popular participation with a kind of popular political knowledge, the wisdom of the multitude. Machiavelli replaces the knowing citizen with the armed citizen as the standard

---

[36] *Discourses*, I-47, I-48. In other examples, we find Machiavelli praising the utility of religion because of its ability to fool the people. For an account of the *Discourses* as civic education, see Whitfield, p. 17.

for participation. In basing participation upon the citizen armed, Machiavelli transforms the problem of popular government from one of knowledge to one of will. Citizenship is tied to a will-ingness to defend the fatherland. In the many examples of virtuous citizenship with which Machiavelli's works abound, citizens are praised for their "stubborn spirits" and obstinate characters. The good citizen becomes the stubborn citizen, but we are left wondering about the relation of free beginnings to a kind of knowledge that gives rise to such "stiff-necked" patriots.[37]

In a remarkable passage in *The Prince*, Machiavelli provides us with a clue. "In republics," he writes, "there is more life, more hate, greater longing for revenge; they are not permitted to rest—nor can they be—by the recollection of their ancient liberty." The sentence says much. We are told that in republics there is great energy; that this activity is related to the remembrance of an ancient liberty; and that this memory has a compelling quality which almost forbids citizens to rest. There is a principle of action here. Like glory, this activity is related to memory. But unlike glory, which links the present and the future, this activity unites the citizen with something in the past. Glory as action involves the seeker in contemplating the pleasing aspect of his own remembrance in future time. Here, Machiavelli is pointing to a kind of activity which emerges out of an ancient remembrance and binds the actor to this unforgotten past. While the posture of the glory-seeker is essentially egotistical or self-referential, the posture that accompanies this second kind of activity seems obligatory and reverential. The republic is best defined in the categories of political activity. Machiavelli is suggesting the existence of a second principle of action upon which the

[37] *History of Florence*, 1241-45, 1246-48. See also Strauss, p. 212. In Machiavelli's transforming the citizen from one who is knowledgeable to one who is will-ful is perhaps the seed of that more complete transformation in Rousseau, where citizenship is defined explicitly in categories of the will.

republic rests. Reverence exists in tension with glory. And while it is the source of activity itself, it operates as a kind of constraint upon glory, preventing its worst abuses. The secret desire of those who seek glory to supplant "the fathers" is repressed in the face of the reverential injunction to "honor thy father." In the context in which Machiavelli uses it here, reverence becomes a kind of activity when the honor of the fathers, or, more properly, the integrity of their legacy, comprehended as "ancient liberty," is violated. This principle in action is what Machiavelli understood as patriotism, the love of that which belonged to the fathers.[38]

[38] *The Prince*, chapter 5. We are reminded of the two Latin verbs for "acting" which Arendt has called to our attention. The first, *agere*, means to begin; to set in motion. The second, *gerere*, means to bear, with a connotation of obligation to one's predecessors. The first is self-referential, while the second has inescapably reverential overtones. See Arendt, *Between Past and Future*, p. 165, and *Human Condition*, p. 189. In her effort to save action, Arendt bases her analysis on the principle of *agere* alone, that is, on natality or new beginnings. In discarding the principle of *gerere*, she discards that which is in tension with natality and which seeks to contain the centrifugal quality of pure innovation in the man and in the state. In contrast, Machiavelli saw the need for a principle that would act as a counterpoise to glory.

Around the problem of containing glory is gathered that constellation of issues which together constitute Machiavelli's rebellion against the Socratic school. The birth of philosophy in ancient Greece followed and, in all likelihood, may have been rooted in the erosion of the earlier principle of political order: the good is the ancient. Reverence as a principle of restraint was already in radical decay; philosophy sought a new principle and found it in knowledge. Plato was particularly antagonistic to action, or, more correctly, to actions—the action of many men. By tying legitimate action to knowledge, Plato believed he could diminish political activity and thereby contain the centrifugal force of unbounded glory-seeking so characteristic of Periclean Athens. But the inevitable result of such a reduction in human action was the concomitant loss of the power generated by acting men (Arendt, *Human Condition*, pp. 199-207). The fragility of the civic fabric was all too apparent when the Platonic republic was forced to confront the problems posed by the external world, that is, by foreign power. Rome was the alternative model in that she had reached political maturity with the equation of the good and the ancient still intact. And unlike the principle of knowledge, which must deny action to the many, reverence, which can be taught, might contain the actions of the many without sacrificing their power. The possibilities of

Machiavelli's teaching regarding free beginnings now becomes more clear. Reverence is a kind of knowledge. It is a knowledge of the things of the fathers and of one's relation to such things. It teaches, comforts, and binds. As such, it is truly a "food" and a "refuge" for a people. A free beginning becomes a legacy bequeathed and, when threatened or stolen, the source of great hatred and vengeance. A city founded in dependence can only bequeath servility (and no one, not even sons, can revere a slave). Machiavelli's investigation into the nature of beginnings becomes a quest for the origins of reverence.

The great importance Machiavelli attaches to reverence and patria, and to their relationship to beginnings, only deepens the mystery that must surround Machiavelli's reluctance to speak about the nature of first things. But Machiavelli's reluctance does not prevent him from telling us something of beginnings. Consequently, we learn that "free cities are built by peoples who . . . are driven by pestilence or famine or war to abandon the land of their birth and to look for new habitation." This condition of homelessness closely parallels the condition we find with the destruction of cities, when "conquered cities are laid waste or their inhabitants driven out, their goods taken from them and they themselves sent wandering through the world." The end of cities gives rise to the preconditions for the founding of new ones, the dispossession and consequent homelessness of a people (the founding of Venice being a classic example). The common condition that all such people share is one of great fear: "Living in the midst of so many persecutions, men bore written in their eyes the terror of their spirits . . . [and] destitute of all aid and all hope, died

---

reverence are reflected in Machiavelli's great interest in foreign policy, in contrast to the ancients. The Machiavellian republic could generate sufficient power so that the external world might not remain simply a source of instability and decay, but might become instead the object of mastery. Machiavelli's great insight lay in his seeing in the Roman experience this potentiality.

wretchedly." We are also told that the knowledge or the memory of "this dread" kept military virtue and honor alive in ancient cities. While such observations remain fragmentary, Machiavelli seems to be saying that free cities are founded through the effort to escape great terror, and that the memory of this pre-political condition is related to the preservation of cities.[39]

Machiavelli's discussion of beginnings in the *Discourses* is radically incomplete, but he returns to the topic of origins again in the guise of a teaching about preservation in the first chapter of Book III. Unlike the first two books, this last book is unaided by preface. Machiavelli's resumption of the topic of origins remains guarded and without introduction. In the case of religions and states, "those changes make for their coservation which lead them back to their origins," or again, later, which "reduce them to their starting points." What follows is a short and ambiguous discussion of the "goodness" of beginnings, a characterization which is hardly borne out in Machiavelli's subsequent examples of such "returns." In Machiavelli's first example, he tells us that "it was necessary that Rome should be taken by the Gauls in order that it should be re-born and in its re-birth take on alike a new vitality and a new virtue." The second example Machiavelli cites is the execution of the sons of Brutus (the killing of sons by a father). While some of Machiavelli's examples of renovation are without violence or terror, of the seven examples which follow the sack of Rome by the Gauls, five involve spectacular executions. Our suppositions regarding the terror out of which cities are founded seem confirmed in Machiavelli's discussion of a return to origins. "Such events," says Machiavelli, "because of their unwonted severity and their notoriety, brought men back to the mark every time one of them happened." The character of such returns seems to be of the sort that would conjure up or bring back to memory

---

[39] *Discourses,* I-1; *Art of War,* p. 623; *History of Florence,* p. 1041.

the terror that was at the beginning. Finally, Machiavelli suggests that such human desolation is a necessary precondition to the founding of peoples and states.

> To show Moses' ability the people of Israel needed to be enslaved in Egypt, and to reveal Cyrus' greatness of spirit, the Persians needed to be oppressed by the Medes, and to exhibit Theseus' excellence the Athenians had to be scattered.

Machiavelli's language could not be more forceful. A people must be enslaved, oppressed, or scattered if the "opportunity" for political foundation is to arise. The association of beginnings with terror seems inescapable.[40]

Earlier, we had supposed that the origins of reverence lay among the first things. Our analysis of Machiavelli's discussions of the beginnings of cities revealed two things: that in the beginning there is terror and that such terror is a necessity in the founding of free states. We are left to wonder at the relationship between reverence and terror. Our suspicion that such a relationship exists is buttressed

---

[40] *Discourses*, III-1; *The Prince*, chapter 26; see also chapter 6. While the meaning of this teaching remains controversial, it can be said with some certainty that Machiavelli did not mean a return to the *form* of things as they once were. This is made clear in criticisms of the Gracchi, as well as in his discussion of the relation of institutions and laws to corruption. See *Discourses*, I-18.

As has been suggested earlier, Machiavelli is a writer with much to conceal. His highest teachings are often contained in his examples, which frequently suggest conclusions at considerable variance from their ostensible meaning. Commentators often fall victim to Machiavelli's rhetorical indirection. This is particularly true of Shumer's treatment of the doctrine of the return to first principles. Taking Machiavelli at his word about "the goodness" of beginnings, Shumer goes on to see the return to origins as a "return to an awareness of a common situation and a dedication to the openness and the need to choose who we are." Such terminology is foreign to Machiavelli's text. Moreover, the gentleness of Shumer's interpretation is part of a tradition that has sought to clean up Machiavelli. However, if Machiavelli's language is dark or full of violence and terror, we suspect that he saw such language as central to his teaching. Indeed, this language must be the starting point of any attempt to understand the meaning of a return to first principles.

by Machiavelli's discussion of Hannibal. In considering Hannibal's ability to unite men of diverse races, Machiavelli writes: "This could not have resulted from anything else than his well-known inhuman cruelty, which, together with his numberless abilities, made him always respected and terrible in the soldiers' eyes."[41]

In his discussion of the notion of the return to origins, Machiavelli suggests that the first such renovation occurred during the consulship of Brutus, that is, after the expulsion of the Tarquins and the founding of the republic. This first return involved a father executing his sons. Their crime was a twofold rebellion: a rebellion against their father and against the fatherland. In the broadest sense, their crime was that of irreverence. And it was "necessary," says Machiavelli, that they suffer the penalty of death.[42]

In Rome, reverence preceded freedom. The riddle of reverence and terror beckons us return to the time of the Roman kings. Machiavelli's striking muteness points toward Livy. Here, Livy's willingness contrasts sharply with Machiavellian reticence.

If a single and recurring theme can be extracted from "the period of the kings" in Livy's history, it is that of irreverence. The conquest of parents by children, the humiliation of fathers, and even the crime of patricide occur both before the founding of Rome and throughout the regal period, building to a crescendo in the tyranny of Superbus. The meaning, as well as the chronology, of the Roman monarchy is framed by the rule of Romulus in the begin-

[41] *The Prince*, chapter 17; see also the discussion of Valentino's execution of his cruel minister, where "the ferocity of this spectacle left those people at the same time gratified and awe-struck" (*The Prince*, chapter 7), and that of the cruelty of Severus, whose qualities "made him, in the sight of both the soldiers and the people, so remarkable that the latter continued to be, as it were, awe-struck and stupefied, and the former respectful and contented." Several pages later Machiavelli insists that it is the "methods" utilized by Severus that are "essential" in "founding" a state (*The Prince*, chapter 19).
[42] *Discourses*, III-3.

ning and that of Lucius Tarquinius Superbus in the end. It is appropriate that we should begin with Livy's remarkable narrative of the death of Romulus. Livy writes:

> Having accomplished these works deserving of immortality, while he was holding an assembly of the people for reviewing his army, in the plain near the Goat's pool, a storm suddenly came on, accompanied by loud thunder and lightning, and enveloped the king in so dense a mist, that it entirely hid him from the sight of the assembly. After this, Romulus was never seen again upon earth. The feeling of consternation having at length calmed down, and the weather having become clear and fine after so stormy a day, the Roman youth, seeing the royal seat empty—though they readily believed the words of the fathers who had stood nearest him, that he had been carried up to heaven by the storm—yet, struck as it were with the fear of being fatherless, for a considerable time preserved a sorrowful silence. Then, after a few had set the example, the whole multitude saluted Romulus as a god, the son of a god, the king and parent of the Roman city; they implored his favor with prayers, that with gracious kindness he would always preserve his offspring. . . . It is surprising . . . how much the regret of the common people and the army for the loss of Romulus was assuaged when the certainty of his immortality was confirmed.[43]

---

[43] Livius, pp. 18-19. Consider these Livian examples of the themes of fatherhood, irreverence, and patricide: Lavinium, the first of the Latin cities, is founded by Aeneas, a hero whose fatherland has been destroyed; Numitor, grandfather of Romulus and Remus, is deprived of his rightful title in Alba Longa by his brother, who thus violates the bequest of their father; after restoring their grandfather, Romulus and Remus desire to build a city that will make Alba and Lavinium (the cities of their fathers) "insignificant"; in need of women, the Romans abduct the daughters of the Sabines, leading to a war between fathers-in-law and sons-in-law. Romulus blames the affair on "the pride of their [the Sabine] fathers," a pride which is ultimately laid low by the Romans; all of the Roman kings

Livy has begun to reveal the meaning of the first terror. The Romans, Livy tells us, were afraid of being "fatherless." As Freud understood it, this fear originated in the child's helplessness, but Freud also knew that such fears were permanently sustained within the human personality by man's consciousness of "the superior (and often malevolent) power of fate." Machiavelli would push this fear back into the pre-political past. In insisting upon the necessity of desolation before a founding, Machiavelli hopes to give rise to a "longing for the father" among an entire people. Such desolation provides the founding father with his "opportunity." It is the terror of helplessness resulting from desolation that turns a people into what Machiavelli calls "matter" upon which one may "introduce a form," and it was slavery, Machiavelli tells us, that disposed the people of Israel to follow Moses. Without terror and desolation, a people will not be sufficiently malleable. Without the plasticity that originates in terror, the founder will be without his opportunity. That Romulus fulfilled the protective role of the father is evident in the people's prayers to him to "always preserve his offspring" and in the diminishing of their fear upon being convinced of "the certainty" of their father's immortality," that is, of his undying protection.[44]

The apotheosis of Romulus was the first act of Roman veneration. It was founded, in part, upon an affection which grew out of their deep need of his power. But Livy also reveals an ambivalence to that power. While the people believed "the words of the fathers" (that is, the senators) regarding Romulus' apotheosis, there was another account of the disappearance of the father of Rome: "I believe that

---

(except Numa, the founder of Roman religion and the only king Machiavelli discusses at length, and his grandson, Ancus) are killed or rumored killed by assassins who are themselves Roman, while Brutus, founder of the Republic, is slain by external enemies.

[44] Freud, *Civilization and Its Discontents*, pp. 19, 71-72. See also *Discourses*, I-1, and *The Prince*, chapters 6, 26.

even then there were some, who in secret were convinced that the king had been torn in pieces by the hands of the fathers—for this rumour also spread." Livy's dual account suggests an emotional ambivalence toward the figure of the founding father. Freud has made us familiar with such ambivalence. The son needs and yet resents the father's power. That power denies the son the fulfillment of his first primal desire, the frustration of which gives rise to the second: the desire to kill the father. Livy's narrative closely parallels Freud's psycho-anthropology. Because of his power, the ur-father was at once loved and hated, envied and feared. Out of hatred and envy, the father was killed and devoured by his sons. But no sooner had their hatred been gratified than the brothers were overcome with guilt and fear. Out of remorse for the deed and out of fear unleashed by their example, this band of patricidal brothers "created the restrictions which were intended to prevent a repetition of the deed. And since the inclination to aggressiveness against the father was repeated in the following generations, the sense of guilt, too, persisted."[45]

The origin of reverence, as Freud would have it, is the guilt suffered as a result of committing the ultimate act of irreverence. If the killing of Romulus was the deed of the fathers only, and thus a private crime, in the destruction of Alba the Roman people were made to share in the primordial crime and thus, presumably, in the consequent guilt also. Livy was well aware of the parricidal implications of the war.

---

[45] Livius, p. 19; Freud, *Civilization*, pp. 78-79, and *Totem and Taboo*, pp. 132, 141. That Machiavelli was familiar with such emotional ambivalence toward the power of father figures is clear from his discussion of the execution of Manlius Capitolinus. "Nor is it any wonder that the Roman populace wanted Manlius Capitolinus back when he was dead, for what they wanted was his virtues, which had been such that his memory evoked everyone's sympathy . . . [but] had Manlius, in response to this desire, been raised from the dead, the Roman populace would have passed on him the same sentence as it did, have had him arrested and, shortly after, have condemned him to death" (*Discourses*, I-58).

Preparations were made on both sides with the utmost vigor for a war very like a civil one, in a manner between parents and children, both being of Trojan stock: for from Troy came Lavinium, from Lavinium, Alba, and the Romans were descended from the stock of the Alban kings.[46]

The destruction of Alba is symbolic, involving not simply military defeat, but the leveling of the city and the forced transplantation of its population to Rome. In effect, Rome razes the house of its father, who is then compelled to live under the rule of the son.

Following the patricidal thread through the Livian narrative, we see its culmination in the rule of the Tarquins, their subsequent expulsion, and the consolidation of the consulate under Brutus. The Tarquins come to embody the primordial crime which is also the crime of Rome. Lucumo, the first of the Tarquins, is twice removed from the land of his fathers. He aspires and succeeds to the Roman throne primarily because he is driven by his wife, Tanaquil. A recurrent theme in Livy's discussion is the ambition of the Tarquin women and the pliancy of the Tarquin men. Within the family government of the Tarquins, the authority of the father is seriously eroded. This characteristic takes on monstrous proportions in Tullia, the granddaughter of the first Tarquin and wife of the last Tarquin, Lucius Tarquinius. Tullia goads her husband, whom she would have king, into rebellion against her own father, Servius Tullius. On his daughter's recommendation, Tullius is murdered.

On this occasion, a revolting and inhuman crime is said to have been committed, and the place bears record of it. They call it the wicked street, where Tullia . . . is said to have driven her chariot over her father's body, and to have carried a portion of the blood of her murdered father on her blood-stained chariot, herself

[46] Livius, p. 26.

also defiled and sprinkled with it, to her own and her husband's household gods, through whose vengeance results corresponding with the evil beginning of the reign were soon destined to follow.[47]

The royal house is literally polluted by the deed. The Tarquins, a family who on Livy's testimony "exhibited an example of tragic guilt," come finally to personify the guilt of the city. In Tarquin the Proud (Superbus), a patricide sits in the seat of the father. It is this rather than the subsequent crime of his son which destines the house of Tarquin for punishment. Because the Tarquins have embodied the guilt of Rome, they threaten to bring to memory that which of necessity must remain forgotten: the primordial crime and the dread of its repetition. Superbus is both father and the killer of fathers. His expulsion becomes at

---

[47] Livius, p. 57. In Livy's narrative of Roman irreverence, the story of Tullia is peculiar in that it portrays the patricide of a daughter. The account of Tullia points beyond the problem of sons to the problem of daughters and to more general difficulties with the principles of Roman authority. Even the otherwise frank Livy seems to understate the motives of the granddaughter of Tanaquil. If the Tarquin women wish their husbands kings, the ambition of Tanaquil/Tullia hides a deeper hatred and contempt of kings. Tullia's rage takes her beyond patricide to desecration, and it is difficult to judge whether she desires more the kingship for her husband or the destruction of her father. Both minister to her ambition, but her ferocity towards her father's corpse suggests a hatred of that authority which can never be hers. Unable to appropriate the substance of authority, Tullia's rage leads her to defile the husk. Such rage, in its white heat, consumes love and guilt alike and knows no fear, thus leaving little ground upon which a new authority might be erected. Tullia's entrance into public life is doubly terrifying, for it threatens to rend the very fabric of political society.

If the example of Tullia suggests the complexity of the Roman ambivalence towards the rule of one man, it was the prodigality of Roman patriotism that especially interested Machiavelli in his investigation into the origins of reverence and political authority. In the Tarquinian house, the Roman ambivalence toward the authority of kings threatened to become a rejection of the principle of authority itself. The expulsion of the Tarquins is a marvelously ambiguous act of reverence and irreverence, but it is more. It also indicates a political conclusion drawn by the Roman people: that kingship as a form of government is inadequate to the task of maintaining the structures of authority in a political order.

once an act of patricide and veneration—the public renunciation of the primordial crime and its secret celebration. In this last devouring of the father, the republic sanctifies paternal authority and restores the commands of reverence.[48] But with the treason of Brutus' sons, the crime of the Tarquins threatens, through its imitation, to pollute the republic as well. "The consulship," Livy writes, "imposed on the father the duty of punishing his own children." The example of their beheading was thus "a striking one . . . for the prevention of crime." So that "its repetition should bring no advantage," it was, indeed, necessary to kill "the Sons of Brutus."[49]

Embedded in the Livian narrative is a conception of political foundation which is rooted in the ambivalent relations of fathers and their "offspring." As history and myth, Livy's narrative preserves but conceals the dreadful origins of the state. Machiavelli, who claims to reveal the meaning of Livy, is denied the cloak of narrative and thus must leave the meaning of the Roman monarchy unspoken.[50]

[48] Livy makes explicit that the revolution wrought by Brutus involved not an assault upon authority, but rather its consolidation and rededication under the consulate. In Livy's words, "the first beginnings of liberty, however, one may date from this period, rather because the consular authority was made annual, than because the royal prerogative was in any way curtailed" (Livius, p. 72).

[49] This sense of "contagion" is quite evident in the treatment of the personal property of the deposed Superbus. Writes Livy: "The consideration of the restoration of the king's effects, for which the senate had formerly voted (prior to the conspiracy of the sons of Brutus), was laid anew before them. The fathers, overcome with indignation, expressly forbade either their restoration or confiscation. They were given to the people to be rifled, that, having been polluted [inoculated] as it were by participation in the royal plunder, they might lose forever all hopes of a reconciliation with the Tarquins." Livy also notes that the harvest from Tarquin's field was thrown into the Tiber, and then continues, "After the tyrant's effects had been plundered, the traitors were condemned and the punishment inflicted" (Livius, pp. 76-77).

[50] While Machiavelli refuses to address directly the deed of patricide, he reveals his understanding of Livy's teaching in several ways. He quotes favorably Livy's "Rome meanwhile grows on the ruins of Alba," but remains silent about that which Livy saw fit to make explicit, Rome's parricide in reducing Alba. In addition to his insistence on the necessity of killing the sons of Brutus, Machiavelli makes the killing of sons and

In Livy, Machiavelli sees not simply an account of the foundation of Rome, but the true origins of all political societies. For Machiavelli, it is anthropological fact as well as theoretical necessity that states are the work of one man. In the eyes of a people, the founder must necessarily appear ambivalent. The vision of the founder is his own. Political creation, Machiavelli insists, is an aesthetic act. In *The Prince*, a book about political aesthetics, Machiavelli says of the greatest founders that Fortune offered "nothing more than opportunity, which gave them matter into which they could introduce whatever form they chose." But unlike the founder in Plato's *Politikos*, Machiavelli does not conceal the terrible necessity of political creation. If the founder is a "redeemer" who is greeted with love, loyalty, devotion, obedience, and homage, he, "above all other princes, cannot escape being called cruel." Fear and reverence are inextricably bound up together in the image of the founder. The emotional ambivalence of a people toward its founder corresponds to his political role. Norman Jacobson sees Machiavelli as teaching in the *Discourses* the necessity of political patricide. In *The Prince*, Machiavelli sees in the murder of the prince the proof, as it were, of the soundness of his creation. It is necessary that the founder both create the state and be devoured by it.[51]

---

the veneration of fathers the quintessential act of citizenship (*Discourses*, I-16, III-22, III-34). Finally, Machiavelli is familiar with the emotional ambivalence involved with powerful father figures. While the Romans, Machiavelli tells us, "hated the name of kings for centuries," they reinvested the consulate with paternal authority. What they hated was the name, not the power, for the name had become soiled with a crime they themselves, of necessity, had to forget. That this hatred lasted for centuries bespeaks a secret fear of that which the Romans sought to repress in themselves. While this reading of Machiavelli remains highly speculative, it is not without some textual warrant, both in Machiavelli and in Livy. Moreover, we believe this reading to be productive of insights into areas of Machiavelli's thought which have heretofore been insufficiently accounted for, particularly the relations of founders to their peoples and the origins of republics.

[51] *Discourses*, I-2, I-9; *The Prince*, chapters 6, 7, 17, 19, 26 (see also chapter 3, in which Machiavelli warns that a new prince will always offend his subjects); Jacobson, *Pride and Solace*, p. 44.

In Livy's account of the origin of the Roman republic, Machiavelli discerns the origins of all republics. In the beginning, political authority is indistinguishable from paternal authority. Founders are invariably the fathers of their people. Kingdoms are older than republics.[52] All republics are, of necessity, founded through an act of irreverence. In the beginnings of all republics lies a forgotten patricide. Machiavelli's silence concerning the killing of fathers (a kind of literary amnesia) is in keeping with his method in the *Discourses*, which is republican not only in content and sentiment, but also in its psychology. The republic is, nonetheless, the political expression of a "band of brothers" who have discovered the power of numbers. Republics are founded in the fraternity of the struggle and preserved by the collective guilt of the fraternal deed. The authority of the father becomes their punishment as reverence is its injunction. The preservation of his legacy becomes their penance, and "they are not permitted to rest—nor can they be" by the recollection of that authority. It is upon this forgotten secret that the constancy of the people is founded. Once the people have begun to love something, says Machiavelli, they continue to love it for centuries. In the devouring of the father, the father's creation is vouchsafed, for the people then become the repository of authority and of ancient things. Hence there is great irony in Machiavelli's advice to founders, for his teaching is oracular: "For men forget more quickly the death of their fathers than the loss of their patrimony."[53]

---

[52] *Discourses*, I-2. Machiavelli is unclear as to whether the first kings were in fact fathers or whether their authority simply was founded on paternal principles. He does make clear, however, that the state emerged through the need for protection, and that such protection was sought in the person of some *one* who was "stronger and more courageous than the rest."

[53] Freud, *Civilization*, pp. 47, 79, and *Totem and Taboo*, p. 146; Strauss, p. 130; *The Prince*, chapter 5; *Discourses*, I-58; *The Prince*, chapter 17. Compare this advice to the Delphic prophecy given to the sons of Superbus and recorded by Livy: "Young men, whichever of you shall first kiss his mother shall enjoy the sovereign power at Rome" (Livius, p. 66). Mach-

Founding Knowledge

The ancient cities had been the works of chance or of a singular virtue. As such, they lacked a true understanding of their origins. Classical political philosophy fared little better in this realm than ancient practice. Even Plato, who delved most deeply into the problems of foundation, was forced to establish his imagined republic upon the fortuitous coalescence of philosophy and power. As the previous discussion sought to demonstrate, republics in particular were necessarily unselfconscious about the true nature of their beginnings. Reverence forbade such knowledge. To the extent that republics like Rome cultivated a knowledge of the first things, the spirit which animated such inquiry was the effort to maintain the equation of the ancient and the good. Writers such as Cato sought at most to forestall or retard the advent of corruption; thus, their knowledge of origins was put in the service of the preservation rather than the founding of republics.[54]

In Machiavelli's time, the ancient republic had long since disappeared, and those republics which still existed were in decline or perennially suffering under the legacy of a bad beginning. If republican politics was to share in the renaissance of things ancient, it required a new understanding of beginnings. Fortune, herself ill-inclined to aid in such a rebirth, must be forced, Machiavelli thought, by a science of foundation. But such a science was something of a paradox, full of difficulties for the republican and dangers for the republic. The preservation of the republic rested upon the equation of the ancient and the good, and yet at the foundation of all states lay a great innovation. Machiavelli well knew that a science of political innovation would serve equally the purposes of those who would destroy

---

iavelli's advice and the oracle's prophecy are interesting complements. Both are concerned with the securing of patrimony, and, as Delphic Apollo speaks of the kissing of mothers, Machiavelli speaks of the forgetting of fathers.

[54] *Discourses*, I-2; Strauss, p. 116.

republics as well as those who would found them. But Machiavelli understood more: that political foundation necessarily involved the destruction of ancient things. The knowledge of the beginnings of republics, the highest knowledge of republics, was, paradoxically, too exalted for republics. In the *Discourses*, a book about the preservation of republics, Machiavelli seeks to preserve the equation of the ancient and the good, and thus speaks of innovation only with reluctance. *The Prince* (which is really a discussion of "the new prince") is about the founding of republics as well as kingdoms, and here Machiavelli speaks endlessly of innovation. The knowledge of citizens teaches how to preserve ancient things. The knowledge of founders teaches how to destroy them.[55]

Such a science is fraught with uncertainties, not the least of which is: for whom is the study of such a science appropriate? Machiavelli would be like Chiron, the Centaur, teaching latter-day Achilleses the foreboding truths of political foundation. Such sons as were given over to Chiron were taught how to be half-man and half-beast. This was knowledge that was not possessed by fathers and that was ultimately irreverent. But who is suited to this knowledge of irreverence? How is Machiavelli to know such students? Such men are "of outstanding brain-power and authority . . . and such men are rare." Lacking the perspicaciousness that accompanies personal instruction or the seclusion of Chiron's cave, Machiavelli sought that limited discretion that is afforded by the covers that separate volumes. In the *Discourses*, Machiavelli makes clear how inappropriate this knowledge would be for such a volume and reserves discussion of it "for a more convenient place": "How dangerous it is to take the lead in a new enterprise in which many may be concerned, and how difficult it is to handle and direct it, and once on its way to keep it going, would be too long and too deep a topic for us to discuss here."

[55] Strauss, pp. 60, 70; Pocock, *Machiavellian Moment*, p. 158.

But even in *The Prince*, Machiavelli would dissuade those not truly suited for the task, warning that "it should be kept in mind that there is nothing more difficult to carry out nor more doubtful of success nor more dangerous to manage than to introduce a new system of things." That history has too often linked the name of Machiavelli with evil testifies to his limited success in this enterprise of discretion. Teaching from afar, and yet faced with what seemed the necessity, even the urgency, of such knowledge, Machiavelli spoke about political foundation with an openness perhaps unequaled before or since.[56]

If it may be said that the knowledge of political preservation involves the maintenance or enhancement of political memory, the knowledge of political foundation is the art of political amnesia. To found a state is to start again at the beginning. The political timepiece is reset and ticks off the first minute. Political time begins with the foundation and other times are forgotten or are taken *out of time*, their events disembodied and seemingly unrelated to living men.[57]

In the *Discourses*, a book whose form and content are about remembrance, Machiavelli treats the nature of forgetting in only one chapter (II-5), and this with an air of incongruity about it. Of oblivion, Machiavelli says:

The records of times gone by are obliterated by diverse causes, of which some are due to men and some to

---

[56] *Discourses*, I-53, III-35; *The Prince*, chapter 5.

[57] Rousseau, no mean student of the problems of foundation, was aware of the importance of political amnesia and political time. In his *Social Contract*, he writes: "Just as men's minds are unhinged and their memory of the past erased by some illnesses, so there sometimes occur during the lifetime of States violent periods when revolutions have the same effect on peoples as do certain crises on individuals; when horror of the past is equivalent to amnesia, and when the State, set afire by civil wars, is reborn so to speak from its ashes and resumes the vigor of youth by escaping from death's clutches. Sparta in the time of Lycurgus and Rome after the Tarquins were like this" (Rousseau, *On The Social Contract*, pp. 70-71).

heaven. . . . The causes due to heaven are those which wipe out a whole race and reduce the inhabitants in certain parts of the world to but a few. This is brought about by pestilence or by famine or by flood and of these the most important is the last alike because it is more widespread and because those who survive are all of them rude mountaineers who have no knowledge of antiquity and so cannot hand it down to posterity. . . . That these floods, pestilences and famines happen, I do not think anyone can doubt, for plenty of them are recorded everywhere in history, their effect in obliterating the past is plain to see.[58]

Of the causes due to heaven, Machiavelli lists three: pestilence, famine, and flood, the last of which, Machiavelli asserts, is the most important because of the extent and character of the obliteration it causes. We are then told that history records many such instances of these catastrophes and that their obliterating effects are "plain to see." Now, while there have been many incidences of pestilence and famine recorded by history, there has been only one flood which corresponds to Machiavelli's description. And while famine and pestilence are great catastrophes, their effect in obliterating the past is not necessarily plain to see. For Machiavelli, the flood (which need not have happened at all) is a metaphor for catastrophe and is useful precisely because it makes "plain" what would not be plain otherwise, the relation of forgetting to catastrophe.

Excluding flood, we are left with pestilence and famine which, we recall, were linked together earlier (*Discourses* I-1) and were accompanied by war. This earlier trilogy forced peoples "to abandon the land of their birth" and to build new cities. And it is such peoples, says Machiavelli, who build "free cities." We also discovered that it was the desolation of such catastrophes that gave founders their "opportunity." We now see that catastrophes are accompanied

[58] *Discourses*, II-5.

by a *forgetting*, and we suspect that such amnesia plays a role in making a people suitable material for a founder. We also are now able to clarify that first distinction pertaining to beginnings that Machiavelli seems to discard: whether a city is founded by natives or by foreigners. Foundings are preceded by a forgetting. If some peoples must literally abandon the land of their fathers and be condemned to wander, natives who have forgotten their fathers are also, metaphorically speaking, cast out into the world and forced to wander. Machiavelli uses the distinction to call attention to the foreign quality of a new people and to "the leaving" or wandering that precedes all foundations.[59]

The trilogy of pestilence, famine, and war includes things human and divine, for if pestilence and famine are the chastisements of God, it is through war that men chastise one another. Of the human causes of obliteration, Machiavelli names two in *Discourses* II-5, "changes in religious institutions and in language." At first appraisal, these seem quite different from "war." Even Machiavelli's example of the Christian assault on pagan theology is at best ideological war and bears little resemblance to the sense of desolation conveyed in chapter I-1. But in *The History of Florence*, we find changes in religion and language unified in a vision of war. Here, we discover what for Machiavelli was both the paradigmatic example of the human causes of forgetting and the only looking glass in which he could see the beginnings of cities. This was the single most traumatic series of events in the political and psychic history of western civilization, the barbarian invasions and the fall of Rome. It was this vision of "so many persecutions [where] men bore written in their eyes the terror of their spirits" that informed Machiavelli's search for a science of political foundation. It was also there that Machiavelli discovered the political implications of desolation and uprootedness.

---

[59] *Discourses*, I-1; Harvey Mansfield, Jr., "Necessity in the Beginnings of Cities," in Parel, p. 110.

The power that this image had for Machiavelli is captured in his prose.

> In those times Italy and the other Roman provinces suffered, for they not merely changed their government and their Prince, but their laws, their customs, their way of living, their religion, their speech, their dress, their names. . . . [And] in addition to the countless ills they suffered, a good part of them lacked the power to flee for aid to God, in which all the wretched are wont to hope, because the greater part of them, uncertain to what god they ought to turn, destitute of all aid and all hope, died wretchedly.[60]

This was the time of the great forgetting, the human equivalent of the Great Flood, when quite literally everything that had belonged to men and had once belonged to their fathers—their gods, their lands, their laws, their language, their culture, even their names—was taken from them. And as if to emphasize the political lessons contained in this profound deracination of western man, Machiavelli concludes:

> Individually and still more in total these things when merely thought about and not seen and suffered, are enough to terrify the firmest and steadiest mind. From this came the destruction, the origin and the expansion of many cities.

[60] *History of Florence*, pp. 1040-41. To call added attention to the role of language in obliterating the classical memory of western man, Machiavelli writes: "Among these ruins and these new peoples originated new tongues, as appears in the languages now used in France, in Spain, and in Italy; these are mixtures of the native languages of these new peoples and the ancient Roman, that make a new sort of speech. Besides this, not merely have the provinces changed their names, but so have the lakes, the rivers, the seas, and the men, for France, Italy, and Spain are full of names that are new and wholly unlike the ancient ones." Machiavelli seems to be saying that when things cannot be named they cannot be preserved or passed on, and thus are consigned to oblivion. In this regard, changes in language, much more than changes in religion, seem to be the most powerful cause of forgetting.

All this remains unspoken in *Discourses* II-5, the language of which is gentle and unassuming. And while Machiavelli speaks of the founders of religion and of the obliteration of the past, the relationship between political foundation and forgetting is not made explicit. Instead, Machiavelli offers a "reasonable" account of why forgetting is a good thing, drawing on an organic analogy.

> As in the case of simple bodies, when nature has accumulated too much superfluous material, it frequently acts in the same way and by means of a purge restores health to the body. Similarly in the case of that body which comprises a mixture of human races, when every province is replete with inhabitants who can neither obtain a livelihood nor move elsewhere since all other places are occupied and full up, and when the craftiness and malignity of man has gone as far as it can go, the world must needs be purged in one of these three ways (famine, pestilence, or flood), so that mankind being reduced to comparatively few and humbled by adversity, may adopt a more appropriate form of life and grow better.

Machiavelli began this chapter by noting that the causes of forgetting are both human and divine. As he nears the end, he himself seems to have forgotten about human causes and speaks only of divine ones. This last passage begins with the suggestion that to forget is a good thing, because it purges old memories which have become "superfluous," much like bodily waste. Falling then into a providential argument and using imagery reminiscent of the discussion in Genesis of the necessity of the Flood, Machiavelli describes a world filled with too many people and too great an evil, and which consequently "must needs be purged." Machiavelli has used analogy well, but the careful reader will observe his deception. Memory, unlike the world (or the body), is never "full up." To be sure, forgetting is often necessary if human beings are to "adopt a more appropriate form of life," but this is a *political* necessity. Here, however, Machiavelli has linked such necessity with divine causes only—those outside the control of men. He has chosen to "forget" about the human causes of forgetting, and has disguised the political necessity of such amnesia in the language of divine necessity. But unwilling to conclude without leaving a clue to his real teaching, Machiavelli writes:

> There was, then, as we have said above, a time when Tuscany was a powerful country, full of religion and of virtue, with its own customs and its own language, all of which we know was wiped out by the power of Rome, so that of it, as has been said, there remains naught but the remembrance of its name.

The memory of Tuscany was obliterated, not by heaven, but at the hands of men. This knowledge, which is carefully concealed in the *Discourses*, is made explicit in *The Prince*. If a knowledge of the human causes of forgetting is dangerous to republics, whose preservation is founded upon remembrance, such a knowledge is central to those who would found political societies and begin political time anew.[61]

Machiavelli's teaching on the nature of political memory and the methods by which it may be destroyed is contained in the first part of *The Prince*. In the first chapter, Machiavelli begins with a taxonomy of states, the principle of which, it soon becomes clear, is the peculiar character of a state's political memory. The implications of this taxonomy are developed in chapters 2 through 5.[62] Chapter 2 is at once

---

[61] *Discourses*, II-5.

[62] Pocock sees in this first section of *The Prince* a discussion of the relation of the new prince's power to the customary structure of society (*Machiavellian Moment*, pp. 156-82). In this section, Machiavelli speaks of ancestral practices both as custom and as recollection. What Pocock would combine under the heading customary structure, however, we would differentiate. While a full discussion of this difficulty must await our treatment of Burke, suffice it to say that custom involves *behavior* whose beginning is by definition "out of memory," while political memory in-

advice to hereditary princes and a warning to those who would despose them. In "the remote origin and long continuance" of such sovereignty, the subjects of the hereditary prince remember only his family and "naturally . . . wish him well," provided he refrains from transgressing "the customs of his forefathers." In mixed princedoms, that is, in conquered dominions "acquired [and] united to an old state belonging to him who gains them," the new dominions "are either in the same region and of the same language or they are not." When the conqueror and the conquered share the same language and political culture, the new prince "needs only to wipe out the line of the prince who was ruling them" and leave them in "other things" undisturbed, and men will "continue to live quietly." But, Machiavelli warns, "when new states are conquered in a province different in language, customs and institutions, then difficulties arise" and new princes are advised to go and live there or send colonies. In other words, if the language, customs, and institutions of the conquered dominion are different from those of the new prince, his new laws and institutions, his very language, bring to memory daily a more ancient way of life which not only denies his regime legitimacy, but also is the source of perennial disorder. The best solution involves some kind of cultural hegemony that will eventually erase the memory of his innovation (presumably through a process of cultural amalgam).

Chapter 4 contains a variation on the theme of the hereditary ruler as the vessel of memory, which we see emerge in chapters 2 and 3. In this chapter, Machiavelli makes his famous contrast between the Turkish sultanate, where one

volves the remembrance of the *actions* of men, the most important of which are the first actions or the beginning. Pocock is not without some justification, particularly in regard to chapter 2, in which the description of the old way of life is characteristically customary, but increasingly, through chapters 3, 4, and 5, the active memory of an ancient past clearly replaces the immemorial character of ancestral practice as the factor which inhibits new princes in becoming "secure possessors."

need only kill the sultan and extinguish his family line, and "states organized like that of France," where the hereditary rule of numerous families in as many provinces makes such extinguishing impractical and whose continued presence is thus always a source of rebellion. Such dominions, says Machiavelli with an economy of statement characteristic of *The Prince*, "can be held only with great difficulty."

> This was the cause of the numerous revolts of Spain, of Gaul, and of Greece against the Romans, resulting from the numerous princedoms in those lands; for as long as there continued any tradition of them, always because of it the Romans were uncertain in their possession; but when that tradition was wiped out by the power and permanence of the Empire, they became secure possessors there.[63]

We come finally to chapter 5. Its title is more revealing than those that have preceded it: "How States Or Principalities Are To Be Managed That, Before They Were Conquered, Lived Under Their Own Laws." This chapter is a discussion of the most extreme case in which ancient memories impinge upon the new prince; it is thus most revealing of the nature of political memory in general, and the culmination of that line of argument which Machiavelli began in chapter 2. But chapter 5 is also a comparison of the nature of political memory in free cities with that of cities unaccustomed to freedom; thus, it is in sharp contrast to the three preceding chapters. Machiavelli begins by arguing that there are three ways to hold such cities: "The first: lay them waste. The second: go to dwell there in person. The third: let them live under their own laws," being satisfied with tribute. But these last two are quickly discarded.

> Because in truth there is no certain way for holding such states except destruction. And he who becomes master of a city used to being free and does not destroy

[63] *The Prince*, chapter 4.

her can expect to be destroyed by her, because always she has as a pretext in rebellion the name of liberty and her old customs, which never through either length of time or benefits are forgotten. And in spite of anything that can be done or foreseen, unless citizens are disunited or dispersed, they do not forget that name and those institutions, and in any emergency instantly they run back to them.[64]

In principalities, political memory is contained in the person of the prince, or, more correctly, in his family line. Blood is the means through which the past and the present are united. The hereditary rulers of such states are, in a sense, the vessels of their communities' collective memory. In all such situations, Machiavelli advises the new prince to wipe out the family line, for, without a living representative of their historic rulers to embody the nation, the people of such a community seem literally to forget who they are. In republics, political memory is not nearly so fragile. The memory of their ancient institutions is somehow etched into the minds of every citizen, impervious to the benevolence of princes or the ravages of time, passed on from father to son even in the face of tyranny. Freedom,

[64] *The Prince*, chapter 5. The power of political memory is eloquently described in *The History of Florence* in the speech of a Florentine signor to the Duke of Athens (and soon to be tyrant of Florence): "You seek to make a slave of a city that has always lived free. . . . Have you considered how important and how strong in a city like this is the name of liberty, which no force crushes, no time wears away, and no gain counterbalances? . . . That there is not time enough for destroying our desire for liberty is most certain, because in a city one often sees it taken up again by men who never have experienced it, but merely because of the tradition their fathers have left them, they continue to love it; therefore when it has been regained, with the utmost stubbornness and peril they preserve it. And even if their fathers have not recalled it, the public buildings, the offices of the magistrates, the insignia of the free organizations recall it. Of a certainty the citizens will perceive the meaning of these things with the utmost longing" (p. 1123). If the people of Florence proceeded to give up their state to the Duke, it only demonstrated what Machiavelli already knew, that Florence suffered from radical dysfunctions in her political memory.

the legacy of the first father, is never forgotten, but leaves an indelible mark, extending and deepening political memory until it is the consciousness of a whole people. In such a city, the streets, the walls, the public buildings, the names are all teachers of rebellion, so much so that this passage also contains a grave warning, perhaps the most grave of any uttered by Machiavelli, and intended to impress upon the prince an equally grave necessity: "And he who becomes master of a city used to being free and does not destroy her can expect to be destroyed by her."

In some rare advice offered to the new prince in the *Discourses*, Machiavelli clarifies the meaning of this awful necessity.

> The best thing he can do . . . , given that he be a new prince, is to organize everything in that state afresh; e.g. in its cities to appoint new governors, with new titles and new authority, the governors themselves being new men; to make the rich poor and the poor rich, as well as to build new cities, to destroy those already built, and to move the inhabitants from one place to another far distant from it. . . . His aim should be to emulate Philip of Macedon . . . [of whom] a writer says that he moved men from province to province as shepherds move their sheep.

The new prince who would be a true founder must destroy the political memory of his people. Particularly in the case of cities accustomed to living in freedom, the new prince must, like those great catastrophes which are his teachers, take from men all that is theirs, leave nothing to which memory might attach itself, and force them to leave the land of their birth and wander again, to establish new cities in new places with new names. Machiavelli himself seems to recoil from the terrible logic of his argument: "It behooves, therefore, every man to shun [such methods], and to prefer rather to live as a private citizen than as a king with such ruination of men to his score."[65]

[65] *Discourses*, I-26; see also II-23.

In later chapters (6 and 26), the architectonic quality of intentional desolation is modified but not abrogated. In these chapters, Machiavelli emphasizes that, if the founder is to be given his opportunity, a fortuitous desolation prior to the appearance of the founder is necessary. If the founder desolates, he must first have material that is malleable, an anomic people whose memories are in disarray. The ruling image becomes that of Moses, for whom "it was necessary . . . that the people of Israel be in Egypt, enslaved and downtrodden by the Egyptians, so that to escape from bondage they would prepare their minds for following him," but who also, to establish his new law and cause the people of Israel to "forget" their golden calf, unleashed the swords of Levi upon them and forced them to wander in the wilderness a full forty years until all of that "evil generation" were gone.

The founder is, above all, the master of the knowledge of memory. And if he conceals and distorts the past "in his own fashion so as to establish his own reputation, . . . the result [is] that there will remain to his successors just so much as he has chosen to record and nothing more." In his effort to assure his own glory, the founder uses the knowledge of remembering and forgetting to erase or to make horrid that which came before him. As such, the founder is, if often unwittingly, the benefactor of civilization, allowing it to "adopt a more appropriate form of life and grow better."[66]

---

[66] *Discourses*, II-5. See also Freud, *Civilization*, pp. 15-16, 46, and *Totem and Taboo*, pp. 18, 21, 25, 30. In Freudian terms, the founder becomes the agent of collective psychic repression and its accompanying amnesia. It is significant that only after the "evil generation" had died out, but before the Israelites entered the land of the Promise, Moses made known to his people that which could not be touched. The Israelites had never completely forgotten their totemic calf, but the holy dread inspired by Moses transformed that memory from something sacred into something unclean. What had been a god had become a demon.

Machiavelli's example of the Flood portrays men who are without a "memory trace" of the past, and thus have not truly forgotten for they had never remembered. But the accompanying examples of lesser catastrophe are indeed about men who have known and then repressed a past. Such discussions are quite similar to Freud's understanding of the phe-

The grand claims of Machiavelli's new science of political foundation found inspiration in the Mosaic "dream of a nation of warriors wrought from a dejected multitude of slaves." If other republican theorists had sought through remembrance to preserve an ancient virtue, Machiavelli's investigations into the nature and origin of memory and oblivion revealed what he thought to be the very source of virtue and corruption itself. Armed with this knowledge, the Machiavellian theorist could see in the malaise of emergent modernity hope where there had been only despair and opportunity in what once had seemed but decay.[67]

Virtue, Corruption, and Remembrance

"Those who read of the origin of the city of Rome, of its legislators and its constitution, will not be surprised that in this city such great virtue was maintained for so many centuries." With these words Machiavelli opens his *Discourses*. The character of a city's virtue, as well as the longevity of that virtue, depends upon her beginnings. This is the first principle of the *Discourses*, the first chapter of which begins with a distinction: there are two kinds of cities, "free cities" and those that "are not at the outset free . . . [and] it was thus that Florence came to be built." At the beginning of the next chapter, Machiavelli delimits his inquiry.

---

nomenon of "organic repression." Freud's investigations into the nature of repression are suggestive in regard to the mental processes by which things are at once forgotten and yet preserved in ritual or through some inverted form. In many ways, this dialectic of memory and amnesia parallels Machiavelli's equally complex discussions of the relation of remembering and forgetting to the founding and preserving of political societies. Finally, however else they differ, Freud and Machiavelli share a recognition of the necessity of forgetting as well as remembering as the foundation of human improvement.

[67] Jacobson, p. 31. For discussions and examples of the relation of virtue and corruption to remembering and forgetting, see *The Prince*, chapters 6, 11, 12, and *Discourses*, II-11, II-19.

I propose to dispense with a discussion of cities which from the outset have been subject to another power, and shall speak only of those which have from the outset been far removed from any kind of external servitude, but instead, have from the start been governed in accordance with their wishes, whether as republics or principalities.

That the *Discourses* concerns itself with cities that were in the beginning free and that Florence is not such a city suggests a relationship between the *Discourses* and *The History of Florence*. Although multifaceted, the fundamental relationship between the two works involves the complementary investigations into the source of virtue and the source of corruption in republics; ancient Rome and modern Florence are exemplary in this regard.[68]

This contrast between ancient Rome and modern Florence is muted somewhat by Machiavelli's great affection for his native city and by his desire "to please everyone," but if *The History of Florence* is composed by a loyal son, its critique remains necessarily a radical one, for the Florentines are a people "who cannot keep their liberty, and yet cannot endure servitude." While Machiavelli offers no commentary on this observation in the Florentine histories, he had said in the *Discourses* that, among a people who were not suited to the civic life of either a monarchy or a republic, all things should be made new. In *A Discourse on Remodeling the Government of Florence*, Machiavelli is more blunt: "When things are not well-organized, the less there

---

[68] *Discourses*, I-1, I-2. Machiavelli hints at such a comparison in his history: "And if describing the things that have happened in this corrupt world, I do not tell of the bravery of soldiers or the efficiency of generals or the love of citizens for their country, I do show with what deceptions, with what tricks and schemes, the princes, the soldiers, the heads of republics, in order to keep that reputation which they did not deserve, carried on their affairs. It is perhaps as useful to observe these things as to learn ancient history, because if the latter kindles free spirits to imitation, the former will kindle such spirits to avoid and get rid of such abuses" (*History of Florence*, p. 1233).

is left of the old, the less there is left of the bad." Florence
had suffered as a result of her servile beginnings, plagued
by political instability. Florentine social structure had become suited to a republic, having decimated her nobility
and grown increasingly egalitarian, but she stood in need
of radical reordering and a wise lawgiver.[69]
In the Preface to *The History of Florence*, after faulting his
predecessors for not dealing adequately with "civil strife
and internal hostilities, and the effects these have produced," Machiavelli reveals his intentions.

> If any reading is useful to citizens who govern repub-
> lics, it is that which shows the causes of hatreds and
> factional struggles within the city, in order that such
> citizens, having grown wise with the suffering of others,
> can keep themselves united.[70]

The political disease from which Florence suffered is well
known to republican thinkers ancient and modern, and it
is at the center of their discussions of political decay. It is
the problem of faction. Traditionally, and in the broadest
of terms, faction has indicated a condition of disunity under
which groups of citizens seek a private good or the good
of a part rather than the common good or the good of the
whole.
In promising to reveal the causes of such corruption,
Machiavelli anticipates his argument, hinting that faction-
alism is related to internal "hatreds." Machiavelli speaks
often of love and hate, and of particular interest to him is

---

[69] *History of Florence*, pp. 1030, 1128, 1138, 1141, 1147; *Discourses*, I-26
(see also I-55); *A Discourse on Remodeling the Government of Florence*, p. 107.
Having great affection for his native land, Machiavelli is at pains to record
that which was best in Florence's past: her potential for greatness, her
good military and civic institutions, and citizens with "great nobility of
mind" (pp. 1086, 1283). While in the *Discourses* Machiavelli frankly admits
the servility of Florentine origins, in the Histories these origins are left
in doubt (p. 1081). Nonetheless, he is compelled to recall Florence at her
worst, a world without courage, virtue, or patriotism. See also Harvey
Mansfield, Jr., "Party and Sect in Machiavelli's Florentine Histories," in
Fleisher, *Machiavelli and the Nature of Political Thought*, p. 240.
[70] *History of Florence*, pp. 1030-31.

the resilience of such sentiments when they are ancient. A chapter heading in *The History of Florence* proclaims: "Old Love and Old Hate Not Easily Canceled." In *The Prince* we find a similar teaching: "To believe that new benefits make men of high rank forget old injuries is to deceive oneself." The resilience of "ancient affection" and "ancient enmity" results, as we might expect, from their being so firmly entrenched in the memory. Such enmities are passed from one generation to the next, becoming, as it were, a "hereditary hate."[71]

Machiavelli saw in the unforgettable character of these ancient enmities the source of the continual divisions with which Florence was perennially plagued. The recurring theme of Machiavelli's narrative of Florentine faction is the role of memory in maintaining and reviving such divisions. We are told that after the struggle between Guelf and Ghibelline an unsuccessful effort was made to reunite the city, but it failed because the people "remembered too clearly" and could not "blot from their memory" the Ghibelline tyranny. Later, when old divisions seemed to have nearly "fallen into oblivion," the Ricci family easily revived the old hatreds in their struggle with the Albizzi. In *The Prince* and the *Discourses*, Machiavelli had hinted at a relationship between corruption and dysfunctions in the political memory of a people. In *The History of Florence*, the book in which Machiavelli most thoroughly discusses the problem of political corruption, that relationship is made explicit.[72]

In the Preface to his history, Machiavelli had suggested that only by returning to the beginnings of these divisions could the nature of faction truly be understood. The oldest and most enduring of Florentine factions, whose "imitation" was a blueprint for all subsequent divisions, was that of Guelf and Ghibelline. In tracing the origin of this division, Machiavelli pays little heed to the political or religious differences between the two factions, emphasizing instead

[71] *History of Florence*, pp. 1245, 1261; see also *The Prince*, chapter 7.

[72] *History of Florence*, pp. 1065, 1090, 1142-43, 1188; see also *The Prince*, chapters 1, 11, 12, and *Discourses*, II-11, II-19.

a dispute among several families which arose over a point of honor. A son of the Buondelmonti renounced his plan to marry a daughter of the Amidei and the Amidei responded with violence. Machiavelli remarks that the Buondelmonti thought it "easy to forget an injury." Within this trifling anecdote is an important truth about the Florentine state. The origin of Florentine faction lay in disputes among her great families. The hatred which sprang from one injury was made venerable after time and remained not only undiminished, but was continually fed by fresh injuries. Subsequent divisions imitated the first in that they too had their origins in the ancient antagonisms among families.[73]

The great family, with its overriding concern for its own well-being, has all the marks of a political faction. In the *Discourses*, Machiavelli observes that when Rome was a "good city," the kin of Manlius Capitolinus did not come to his aid, refusing to foment internal disorder out of "love of country." Rome stands in contrast to Florence, where "friends and relations protected every noble" from the law. Machiavelli's opposition of "love of country" to "love of blood" is the standard by which a city is judged "good" or "bad." If Machiavelli was not the first to see in the loyalty of blood kin a rival to public things and a threat to the well-being of the community, he poses that opposition more completely than anyone before or after him. Brutus, the prototypical citizen of the *Discourses*, must kill his sons to preserve the republic. The choice could not be drawn more starkly. In the *Discourses*, the killing of sons is a recurrent theme; in each case it is seen as necessary to maintain the virtue or integrity of the city. Metaphorically, the killing of sons becomes the quintessential civic act, the choice between blood and nation posed in its most extreme form.[74]

[73] *History of Florence*, p. 1085, 1099-1100, 1141-42, 1221-23. Speaking of that first division and with characteristic understatement, Machiavelli says, "I think it not useless to record the families that belonged to the two parties."

[74] *Discourses*, I-16, III-8, III-22, III-34; *History of Florence*, p. 1094. Brutus

For Machiavelli, this opposition is complete, because both the clan and the nation are, in a manner of speaking, structures of remembrance which necessarily compete for the minds of men. What appeared in *The Prince* as simply two kinds of collective memory, one tied to blood relations, the other to civic relations, are now seen as rivals. Families, as well as political communities, are vessels of memory, but familial remembrance somehow consumes the memory of public things upon which the vengeance of citizens and the integrity of the republic are founded. (The familial factions of Florence were perpetually conspiring with foreigners against the fatherland.) As kinship and citizenship are rival ways of integrating the present with the past, so blood and glory are rival forms of human preservation, contending, as it were, for the future. Brutus gains a lasting immortality through the act of destroying his own seed. In the *Mandragola*, Machiavelli bitterly mocks an inversion of Brutus in his characterization of Messer Nicia. Out of his "longing" for children, Nicia consents to the murder of a fellow-citizen. Nicia has his heart so set on fatherhood that "he has forgotten every other good." His desire for the preservation of his flesh has caused him to "forget the fatherland." Against those enamored of the immortality of the seed, Machiavelli observes that "heirs soon [begin] to degenerate as compared with their ancestors," surpassing their fathers not in "virtuous deeds," but only in "extravagance, lasciviousness, and every other kind of licentiousness." He who would preserve the highest part of himself should trust in the memory of his people rather than in his offspring, as did Brutus, for through the memory of his deed Brutus spawned generations of loyal "sons."[75]

is imitated in this by Manlius Torquatus. Indicative of the power of blood in Machiavelli's view is his observation that Castruccio never married lest love of children prevent him from showing due gratitude to the blood of his benefactor.

[75] Machiavelli, *Mandragola*, p. 27; *Discourses*, I-2, III-34. For a discussion of the family as a vessel of memory, see *Discourses*, III-46.

Machiavelli's fierce assault upon the notion of blood is a measure of the power he believed it to wield in men's minds. If as a means of both preserving the past and insuring the future it depends upon the fortuitous continuation of offspring and is thus always precarious, its appeal lies in its utter materiality. The relations with progenitors and descendants which are established through "deeds" alone will always seem less real than those relations founded upon blood. Moreover, the reverence and immortality which belong to the political community, unlike the reverence and immortality promised by a community founded upon blood-tie, rest upon the integrity of the nation; that is, they rest upon human artifice and depend for their survival upon human will.[76] Thus, political foundation and the state are, for Machiavelli, not simply unnatural; indeed, they are at war with nature. The state must seize and make its own that authority which originally rested with blood. The substitution of the collective father for innumerable petty patriarchs is the result of a political deed. Machiavelli seeks not the elimination of the paternal principle, but rather its consolidation, making patriarchs brothers and fellow-citizens. Machiavelli's Theseus is much in evidence here, uniting that which had been previously "scattered."[77]

[76] In recalling the revolt of the wool guild and other lower class elements, Machiavelli discusses the tendency of relations founded upon blood to submerge the noble deed as a standard by which to judge men. The concrete quality of blood relations is made apparent in the equality of the flesh that the speaker proclaims and the great appeal it enjoys among the dregs of the nation. Machiavelli's proletarian agitator is able to call into question the authority of the hereditary aristocracy simply by placing that authority, founded as it is upon blood, on its head. The utter materialism of the hereditary argument makes it easy prey for the materialist egalitarianism Machiavelli puts into the mouth of his agitator: "And do not be frightened by their antiquity of blood which they shame us with, for all men, since they had one and the same beginning, are equally ancient; by nature they are all made in one way. Strip us all naked; you will see us all alike; dress us then in their clothes and they in ours; without doubt we shall seem noble and they ignoble, for only poverty and riches make us unequal" (History of Florence, p. 1160).

[77] McWilliams, p. 25; The Prince, chapters 11, 26. Machiavelli's view

The foregoing discussion suggests that a bad beginning involves the incomplete consolidation of authority in the state, or a *fatherless origin*. In the *Discourses*, Machiavelli argues that the difficulties which plague cities like Florence result from a bad beginning. In *The History of Florence*, the poverty of Florentine civic life stems from a factiousness rooted in blood loyalty. We are reminded that Florence was founded in servility and safety, without that necessity that would have compelled her to become united and to suppress the arrogance of the families. In a speech by one among a group of citizens "moved by love of country," the fatherless origins of Florence and the need for a more thorough consolidation of political authority are hinted at.

The love we bear, reverend Signors, to our native city has first made us assemble, and now makes us come to you to talk of that evil which is already great and which is all the time increasing in our republic, and to offer ourselves as ready to assist you in getting rid of it. . . . From the time when this region withdrew itself from under the power of the Empire, its cities, not having a strong rein to guide them, have organized their states and governments not as free but as divided into factions. . . . The result is the avarice the citizens display, and their thirst not for true glory but for despicable honors depending upon hates, enmities, disputes, factions. . . . It is given from on high, in order that in human things there may be nothing either lasting or at rest, that in all republics there are fated families, born for their ruin. Our republic, more than any other, has abounded in these, for not one but many have stirred up and distressed her. . . . We have not reminded you of our corrupt habits and our ancient

---

opposes the political anthropology of Aristotle, in which the state emerges organically out of kinship groups. But neither does Theseus establish his authority by laying low the ancient clans. Rather, he detaches that authority from the patriarchs and makes it his own, becoming "a father" to his people.

and continual divisions in order to frighten you, but to remind you of their causes and to show you that, just as you can remember them, we remember them, and to tell you that the example of those ought not to make you despair of restraining the present ones. Because in those ancient families power was so great, and so great the favors that they had from princes, that legal methods and ways were not strong enough to restrain them. But now that the Empire has no power over us, the Pope is not feared, and all Italy and this city are brought to such an equality that by herself she can govern herself, the difficulty is not great.[78]

These "fated families" have been the bane of Florentine political life. And if in the beginning the great families were not sufficiently humbled, the time is now right for a new beginning. Machiavelli puts this revolutionary teaching in the mouth of a nameless patriot, who reveals the secret underlying all of Florence's civil strife, but only as a prelude to overcoming the legacy of ancient hatreds. And what this citizen would do through his speech, Machiavelli would do through his history. "Remember," teaches Machiavelli, "so that you may forget." But the therapeutic intent of *The History of Florence* is informed by Machiavelli's realism. Men will not forget of their own accord, and ancient enmities are not canceled with ease. The therapeutic remembrance of which *The History of Florence* consists is only for those few "free spirits" who might yet rid Florence of "such abuses."[79]

Thus, the problem of Florentine corruption has resolved itself into the problem of new beginnings which, in its turn, becomes the problem of revolution. Yet Machiavelli himself is an unobtrusive revolutionary. A judicious writer, in his book on Florence he is extraordinarily so. *The History of Florence* had been commissioned by a Medici pope, and

[78] *History of Florence*, pp. 1145-47.
[79] *History of Florence*, p. 1233.

Machiavelli was a man of discretion. In the first chapter of Book VIII, which records the circumstances surrounding a Florentine conspiracy against the Medici, Machiavelli observes only the futility of such conspiracies. But in the last chapter of the preceding book, a different view of conspiracies is made known. A conspiracy against the Duke of Milan was begun by one Cola Montano, "a lettered and ambitious man" who called "glorious and happy [those] whom nature and fortune had permitted to be born and live in a republic, and explaining that all famous men were brought up in republics and not under princes." Montano drew his pupils into the conspiracy with the promise of an everlasting fame for those who founded republics. Like Chiron in *The Prince*, Montano would be the teacher of founders. This Cola Montano is but a shadow of Machiavelli himself, and his cameo appearance here points to a relationship between the theorist and political foundation which Machiavelli has been careful to conceal. And if Montano failed, yet another might succeed, for in Tuscany there is "so great an equality that a wise man, familiar with ancient forms of civic government, should easily be able to introduce there a civic constitution. But so great has been Tuscany's misfortune that up to the present nothing has been attempted by any man with the requisite ability and knowledge."[80]

The Theorist and the Pursuit of Glory

Good foundations require knowledge. True founders are men of "rare" and "outstanding brain-power." The knowledge of political foundation is among the most exalted, for "the maker" of political things builds for the ages. The founder must penetrate the curtain drawn round the future. Those without the almost prophetic gift of foresight are "not truly wise" and "this power is given to very few."

[80] *History of Florence*, pp. 1378-82; *Discourses*, I-55.

In many ways the first modern and the defender of the demos against the aristocratic bias of the tradition, Machiavelli remains, in this, a Socratic.[81]

In the allegory of the cave, Plato had suggested that the city was irremediably a world of illusion. It was left to Machiavelli to develop fully the implications of this fact for political creation. In Plato, the opposition of appearance and reality was mediated through the doctrine of right opinion. If the many were incapable of knowledge, they could be told appropriate myths and noble lies which partook of the truth and which placed them in a proper relation to it. For Machiavelli the opposition of the two worlds is more complete.

> In general men judge more with their eyes than with their hands, since everybody can see but few can perceive. . . . The mob is always fascinated by appearances and by the outcome of an affair; and in the world the mob is everything; the few find no room there when the many crowd together.

In the political world, there are only ordinary people. And in this world there is only appearance. The political art does not involve mediating between this world and a higher reality, but rather constructing this world through the creation of images—that which men can see. Plato's philos-

---

[81] *Discourses*, I-55, *The Prince*, chapter 13. In the founding of states, knowledge comes close to being virtue and such virtue is very rare. It might even be said that Machiavelli develops more completely than his predecessors the creative impulse implicit in many of Socrates' analogies to the art of rulership. Socrates draws his examples from both the theoretical and the applied arts, but the suggestion of the *Republic*, that the philosopher is compelled to bring theory into the world and mix it with matter, raises questions about the status of such an impulse in Plato's political philosophy. In any case, whatever architectonic suggestions there may be in Plato's work, they are muted by the philosopher's need to wait upon fortune and the unlikely coalescence of philosophy and political power. It is Machiavelli who is alive with the creative impulse. In what amounts to a kind of Platonic inversion, Machiavelli's founder is almost compelled by some inner need to bring a political world into being. Thus, it is Machiavelli who is the first great theorist of political fabrication.

opher is ill-equipped by temperament for such tasks, preferring the penetration of images to creating them.[82]

It is the historian and not the philosopher who fabricates a world, and it is this aspect of history that has such great appeal for Machiavelli. Machiavelli notes how historians alter the record of the past, omitting certain things or transforming rumor into fact. If history had often been impressed into the service of conquerors and tyrants, it might just as fruitfully be used by theorists and founders. In the Preface to Book II of the *Discourses*, in which Machiavelli calls the truth of histories and memories into question, he examines his own use of the past:

> Indeed, if the virtue which then prevailed and the vices which are prevalent today were not as clear as the sun, I should be more reserved in my statements lest I should fall into the very fault for which I am blaming others.

But, as Machiavelli had said only one page before, man can never have a perfect knowledge of times "long since past." That Machiavelli's vision of the past is "as clear as the sun" suggests much, for as the sun enlightens it also blinds, particularly when one looks directly into it. Machiavelli is "the survivor" from the flood who conceals and distorts his knowledge of ancient things "in his own fashion so as to establish his own reputation and that of his family." Machiavelli's family is that of republics, and he uses his knowledge of the past to reestablish republicanism in the world. To succeed, however, he must teach others this republican history. Machiavelli continues his preface:

> But as the fact are there for anyone to see, I shall make so bold as to declare plainly what I think of those days and of our own, so that the minds of young men who read what I have written may turn from the one and prepare to imitate the other.

[82] *The Prince*, chapter 18.

95

As grandparents have always known, the young in particular are ever fascinated with tales of the past. Machiavelli would enlist this natural fascination in the cause of his new political art.[83]

Strauss observes that, after Livy, Machiavelli praises Xenophon above all other ancient writers, and in particular Xenophon's *Education of Cyrus*. This biography of Cyrus is said to have had a great impact upon the young Scipio who, we are told, modeled himself on this image of the Persian prince. That Scipio sought to imitate Cyrus and that this Cyrus was in large measure the creation of Xenophon is not lost on Machiavelli. Through his "history," Xenophon had become the teacher of Scipio, reaching out from the grave to mold the young Roman's character. *The Education of Cyrus* became the education of Scipio. The historian (like the founder) can reach into the remote future.

Unlike philosophy, which had seemed most impotent when in the world, "history," or what men believed to be the past, could shape their actions in the present and thus create the future. History in the hands of the theorist becomes an art, not a science, and, as Strauss observes, Machiavelli's use of historical material is "artful." The creation of a political world particularly involves the manipulation of the images of the past. Machiavelli promises to make his new prince "appear long-established." The theorist must seek to manipulate the memory of his audience. Machiavelli's Castruccio is likened to Xenophon's Cyrus, and Machiavelli makes explicit the breadth of the theorist's warrant: "I have chosen to bring him back to the recollection of men, since I have found in his life many things . . . that are very striking." Machiavelli enjoins his readers to imitate the ancients, but only after the ancients are painted in decidedly *Machiavellian* hues.[84]

History's persuasive potential is not unlike that of the old religion; as Numa had "conversations" with a nymph,

[83] *Discourses*, II-Preface, II-5.
[84] Strauss, pp. 45, 290; *Castruccio Castracani*, p. 564; see also *The Prince*, chapter 24.

so the theorist converses with the ancients. Paradoxically, history, because it pretends to be the record of human action in the past, persuades where philosophy does not. To Machiavelli's ordinary people, history seems *real* while philosophy appears to "the mob" in characteristically hypothetical garb. Philosophical knowledge had always rested upon self-knowledge, but Machiavelli knew that the Delphic injunction must always remain an impenetrable mystery to ordinary people. Such people seek themselves in the world, looking for their reflection in those who came before them. This is not less true of whole peoples, for a people will look to its own past in search of its collective identity. Thus, Machiavelli writes of his people: "If to imitate the Roman way seems to be difficult, that of the Tuscans of old should not appear so difficult especially to the Tuscans of today."[85]

Classical political philosophy with its new principle of order had sought to restore the city, but the city refused to acknowledge her. Unable to attach herself to a worldly power, philosophy could only found republics in speech. Machiavelli's "new way" involved an investigation into the linking of theory and power. He saw at once that the people are the source of the greatest power, and that their political world is one of appearances. The founder who would gain access to that world and make its power his own must master the art of political appearances. Machiavelli instructs his new prince: "Everybody sees what you appear to be, few perceive what you are, and those few do not dare contradict the belief of the many, who have the majesty of the government to support them." By destroying and manipulating old memories and by creating new ones, the founder creates the horizon of a common world. The republic becomes possible and grows out of the unity of this common "past."[86]

[85] *Discourses*, II-4; *The Prince*, chapter 18.

[86] *The Prince*, chapter 18. Commenting on the necessity of Rome's regal beginnings in providing for the maturation of the people before they acquired their liberty, Livy observes: "For what would have been the

If the founder conjures mnemonic illusions, he himself is not free of illusion. Jacobson has observed that "there is none so blind as will not see. Such a one is the man of monumental political ambitions." The "man of monumental political ambitions" is driven by a passion for immortal glory and by the secret desire to eclipse his father's memory. The theorist knows this passion and uses it to seduce the new prince. Machiavelli writes to Giulio de' Medici (Clement VII): "God has given to your house and to Your Holiness in person . . . [the] power and material for making yourself immortal, and for surpassing by far in this way your father's and your grandfather's glory." In the hope for and vision of a future, the eyes of the man of monumental ambition are riveted upon the past, upon those who have achieved what he seeks. Desiring to overthrow the past and achieve unrivaled glory, he is strangely possessed by what came before. Tempted by the vision of "Cyrus' glory," the new prince is easily led to play Scipio to Machiavelli's Xenophon.

No one should be astonished if in the following discussion of completely new princedoms I make use of the most outstanding examples; since men almost always walk in the path made by others and conduct their affairs through imitation, although they are not altogether able to stay on the path of others nor arrive at the ingenuity of those they imitate, a prudent man

consequence, if that rabble of shepherds and strangers, runaways from their own peoples . . . freed from all dread of regal authority, had begun to be distracted by tribunical storms, and to engage in contests with the fathers in a strange city, before the pledges of wives and children, and the affection for the soil itself, to which people become habituated only by length of time, had united their affections? Their condition not yet matured would have been destroyed by discord" (Livius, p. 72). Regal authority created the conditions out of which a multitude of strangers and runaways was shaped into a single people who could love the Roman soil. Rome succeeded in creating a common past out of a diversity of pasts, and then maintained the unity of the state by appealing to this *new* past.

should always take the path trodden by great men and imitate those who have been most outstanding.

The injunction to imitation gives the theorist access to the new prince. Later, Machiavelli reiterates his teaching: "Above all he should do as some outstanding man before him has done [that is, Scipio], who decided to imitate someone who has been praised and honored before him and always keep in mind his deeds and actions." If the theorist is to succeed, he himself must imitate Xenophon and become a historian, the final arbiter of praise and blame.[87]

Machiavelli seeks not only to make the new prince his instrument, but also to perpetrate a great fraud upon him. In need of the prince and yet fearing the envy of such a man, the theorist wraps the methods "he devises" in the mantle of the past. Like Callimaco in the *Mandragola*, who succeeded in deceiving Nicia by disguising himself as a fool, Machiavelli presents himself to the prince in the guise of "a man of low and humble station." For like Brutus (who also "played the fool"), the theorist must bide his time. Blinded by the contemplation of his own immortality, the new prince is devoured by his own creation while the theorist steals to the pinnacle of glory. The prince suffers from the myopia that attends his position. Standing on "places high above," he can only survey "the plain." He becomes the victim of his vantage point. Only the theorist, founding as he does from afar, can survey at once the plain and the highland.[88]

The seduction of the new prince by the theorist rests

[87] Jacobson, p. 48; *Remodeling the Government of Florence*, p. 114; *The Prince*, chapters 6, 14. In a similar vein, Nietzsche sees in "monumental history" the source of the great deed and the inspiration for him who would build for the ages, but he insists that, for such history to be efficacious, the past must be identified with the present by hiding differences in circumstance from the eyes of the actor (Nietzsche, pp. 14-19).

[88] *The Prince*, Dedication. The theorist keeps from the prince the knowledge of the superiority of the people in preserving the state, as well as the knowledge that his "success" must lead to his (or his family's) demise. See also Strauss, pp. 25, 268.

upon the conviction that the highest glory is gained by the founders of states. Little is said in *The Prince* to dispel such convictions. But in the *Discourses*, Machiavelli raises the issue of the nature of glory, asking whether Romulus or Numa is more to be praised: "So that if it were a question of the prince to whom Rome was more indebted, Romulus or Numa, Numa, I think should easily obtain the first place." Numa's superiority rests upon the importance of his teaching and the difficulty of its accomplishment: "For, where there is religion, it is easy to teach men to use arms, but where there are arms, but no religion, it is with difficulty that it can be introduced." Machiavelli is silent about the most difficult teaching, but he would be the mentor of founders. As such, Machiavelli lays claim to the highest glory for himself: "No one is so much exalted by any act of his as are those men who have with laws and with institutions remodeled republics and kingdoms." Machiavelli claims the highest glory not as the founder of a single republic, but as the restorer of the republic in the world. His claim rests upon the nature of his knowledge, the rarity of his gift, for if there "have been few who have the opportunity to do it," there have been only "very few who have understood how to do it." And while Machiavelli tells his new prince to keep to paths that are well beaten, Machiavelli seeks praise down paths "as yet untrodden."[89]

The reverence Machiavelli promises Lorenzo in the "Exortation" he secretly desires for himself. And if "Aristotle, Plato and many others" could only "form a republic . . . in writing," Machiavelli hopes to be the founder of many "in reality." The ancients, he thinks, failed for lack of power.

---

[89] *Remodeling the Government of Florence*, pp. 113-14; *Discourses*, I-Preface, I-11; see also *The Prince*, chapter 26. Ostensibly addressing Lorenzo, Machiavelli says that nothing brings as much honor to a newly rising man as do new laws and new methods invented by him. These things, when they are well established and carry with them the idea of greatness, will make him worthy of reverence and admiration. For further discussion of the limits of imitation, see Chapter 22 of *The Prince*, on the three types of "brains," and *The Art of War*, p. 721, on "inventiveness."

Machiavelli has learned from them. Theory has been strapped to the back of the man of monumental ambition and will ride his passion to its realization. Machiavelli knows this passion. It is his own. He too would be immortal, and he secretly wishes to slay his "fathers" (or to supplant Socrates and Jesus). He is at once the new Prince and the new Prophet, hoping that, when men remember, the name of Machiavelli will be "the first to be praised."[90]

[90] *Remodeling the Government of Florence*, pp. 113-14. The figure of Jesus looms particularly large in Machiavelli's work. Machiavelli's restoration of the republic and its pagan foundations would invert the teaching of Christ, as other men will then begin to love their country more than their souls. It is necessary that Jesus be overthrown, for he has stolen the praise of men. As Machiavelli observes, praise of founders is second only to praise of those men "who have been gods" (p. 114).

THREE

EDMUND BURKE:
POLITICAL ORDER
AND THE PAST

Remembrance and Rebellion

Of Edmund Burke, John MacCunn said, "His very name is a symbol of reverence towards all that is old and venerable." If others have not always shared MacCunn's admiration or joined in his praise of the Right Honorable Mr. Burke, few have disagreed with his assessment of Burke's attitude toward the past. Perhaps no other political theorist has had the past respectfully on his lips more often than had Edmund Burke. Burke never seemed to tire of reminding his readers that all that is good in politics is that which is "inherited; . . . a patrimony derived from their forefathers." To successive generations of political thinkers who have called themselves conservatives, Burke has seemed a bastion against those who sought to tear down the old and the tried in favor of the new and the untried. There is much truth in this view of Burke, a view which, like Burke's beloved "custom," has become venerable with age. In this essay, we will attempt less the overturning than the modification of such dogmas. It will be argued that Burke attempted not simply to defend the past against ruthless innovators who never looked back (which he did), but also that, in Burke's view, the past itself had become infected with the spirit of innovation, and that he sought a new relation of past and present that would rid the past of its problematic character.[1]

To this day, Burke is best remembered for his fulminations against the French experiment of 1789. But as Isaac Kramnick has cautioned, any understanding of Burke must come to terms with his "English aspect." The fundamentals of Burke's thinking regarding politics were formed long before 1789; indeed, they emerged directly out of Burke's understanding of the English political experience. Many commentators have acknowledged Burke's debt to the constitutional and common law traditions, but few have recognized the extent of that indebtedness.[2]

In the seventeenth century, England was torn apart by what amounted to (at least on the doctrinal level) a dispute over the character of her past. The struggle, which was to culminate in what is commonly known as the Puritan Revolution, was over the locus of sovereignty in the English constitution. Parliamentarians, monarchists, and radicals all appealed to the past in an effort to vindicate their particular claims. The older but "naive" notion of "the king in parliament" seemed increasingly inadequate during the first half of the seventeenth century, when political conflict more often than not pitted the king against parliament. While "parliament men" defended their historical rights, apologists for the absolutist pretensions of the Stuarts pointed to the Conquest of 1066 and argued that all so-called rights were in fact privileges enjoyed at the will of the king. Parliamentarians, borrowing a page from the common lawyers who had long argued the immemorial character of the com-

[1] MacCunn, *The Political Philosophy of Burke*, p. 92; Burke, *Reflections*, p. 36. [Hereafter in this chapter, works by Burke are cited by title, volume (where appropriate), and page number(s) only.]
[2] Kramnick, *Edmund Burke* (hereafter cited as Kramnick [1]), Preface.

mon law, claimed for their institution an antiquity "time
out of mind" (and thus predating the Norman Conquest).
If Parliament defended its rights by claiming for them an
unbroken continuity which stretched back into a dark and
impenetrable Saxon past, anti-monarchical radicals spoke
of a golden age of Saxon liberty, viewing the Conqueror
and all those who rested their claims upon his as usurpers
and tyrants. As Burke himself observes:

> The spirit of party, which has misled us in so many
> other particulars, has tended greatly to perplex us in
> this matter. For as the advocates of prerogative would,
> by a very absurd consequence drawn from the Norman
> Conquest, have made all our national rights and lib-
> erties to have arisen from the grants, and therefore to
> be revokable at the will of the sovereign, so, on the
> other hand, those who maintained the cause of liberty
> did not support it upon more solid principles. They
> would hear of no beginning to any of our privileges,
> orders, or laws, and, in order to gain them a reverence,
> would prove that they were as old as the nation; and
> to support that opinion, they put to the torture all the
> ancient monuments.[3]

The seventeenth century had raised the question of which
institution was the bearer and defender of the past. Men
fought over the past, for with the past went power and
legitimacy. The very fabric of English political life had been
rent horribly through an exercise in political memory. After
1660, all such political-historical questions were viewed as
subversive. Even after 1688, the Whigs would have no part
of this notion lest 1648 and the Commonwealth return; they

---

[3] Pocock, *The Ancient Constitution and the Feudal Law*, especially pp. 126,
233; "An Essay Towards an Abridgement of English History," in *The Works
of the Right Honorable Edmund Burke*, vol. 7, pp. 478-79. It is significant
here that both Hobbes and Locke, in their efforts to reestablish sovereign
power, shunned any appeal to the past, "solving" the problem of the
past by raising the debate above history and placing it on the plane of
nature and reason.

preferred "the myth of confirmation" of *immemorial* liberties to any appeal to origins. At the center of the problem
of England's political memory lay, in Burke's words, a "dispute not yet concluded, and never near becoming so."[4]

The horror of civil war had proven to Burke's satisfaction
that to look in "dark places" could only give rise to pain.
But the radicals and dissenters of Burke's England (often
the biological as well as the theological and ideological descendants of Cromwell's Roundheads) had not so learned
from the suffering of the nation. The problem with these
radicals, Burke insisted, was their love of discussing "the
foundations on which obedience to government is founded."
Such historical prying was bound to turn up something for
any faction to "talk up." It was radicals, the likes of Richard
Price and Joseph Priestley, who always had the word
"origins" on their lips. Even Thomas Paine, with all his
talk of natural right, could not resist an occasional backward glance.

> It is very well known that in England the great landed
> estates now held in descent were plundered from the
> quiet inhabitants at the Conquest. The possibility did
> not exist of acquiring such estates honestly. If it be
> asked how they could have been acquired, no answer
> but that of robbery can be given. . . . Blush aristocracy
> to hear of your origins for your progenitors were
> thieves.[5]

[4] Quoted in Kramnick [1], p. 149. From the Whig perspective, the dispute over the locus of sovereignty had given rise to two tyrannies, that
of the Stuarts and that of Parliament. In 1660 and again in 1688, England
sublimated the problem of sovereignty, preferring political peace to theoretical or historical clarity. After 1688 (Locke's *Second Treatise* notwithstanding), the Whig justification of the Glorious Revolution refrained from
any mention of origins or the original contract, for the concept could not
be cleansed of the idea of popular sovereignty. See Pocock, *Ancient Constitution*, pp. 230-33.

[5] *On the Sublime and Beautiful*, pp. 322-23; Kramnick, *The Rage of Edmund
Burke* (hereafter cited as Kramnick [2]), p. 36; Thomas Paine, quoted in
Kramnick [2], p. 148. In a frank criticism of the Protestant lords of Ireland,
Burke reveals that he is in secret agreement with Paine, accusing these

England's first effort at remembrance had ended in civil war, regicide, and a dangerous breach in the continuity of her institutions. These only compounded the problematic character of her political memory, adding their unforgettable precedents to a past already fraught with difficulty. Men were "imitative animals," thought Burke. Thus, history "may, in the perversion, serve for a magazine furnishing offensive and defensive weapons for parties in church and state, and supplying the means of keeping alive or reviving dissensions and animosities, and adding fuel to civil fury." The analogy to military ordnance was, in Burke's view, particularly appropriate. If men were generally "imitative animals," both Burke and the radicals understood the power of ancient example, particularly in a nation in which looking to the past was "a habit of the mind." Dissenting ministers never failed to give "anniversary sermons" commemorating the Revolution of 1688 and to use the occasion as a pretext for drawing out what to their minds were the "democratical" principles of '88. In such an enviroment, Burke thought even the remembrance of "the cautious and deliberate spirit" of the men of 1688 was inflammatory.[6]

Burke knew that the dissenters were the backbone of the English republican faction, and that these eighteenth-cen-

---

lords of wishing "to let time draw his oblivious veil over the unpleasant modes by which lordships and demesnes have been acquired in theirs, and almost in all other countries upon earth." Ironically, the complaint against Protestant lords in Ireland by Burke, Irish patriot, becomes the very foundation by which Burke, savior of the ancient regime, would shore up the foundations of social order. It is this same "oblivious veil," castigated here, which Burke praises as the "politic, well-wrought veil" drawn by Lord Somers over the Revolution of 1688. See Kramnick [2], p. 179, and *Reflections*, pp. 20-21.

[6] *Reflections*, pp. 71, 162. For the human tendency toward imitation, see "Hints for an Essay on the Drama," in *Works*, vol. 7, p. 145. Later, English radicals and dissenters would also commemorate the fall of the Bastille (July 14). Burke noted with dismay the tendency of such "festive anniversaries" to keep alive the spirit of institutions (see "Thoughts on French Affairs," in *Works*, vol. 4, p. 369).

tury republicans had forgotten neither the Commonwealth nor their "ancestors of ambition."

> These gentlemen of Old Jewry, in all their reasonings on the Revolution of 1688, have a Revolution which happened in England about forty years before and the late French Revolution so much before their eyes and in their hearts that they are constantly confounding all the three together.

Kramnick has suggested that Burke was preoccupied with 1688, but this is only apparently so. It is true that while Burke speaks often of "the Glorious Revolution" and "the Revolution of 1688," he rarely speaks directly of 1648. More interesting is his refusal to name that "Revolution which happened in England about forty years before." It is not his frequent allusion to 1688, but rather his inability to utter the name of that earlier revolution, which bespeaks a curious historical fixation. While its name remains unknown, the images of 1648 seem to force themselves upon Burke and are everywhere scattered throughout his speeches and writings. In a speech before the House of Lords, Burke, "foaming like Niagara," creates for his auditors a horrific vision in which the events of July 14 (the day on which the Bastille was taken, and afterwards commemorated by English as well as French republicans) are united with the memory of the Rump in what must have seemed to such venerable peers a nightmare of republican excess.

> [These dissenters, having] met to commemorate the fourteenth of July, shall seize the tower of London and the magazines it contains, murder the governor and the mayor of London, seize upon the king's person, drive out the House of Lords, occupy your galleries and thence, from a high tribunal, dictate to you.[7]

---

[7] "Thoughts on French Affairs," p. 324; *Reflections*, pp. 18, 193; Kramnick [2], p. 151. The reference to Burke's effusive oratorical style is Dr. Johnson's, on Boswell's authority, and is quoted in Kramnick [2], p. 180.

The events of 1648 culminated, of course, in the execution of Charles I. And it was the images of regicide which appeared before Burke most frequently, seeming almost to haunt him. If Burke cautioned others to disregard the "ghosts" of the past, it was because he himself knew the terror of such "apparitions." Burke was probably right in accusing republican dissenters of secretly commemorating the thirtieth of January in their anniversary sermons, but their preoccupation was unquestionably his own. Dr. Price, Burke reminds his readers, is no "innovator," but "only an imitator," one who "follows a precedent," that set by Reverend Hugh Peters (one of the regicides) who, riding before a condemned Charles I, enjoyed "a triumph as memorable as that of Dr. Price."[8]

It was a sermon of this same imitator, the Reverend Richard Price, which called forth *Reflections on the Revolution in France* from Burke's pen. Burke confronts Price's sermon directly in the very beginning of that document.

That sermon is in a strain which I believe has not been heard in this kingdom, in any of the pulpits which are tolerated or encouraged in it, since the year 1648, when a predecessor of Dr. Price, the Rev. Hugh Peters, made the vault of the king's own chapel at St. James's ring with the honor and the privilege of the saints, who, with the "high praises of God in their mouths, and a two-edged sword in their hands, were to execute judgement on the heathen, and punishments upon the people; to bind their kings with chains, and their nobles with fetters of iron."

Burke would not, nay, Burke could not forget the deed of 1648. The regicide seared the consciousness, defying all efforts at purgation.[9]

---

[8] *Reflections*, p. 75; see also p. 163.

[9] *Reflections*, p. 12. Dickens's description of the regicide is suggestive: "The King's last word, as he gave his cloak and the George . . . to the Bishop, was 'Remember!' He then kneeled down, laid his head on the

In refuting the claim of those who insisted that the Revolution of 1688 had established, at least in principle, the doctrine of elective monarchy, Burke is unable to resist the patricidal analogy: "Do these theorists," asks Burke, "mean to imitate some of their predecessors who dragged the bodies of our ancient sovereigns out of the quiet of their tombs?" Indeed, the English radicals and dissenters of the eighteenth century had predecessors, but these predecessors were not the men of '88. Burke accuses the English republican faction of looking upon the events in France as a civil war and of drawing a parallel between such events and "our late civil war." But Burke himself cannot help but draw the same parallel as he conjures up the ironic vision of an army of English republicans singing the Marseillaise Hymn as they parade before the statue of Charles I at Charing Cross.[10]

The killing of a king, the carnage of civil war, these were things which seemed forcibly to dominate Burke's memory. He imagined (we suspect quite correctly) that similar phantoms lurked in the memory of the nation. Often on his lips and ever before his eyes, Burke recoiled in horror from such a past. These were the images that informed Burke's understanding of political modernity. Modernity, thought Burke, was characterized by a new kind of conflict. To be sure, there had always been political conflict (as there had always been opposing interests). But the older form of conflict had been rooted in those interests "which arose from . . . locality and natural circumstance." Modern po-

---

block, spread out his hands, and was instantly killed" (*Dickens Works*, p. 100). It was as if the last words of a condemned king had become a curse, surviving his beheading perhaps even conquering that ignominy—a kind of political spectre come to haunt Burke and the nation.

[10] *Reflections*, p. 25; "Fourth Letter on the Proposals for Peace with the Regicide Directory of France," in *Works*, vol. 6, pp. 94, 102. The desecration to which Burke refers was that of the tombs of many kings and lords (as well as many churches) at the hands of the more zealous among Cromwell's soldiers. The legacy of this desecration became no less memorable (as it remained everywhere visible) than that which it sought to efface.

litical conflict, which first made its appearance with the
Reformation, was founded upon disputes which were essentially doctrinal. The year 1648 (which Burke, no less
than Thomas Hobbes, saw as the political consequence of
the English Reformation) was at base a theoretical dispute
over the nature and origin of sovereignty. The "litigatious
spirit" of theologians had spilled over into political life.
The effect of such disputes was to introduce into communities "theoretic interests" which, by dividing the opinions of fellow-citizens, undermined the bedrock of political
order and sowed the seeds of civil discord. Thus, the peculiar problem of modern politics was unity while its peculiar malady was civil war.[11]

Burke was particularly concerned with the "contagion"
of the modern disease. In the past, the political order and
public opinion had been inoculated against such flights of
abstract reason by the unanimity of tradition. There had
always been theories and utopias, those of Plato and Thomas
More being only the most noteworthy, but modern doctrine had somehow become "armed." Ancient theory was
but the imaginings of philosophers and thus without power.
Modern politics, by contrast, is characterized by the heretofore unknown alliance of the intellectuals and the multitude, with the consequent *democratization* of theory. While
these new theories speak to the people's deep desire for
well-being, this is not what moves the people. Unlike the
philosopher, the multitude is engaged not by naked theoretical beauty or by the symmetry of rational design, but
by "a thing feasible in practice." (Of French practice, Burke
had warned that men ought not to "see" such things.)[12]

[11] "Thoughts on French Affairs," pp. 319-23. On at least one occasion,
Burke finds an analogous situation in antiquity, suggesting that the struggle between Athens and Sparta was ultimately a struggle between the
rival ideologies of "democracy" and "aristocracy." But whether the emergence of ideological struggle at the time of the Reformation is a wholly
new phenomenon or a recurrence of that which, in Burke's estimation,
destroyed Hellenic political life, it is the "theoretic" nature of modern
conflict which, in Burke's view, is its distinguishing feature.

[12] "Three Letters on the Proposals for Peace with the Regicide Direc-

While doctrine remained imagined only, it was weak, unarmed. Abstract theory had become "armed doctrine" by insinuating itself into history and thus entering the realm of possibility. The past, once a unified fabric, was, like the community itself, broken up, cut into pieces. Tradition had spoken with one voice, but the discovery of history had made the past problematic. Radicals and dissenters now had "predecessors." History was full of rebellious, even regicidal, "precept." The past had become a place of terror, filled with "massacres which cannot be remembered without horror."[13]

The Burkean vision was instructed by this remembrance of "massacres" and "horror." Yet the past could not be given up, for it alone stood in the way of unbridled innovation and the disintegration of the social fabric. Only oblivion, thought Burke, could save both himself and the nation. Burke would seek a new relation of past and present, free from the torment of remembrance. But, as Burke knew, such a principle could be spoken only as a plea (or an incantation): "Let the memory of all actions in contradiction to that good old mode . . . be extinguished forever."[14]

Custom and Oblivion

Lord Acton once complained of Burke that "he looked for what ought to be in what is." Others have concurred in Acton's assessment. Thus, Strauss sees Burke as extracting wisdom from what is and assuming "that the model constitution was actual in his time." Unlike later theorists of

---

tory," in *Works*, vol. 5, pp. 259-60; "Thoughts on French Affairs," p. 358; "On the Policy of the Allies," in *Works*, vol. 4, p. 427.

[13] "On the Policy of the Allies," p. 468; "Fourth Letter," p. 21.

[14] "Speech on American Taxation," quoted in Kramnick [1], p. 23. Likewise, Burke looked upon forgetting as a necessary component of his political theory. This was the guiding principle of his effort at "conciliation" with America. And as we shall see, the theoretical kernel contained within the notion of a "memory . . . extinguished" would find its way into Burke's discussion of custom also.

European conservatism, Burke appears not as the embittered reactionary but as the clarion defender of the status quo. There is undoubtedly much evidence for this view. While Burke resisted efforts at reformation of the franchise, for example, he remained a lifelong defender of the principles of the Glorious Revolution. And while his political enemies often accused him of papist sympathies (his Irish descent and Catholic mother, as well as his own defense of Catholic toleration in Ireland, providing much fodder for enemy cannons), Burke was no Jacobite.[15]

Yet, despite protestations and deeds to the contrary, there is something of the reactionary in Burke. Underneath the doctrine is a mood, a sensibility, a secret longing to go back to that "age of chivalry" which had been the "glory of Europe," to an earlier time, before modernity and her "sophisters, economists, and calculators" had callously ripped those "pleasing illusions" from the face of the world. The nineteenth-century defenders of the ancient regime, men of almost effete sensibilities, recognized in Burke a kindred spirit. And yet Burke was no reactionary of the common stripe. Both he and the nation had eaten of the apple and they remembered. Between the eighteenth and the sixteenth centuries stood the seventeenth, and it fiercely resisted oblivion. Burke sought a return of a different order, not to the actual conditions of the past as such (which were not likely to be recovered and, had they been, would have smacked too much of innovation themselves), but to the pre-modern mind—a mind free from the taint of memo-

---

[15] Strauss, *Natural Right and History*, pp. 319-21. Even on their face, the conclusions of Lord Acton and Strauss are problematic, for Burke was not the only one to appeal from an "is" to an "ought." As the entire first section of the *Reflections* demonstrates, radicals, no less than Burke, appealed to the principles of the present constitution for support. The "is" of which Acton and Strauss speak was a highly controversial one indeed. The question was not whether the constitution ought to be changed, but rather what the nature of the constitution was, and this could only be settled by appeals to the past. See also Pocock, *Ancient Constitution*, p. 46.

rable innovation. In his "Essay Towards An Abridgement of English History," Burke shows considerable interest in the several great innovations in England's past (the Roman conquest, the introduction of Christianity, and the Norman Conquest), all of which "unsettled everything," and in how these memorable discontinuities fell again into "darkness." Like other English "men of speculation," Burke would "employ [his] sagacity to discover the latent wisdom" which prevailed in the English past. In this past, Burke sought the key to oblivion. In the idea of *custom*, Burke believed he had found it. Thus, Pocock is correct when he says that the notion of custom "offered a means of escape from the divorce of past and present" which plagued those who had discovered history. Such an escape might prove an inoculation against the fears and horrors hidden in memory.[16]

The idea of custom did not present itself to Burke as the mere distillation of contemporary English political life. In a truly customary society, the force of custom operates upon men "insensibly." It appears to men not as a thing to be known or examined, but as an atmosphere in which men move, or, in Burke's words, "like the air we breathe in." Anthropology, even that most reverent variety to be

---

[16] *Reflections*, pp. 87, 99; "Abridgement of English History," especially pp. 234, 264, 381; Pocock, *Ancient Constitution*, p. 14. What is being suggested here is at least mildly heretical, for it casts Burke in the role of the theorist. Many commentators point to Burke's abhorrence of the very word *theory*. They often argue also that Burke's teaching is simply that political wisdom *is* abiding by ancient usage. We insist, rather, that Burke thought this no longer possible in the original sense and thus sought a higher understanding of the nature of custom—the *idea* of custom—in an effort to pave the way for its return. Finally, on the question of theory, we appeal to Burke himself, who taught not that theory should be shunned, only that the "touchstone" of theory was practice, and who rooted his own theory deep in English practice. Admittedly a novel reading of Burke's approach to custom, it nonetheless points to a solution of a nagging problem in the traditional interpretation. Even admirers such as Russell Kirk, the contemporary Burkean scholar, have pondered the dilemma of custom after men have eaten of the apple. But Kirk fails to see that this dilemma was also Burke's. See Russell Kirk, "Burke and the Philosophy of Prescription," in Kramnick [1].

found in the work of Coke, Blackstone, and Burke, is always a post-customary science. Pocock insists that the antiquarian sensibilities of the English common lawyers were a habit of mind already ancient in Coke's time. Be that as it may, 1648 had vitiated all such habits. When Burke picked up again the jurisprudential thread of English political thought (which had been discarded by Hobbes and Locke in favor of *naturalistic* solutions), he did so consciously because he discerned in that tradition potential solutions to contemporary political difficulties. Despite the interpenetration of jurisprudence and political theory in the English tradition, the conservatism of the legal mind and of reasoning grounded in precedent is of a different order and springs from different needs than the ideology of modern conservatism.[17]

A highly developed and refined theory of custom was readily available to Burke. Over a century and a half of debate among common lawyers and constitutional scholars concerning the origin and operation of England's customary or common law had given rise to a self-conscious understanding of the nature and place of custom in English practice. As anonymous editor of the literary and political journal, the *Annual Register*, Burke had been steeped in the subtleties of English constitutional scholarship. While such scholarship had contributed to the destruction of that atmosphere in which customary right flourishes, a profound understanding of custom's nature and value, Burke thought,

---

[17] "Three Letters," p. 310, Pocock, *Ancient Constitution*, p. 39. While they may seem a small, even pedantic, quibble, the historical work of scholars such as Pocock and Quentin Skinner, with its emphasis upon threads of ideational continuity and the conceptual environments of political theory, secretly conspires to entrap theory within context, thereby robbing it of its claim to vision. Good theory responds to context but is not imprisoned in it. Jurisprudence might very well have been for Burke "the pride of the human intellect" (*Reflections*, p. 108), but its political importance lay not so much in law, as such, as in its *orderliness*, for Burke discovered in the law's method clues to the restoration of order. See also Kirk, in Kramnick [1], p. 140.

might yet pave the way for the eventual restoration of a customary order.[18]

This body of legal and constitutional scholarship had long since identified custom's chief characteristic—its immemorial character. The force or authority of custom is purely prescriptive, that it has been this way since "time out of mind." The man of custom, if asked to justify obedience to custom, will reply only that "these are the ways of our fathers and have always been so." When queried about its origin, custom is mute. This is to say that custom is characterized chiefly by the decay of memory.[19]

The first scholars of the common law had inferred from custom's apparent "beginning beyond memory" that custom had been fixed and unchanging since a time out of mind (often thought to be before the Saxon had emerged from the mist and darkness of the primeval forest). Subsequent scholarship inevitably had revealed that custom was, in reality, not a fixed body of unwritten law, but a growing and changing thing, the product of an evolutionary process of adaptation to, in Pocock's expression, "the consecutive emergencies brought to [a society] by its experience in history." But what had appeared to the seventeenth-century defenders of the ancient constitution as the gravest of admissions—that the origin of right founded upon custom was not, in fact, embedded in a time out of mind—was, for Burke, the very genius of custom. By the end of the eighteenth century, no one could seriously chal-

[18] Burke's later writings attest to his familiarity with Coke and Blackstone (*Reflections*, p. 36). The *Annual Register* took a particular interest in political and constitutional history, as well as in the specific problems connected with the history of Parliament. Blackstone's *Commentaries* came in for special praise. As Kramnick persuasively argues, such idiosyncratic concerns most likely reflected the tastes and interests of the *Register's* young editor. See Kramnick [1], pp. 123, 139, and Pocock, *Ancient Constitution*, p. 242.

[19] Compare this relation to ancient things with that of Machiavelli. Machiavelli, we are told, had "conversations" with the ancients, putting to them questions about their practice and presumably getting some reply. Custom, on the other hand, speaks not.

lenge the idea of historical change. Evolutionary change as well as revolutionary cataclysm had shattered the belief that the present was like the past. The "miracle" of custom was not that it remained unchanged (which it didn't), but that it somehow succeeded in hiding change (even the cataclysmic variety), purging the mind of the memory of dangerous examples of innovation. The appeal of custom was not the fixed character that Burke knew it not to possess, but the appearance of fixity it so successfully created.[20]

Change had become the inescapable political reality. Of change, Burke writes, "there are some fundamental points in which Nature never changes; but they are few and obvious, and belong rather to morals than to politics." Burke's teaching is addressed to the conservative personality. He understood that personality. It was his own. He knew it to be rooted in the moral sensibility that things ought not to change. Burke himself confessed how deeply he hated "to see anything destroyed." He sought to educate that sensibility, teaching it to avoid the pitfalls of resentment and nostalgia which could lead only to political impotence: "We must all obey the great law of change. It is the most powerful law of nature, and the means perhaps of its conservation. All we can do, and that human wisdom can do, is to provide that change shall proceed by insensible degrees." Burke would save the conservative insight in the face of the onslaught of modernity. Here, he redefines the appropriate posture of conservatism and identifies its new task. The past, strictly speaking, is unrecoverable. Some change is perhaps even necessary but in any case unavoidable. However, if we are to save the future, we must hide the fact that the present is not like the past. It is in memory that men become sensible of the fact that the present differs from what came before it. In memory also is the knowledge that the past contains great innovations. As long as such memories remain, revolution will continue to

20 Pocock, *Ancient Constitution*, p. 173.

hide in the shadows of the mind and stalk civilization. The first task of conservatism must be the obliteration of such remembrance.[21]

Burke was not the first to discover that there are several modes in the relation of the present to the past. The sense of flux, turmoil, and change which accompanied the emergence of modernity had, for several centuries past, suggested to the European mind the complexity of that relation. In traditional societies and relatively stable political environments, custom and memory, habit and precept, are united in the equation of the ancient with the good. The memory of ancestors gently fades into myth. Custom begins where commemoration leaves off. All are bound up in the unified fabric of the past. The kaleidoscopic politics of the Italian city-state and the discovery of antiquity had contributed to Machiavelli's exploration of the modes of the past no less than to his theory of fortuna. But if Machiavelli succeeded in differentiating "ancient usage" and "memory," they remained for him, as they had been for the Romans, complementary modes in the relation of men to their past. Only the terrible lessons of civil war and the fragmentation of a once unified past revealed the potential antagonism between custom and memory.

If Hobbes saw the consequences of historical argument for civil peace, John Locke may have been the first to recognize the full implications of a fragmented past. Locke knew that the essence of the relation of past and present is a pedagogic one. The often noted ahistorical character of his political theory is an attempt to factor memory out of politics. The pedagogic role of the past remains, but only as a habitual civility inculcated within the family. Habit or custom becomes the means through which the present is instructed in the mysteries of the past. Even in Locke's state of nature, the Hobbesian Ego's demands for "Grati-

---

[21] "On the Policy of the Allies," pp. 468-69; *Reflections*, p. 160; Kirk, in Kramnick [1], p. 152. See also Mansfield, *Statesmanship and Party Government*, p. 221. Burke's motto, says Mansfield, is "no inquiries."

fication Now!" are mitigated by the knowledge of civility founded upon past experience and a presumed family structure. In the *Second Treatise*, Locke's antagonism to memory is apparent only in the conspicuous absence of history (organized memory) from his justification. But in his more explicit work on education, Locke distinguishes between memory and habit, clearly demonstating his preference for the latter. He begins by noting that unlike memories, which center around the remembrance of a past time, habits have an immemorial beginning in the mind of the child. This *beginninglessness* makes habitual behavior seem "natural." The political lesson is made explicit. "Awe," "respect," and "reverence" are best established through habit. Habits are to be preferred to untrustworthy memory because they do not depend upon "reflection." Thus, they are a superior basis for action (or, more properly, for behavior). Finally, in anticipation of Burke's political theory, Locke lauds the ability of habit to cure behavioral "faults" that presumably result from the problematic character of memory.[22]

Early in his career, Burke revealed his agreement with Lockean pedagogy: "It is by imitation far more than precept, that we learn everything. . . . This forms our manners, our opinions, our lives." Later, this teaching would grow to inform Burke's understanding of the limited utility of history. History may indeed teach, serving as the origin of "habit," but ought never to become the source of "precept." And, like Locke, Burke saw the family as the source of salutary habit: "We begin our public affections in our families. No cold relation is a zealous citizen. We pass on to our neighborhood and our habitual provincial connections." It is the importance of habit for Burke that lies behind the apparent paradox of his uncompromising defense of religious establishment accompanied by his indifference to the substance of religious teaching. Wrongly

---

[22] Locke, *Some Thoughts Concerning Education*, pp. 31-32, 40-42.

accused by advocates of toleration and by dissenters of hypocrisy, Burke could fight for toleration for Irish Catholics while opposing the same for English papists and dissenters alike. The consistency of Burke's position was his defense of habit. Men should be left in religious matters, no less than in political ones, "as they anciently stood." The value of establishment was its foundation on habit. Burke was to insist that the Allied policy toward France must include the restoration to Catholics of the "ancient Catholic religion" and, to Protestants, of the "ancient Calvinistic religion." Like Locke, Burke saw the maintenance of reverence and awe as dependent on habitual obedience. To change ancient usage and "early prejudice" was to open the floodgates to any and all systems "of folly, or impiety, or blasphemy, or atheism." Trusting in no other authority, Burke feared that men free from custom were free of all law save their passions. If the social contract theorists of the seventeenth century had unmasked the "artificiality" of political authority in an effort to restore authority to political life, their eighteenth-century pupils had used this knowledge in their assault upon all established authority. Burke had come to believe that the only solid foundation for authority was habit and the aura of nature with which it surrounded human artifice.[23]

Burke's historical studies had convinced him of the possibility of restoring the habitual, even in the face of unsettling memories. Burke's observations regarding the ability of custom and habit to unite men, even men who have reason to hate one another, are suggestive.

> Men . . . are led to associate by resemblances, by conformities, by sympathies. . . . Nothing else is as strong a tie of amity . . . as correspondence in . . . customs,

[23] *On the Sublime and Beautiful*, p. 235; "On the Policy of the Allies," pp. 452-53, 468; *Reflections*, pp. 88-89, 231; Letter to Richard Burke, Esq., "On the Protestant Ascendency in Ireland," in *Works*, vol. 6, pp. 385-412. See also *Reflections*, p. 104, and McWilliams, p. 28.

manners, and habits of life. . . . They approximate
men to men without their knowledge, and sometimes
against their intentions. The secret, unseen, but irre-
fragable bond of habitual intercourse holds them together.[24]

The power of the customary, of the habitual, is bound
up with the "secret" and the "unseen." Locke's praise of
the habitual had centered around the ability of repetition
to impart to rules or injunctions a seeming naturalness. It
is this same repetitive quality (in Burke's parlance, unbroken continuity) that gives to custom its natural appearance,
that atmospheric quality which causes it to be "unseen."
Customs, Burke knew, were simply the collective habits or
prejudices of a people. Such collective habits were so thoroughly ingrained in a nation as to be indistinguishable from
natural propensities—a kind of "second moral nature."[25]
But Burke knew more. Nature presents herself to human
beings as the embodiment of repetition. The original source
of Nature's power in the human mind is her regularity. In
erecting a politics in "conformity to nature," Burke hopes
to trade on Nature's stock. "Calling in the aid of her unerr-
ing and powerful instincts, [we] fortify the fallible and feeble contrivances of our reason." "Repeating as from a rub-
ric," Burke conjures up Nature's power in support of the
constitution.

Working after the pattern of nature . . . our political
system is placed in a just correspondence and symmetry with the order of the world and with the mode
of existence decreed to a permanent body composed
of transitory parts, wherein, by the disposition of a
stupendous wisdom, molding together the great mysterious incorporation of the human race, the whole,
at one time, is never old or middle-aged or young, but,

[24] "Three Letters," pp. 317-18.
[25] "Abridgement of English History," p. 292.

in a condition of unchangeable constancy, moves on through the varied tenor of perpetual decay, fall, renovation and progression.[26]

The customary political order is linked to the mysteries of the Earth Mother who swallows up the riddle of death in her cyclical vision of "perpetual decay, fall, renovation and progression." On close inspection, Burke's political vision has the dreadful appearance of a mulch pile. In the regenerative vision of Nature's "pattern," decay and death are mollified. Men are likened to "transitory parts" of a "great" and "mysterious" corporation. The awful truth of Nature's "stupendous wisdom" and man's deep fear of being like "the flies of a summer" help conceal the terror of death's reality. Machiavelli had seen in the realm of politics an arena in which men could confront death. Thus, the republic was conceived as a structure of remembrance, the deed a protest against Nature's unalterable sentence. But what had been for Machiavelli the source of political greatness appears to Burke the cause of political destruction. Seeking to rid politics of the deed and deny to men remembrance, Burke pits Nature against politics: "By preserving the method of nature in the conduct of the state," politics is emptied of the uncustomary, the extraordinary, the memorable. Nietzsche understood Burke's "method" all too well: "Dull habit, the small and lowly which fills all corners of the world and wafts like a dense earthly vapor around everything great, deceiving, smothering, suffocating, obstructs the path which the great must still travel to immortality. . . . The monumental ought not arise—that is the . . . watchword."[27]

Against those who would do battle with death, Burke reminds men that "the grave" will heap "its mold upon our presumption" and "the silent tomb" will impose "its law on our pert loquacity." Our "deeds" and our "words"

---

[26] *Reflections*, pp. 21, 38, 39; McWilliams, p. 34.
[27] Nietzsche, p. 15.

are revealed as so much dust. Thus we see that in the guise of maternal warmth and affection is concealed a cruel taunt and a reminder of futility. For behind the mask of the loving Mother is the face of Medusa, emasculating those who would pursue glory and reducing men to impotence. "Love," Burke observed in *A Philosophical Enquiry into the Origin of Our Ideas of the Sublime and Beautiful*, "approaches much nearer to contempt than is commonly imagined." Against man's desire to father a memorial, Burke marshalls the forces of the Earth Mother. Wrapped in the warm embrace of Nature, shielded from the knowledge of nothingness, men forget death and protest no more as the remembrance of past deeds sinks into an oblivion of endless recurrence.[28]

Action and Inheritance

In [the] choice of inheritance we have given to our frame of polity the image of a relation in blood, binding up the constitution of our country with our dearest domestic ties, adopting our fundamental laws into the bosom of our family affections, keeping inseparable and cherishing with the warmth of all their combined and mutually reflected charities our state, our hearths, our sepulchres, and our altars.

Few of Burke's teachings are better known than his insistence upon the importance of considering the fundamental political institutions of a nation as a patrimony received from one's forefathers, and few passages are more revealing of Burke's intention in doing so. As we have observed, the customary had suffered from the assaults of *history*. The historical investigations of its defenders no less than its detractors had eroded the immemorial soil in which custom flourishes and upon which the authority of custom depends. Burke knew better than most the implications of the erosion of custom for England.

[28] *Reflections*, p. 97; *On the Sublime and Beautiful*, p. 250.

Our constitution is a prescriptive constitution; it is a constitution whose sole authority is that it has existed time out of mind . . . Your king, your lords, your judges, your juries, grand and little, are all prescriptive.

All established authority was at stake. Custom was the foundation upon which the entire structure of English political life rested.[29]

As Burke knew, adherence to tradition is intimately bound up with continuity. Prescriptive authority is gravely threatened by any radical breaks in the flow of historical time. Time itself is prescriptive authority's only means of healing breaches in continuity: "Political arrangement, as it is a work for social ends, is to be only wrought by social means. There mind must conspire with mind. Time is required to produce that union of minds which alone can produce all the good we aim at." Time heals all wounds only by calling oblivion to its assistance. Times of change and social upheaval, always threatening to established authority, are particularly so to an authority which rests solely upon a "continued and general approbation." It is this threat which

---

[29] *Reflections*, p. 38; "Speech on the Reform of Representation," quoted in Kramnick [1], p. 149. This remains an interpretive point of some controversy. Few disagree that Burke drew heavily on the historical and jurisprudential traditions which were much in evidence in English intellectual life during the seventeenth and eighteenth centuries. What remains controversial is the character of that indebtedness. An important assumption of our studies here, one we believe warranted both historically and textually, is Burke's prevailing sense of change and his fear of the erosion of tradition. This understanding casts Burke as a theorist who seizes upon elements of the traditional in a conscious effort to recoup the present and save the future. Others have seen Burke as "saturated" with the work of the common lawyers, his work revealing their "habit of mind." Pocock, for example, emphasizes Burke's insistence upon the continuity and contemporaneity of the English adherence to ancient usage as evidence of Burke's belief in the fact. We choose to see such insistence as necessary to the recovery of custom's authority and also, perhaps, as a kind of "whistling in the dark," suggesting Burke's doubts rather than his convictions. Moreover, Burke's preoccupation with discontinuity and a fragmented past are difficult to incorporate into Pocock's analysis. See Pocock, *Politics, Language and Time*, pp. 210, 213, 222, and Kirk, p. 140.

underlay the apparent fragility of tradition in the past several centuries. Conservatives in such times must *play for time*; that is, they must find a means to insure or encourage continued adherence to the ways of the fathers in the face of alternate modes of action or innovation. Among the most thoughtful conservatives, this is not simple nostalgia or reaction, but rather a strategy of buying time to enable the pull of prescription to reassert itself as the memory of actions "in contradiction to that good old mode" fades from the consciousness of a people.[30]

Burke suggests as much in his "choice" of inheritance, in the quotation with which we began. His choice is strategic: "We are not guided," he tells us, "by the spirit of antiquarians [that is, by the spirit of unaided custom], but by the spirit of philosophical analogy." Those other affections which bind men together had been severely shaken; thus, Burke would give to the "frame" of the state "the image of a relation in blood." Burke hopes to shore up English political life by "adopting our fundamental laws into the bosom of our family affections." The turmoil of two centuries had delivered to the traditional mind a succession of violent shocks, undoubtedly more severe for their having been inflicted upon a culture knowing only stasis. Burke, a man of no slight rhetorical ability, knew well the appeal of a "mode of existence" conceived as "a permanent body" and bound together through blood-tie. The constitution would be bound up with that "close affection which grows from common names, from kindred blood." The appeal of blood lay both in the strength of such bonds and, at a time when other bonds seemed weak, in its automatic and inescapable presence. Blood kin are often bound together through affection, but those bonds remain in the face of enmity also. As the adage reminds us, "You can choose your friends, but not your relatives."

[30] *Reflections*, pp. 113, 197 (see also p. 192); "Abridgement of English History," p. 217; Kramnick [1], p. 149.

In times such as Burke's, there is great psychic comfort to be derived from "keeping inseparable and cherishing with the warmth of all their combined and mutually reflected charities our state, our hearths, our sepulchres, and our altars." A master of emotional prose, Burke nurtured the sensibilities of his readers. He knew that what "the heart owns . . . the understanding ratifies."[31]

Burke knew also that his philosophical analogy must circumscribe the energy unleashed by modernity, which continued to menace the already weakened authority of prescription. The common law had revealed the phenomenon of oblivion. Burke returned to the law for the analogy that would be the foundation of his reintegration of past and present. As a body of law, the common law's first concern had always been to establish proprietary rights and, in particular, the transmission of such rights. It was upon this "idea of inheritance" that Burke would establish the political relation. In describing that relation "as a patrimony derived from [one's] forefathers," Burke also revealed the source of the perspective he brought to his investigations.[32]

While the idea of inheritance showed great potential as a means of reconciling past and present, it was not without certain difficulties—difficulties related to those that plagued a fragmented past. The most visible example of inheritance in English institutional life was also that which most clearly suggested the difficulties contained in the idea of inheritance—the Crown. With the exception perhaps of 1648, every

[31] *Reflections*, pp. 38, 87; "On Conciliation with America," p. 160; See also McWilliams, p.37, and Kramnick [1], p. 8. Burke was sensitive to both the necessity of bonds and their precariousness. His defense of the political party was in part founded upon the importance of such bonds. (Burke, after all, was one of those men who left the land of his fathers to seek his fortune in a "new world.") The great pain Burke suffered as a result of his break with Fox and the "new Whigs" suggests how personally Burke was touched by the anomie present in even nascent modernity.

[32] Pocock, *Politics, Language and Time*, p. 211; "Three Letters," p. 326; *Reflections*, pp. 16, 36, 57-58.

threat to political stability in the English past, including the Conquest itself (as well as the abortive invasion of the Spanish during the reign of Elizabeth), had been connected in some way with the problem of succession, that is, with the right of inheritance. Burke's praise of the men of 1688 is, in part, approval of their efforts to fix the character of that succession by keeping it in the Protestant line.[33]

The effect of 1648 was to spread the difficulties inherent in the idea of inheritance to the political culture at large. Just as multiple offspring raise difficulties for a father's patrimony, so a fragmented past raises questions about the character of an inheritance. What *had* the past bequeathed to eighteenth-century Englishmen? Even if Englishmen desired, as Burke insisted they did, "to derive all we possess as an inheritance from our forefathers," the nature of that inheritance was problematic. If the sermons of Richard Price and the proceedings of the Revolution Society revealed anything, it was the uncertain and disputable character of that legacy. And just as the Settlement had sought to remove the dangerous uncertainty of the succession, so Burke sought to cleanse the legacy of the forefathers. Burke knew that that inheritance must be "entailed" if the legacy itself was not to be the cause of political turmoil. While Burke often spoke as if the idea of inheritance was opposed to innovation or to the rejection of the legacy, other phrases reveal more subtle conflicts within the concept of inheritance itself. A warning to his readers not to expose "their sure inheritance to be scrambled for and torn to pieces by every wild, litigious spirit" is suggestive, reminding us of a common literary theme no less common in real life: the destruction wrought by quarreling over the patrimony. (The example of Henry II and his notoriously rebellious and jealous sons springs immediately to our minds, just as presumably, it did to the minds of eighteenth-century Englishmen.) The common law had resolved the problem in

[33] *Reflections*, p. 19.

favor of the eldest male heir (the principle of per stirpes) and against the claims of the younger brothers, and Burke agreed. "They should not think it among their rights to cut off the entail." But Burke knew that the sure possession of the past, unlike property, was not within the power of the magistrate.[34]

The questions of legacy are complex. What is a father's legacy? Is the patrimony only the fortune or the objects of the father? Is it not also a spirit or a memory, and can such things be claimed by one? How can others be excluded? Who really is his father's son? These were the questions that Burke tried to conceal. He sought a metaphorical equivalent of primogeniture in his idea of inheritance, one which might, indeed, give rise to but one representative of the ancestor. He achieved this end by reducing the concept of inheritance to its legal content—the real property of the ancestor. In Burke's analogy, the concept of *estate* is narrowed further to mean the house or the "building" of the father. The ancestral home is quite literally indivisible.[35]

The idea of a father's house as a metaphor for a nation's ancient institutions is not an uncommon theme (Lincoln's "House Divided" being but the best American example); however, Burke's use of the metaphor is decidedly structural. It is the "edifice" of that house that Burke describes, emphasizing aspects such as "walls." "Foundations" take on the appearance of stone and mortar. As Hawthorne, too, understood, there is a kind of power in an ancient edifice. Captivating, it captures the present within a *form*

---

[34] *Reflections*, pp. 35-37.

[35] Burke suggested as much when he wrote that "we transmit our government and our privileges in the same manner in which we enjoy and transmit our property." Burke's strictures against the dividing up of property are but the private side of his opinions regarding the public inheritance: that there should be a single representative of the past. His use of the technical and opposing terms of per capita (equal shares) and per stirpes (single representative of the ancestor) in his discussion of the concept of the inheritance reveals his sensitivity to the theoretical as well as the legal complexities involved. See *Reflections*, pp. 25, 57-58.

of the past. Inside such "castles," the ghosts of ancestors long dead still reign. The metaphor reveals the most important consequence of Burke's conception of patrimony.

We have derived several . . . no small benefits from considering our liberties in the light of an inheritance. Always acting as if in the presence of canonized forefathers, the spirit of freedom, leading in itself to misrule and excess, is tempered with an awful gravity.

Men are "petrified" (Arendt's phrase) when in the "presence" of their "canonized forefathers." It is this immobility (the limiting of action to *acceptable behavior*) that Burke understands as tradition. Action is trapped in the form of the past. The ability of inheritance understood as tradition to take action out of the present intrigued Burke (as it frightened Arendt). Burke observes that the "advantages . . . obtained by a state proceeding on these maxims are locked fast in a sort of family settlement, grasped in a kind of mortmain, forever."[36]

But this conjuring up of the dead hand is itself a language of great fear. Tradition seeks its greatest tyranny as the living force which has sustained it begins to ebb. In the flush of republican confidence, Machiavelli taught that men could *act into* the past, that the past was confirmed in the present through the deed. Machiavelli was unafraid. For Burke, the legacy of such confidence had proven itself to be civil war, massacres, and regicide. Only the most rigid adherence to tradition could save the political world from those innovations and revolutions which lead to disintegration and tyranny. "The evils of inconstancy and ver-

---

[36] *Reflections*, pp. 24, 39-40, 99, 290; See also Arendt, *Between Past and Future*, p. 168. Mortmain means literally "dead hand." Like a last will, tradition pushes an ancient will into the future. Burke quotes the Act which confirmed Elizabeth's claim to the throne: speaking for the nation, members of Parliament submitted "themselves, their heirs, and posterities forever" (*Reflections*, p. 22). Three pages later, Burke quotes Vergil: "Through many years the fortune of the House stands, and grandfathers' grandfathers augment the roll" (p. 25).

satility," thought Burke, were "ten thousand times worse than those of obstinacy and the blindest prejudice."[37]

The ancients and their republican students also had known the dangers of political action: its tendency to "force open all limitations and cut across all boundaries." In all action is "the seed of . . . boundlessness." The ancient legislator had sought to bind action within the walls of piety and reverence. The dynamic of the republic existed in the tension created within these walls. The city knew that it must risk action or die. But if Burke knew that the "atheists" of Paris posed a grave threat to order, action, he feared, would not be fettered even by piety. Order seemed too precarious. "Rage and frenzy will pull down more in half an hour than prudence, deliberation, and foresight can build up in a hundred years." For Burke, as for the exasperated (or fearful) parent, peace was inextricably tied to quiet.[38]

Although the tradition had (with few exceptions) exhibited caution toward and even distrust of the spirit of liberty, the description of liberty as "vice," "folly," and "madness" was not among even the most scrutinizing analyses prior to Burke.[39] In Burke's teaching, activity seems to be a qual-

---

[37] *Reflections*, p. 109.

[38] Arendt, *Human Condition*, pp. 190-194; *Reflections*, p. 196. Burke's fear of the "boundlessness" of action can be detected in his description of the revolutionary spirit, which dared to wage war "with heaven itself" (*Reflections*, p. 10). Conservatism has since confused order with orderliness. Republicanism, in contrast, has always taught that the best political order (at least the best possible political order) is characterized by a certain level of *disorder*. Political *peace* more often than not is indicative of decay in public spiritedness.

[39] *Reflections*, p. 288. Burke is well known for his opposition to abstract principle in politics. While he claims to be a lover of liberty in principle, he insists that, in things relating to human action, "circumstances" are what give a "distinguishing color and discriminating effect" to every principle (*Reflections*, p. 8). This is a venerable argument with classical pedigree, but Burke's use of it belies an antagonism to action and its political embodiment, the republic, which itself borders on abstract principle. Later, in accord with the corollary of circumstance, Burke claims to "reprobate no form of government merely upon abstract principles" and yet, one page later, we find him quoting Bolingbroke (in itself noteworthy, as Bolingbroke's naturalism was the first victim of Burke's rapier wit in

ity upon which the forces of destruction have a monopoly. Regardless of the personification of the moment, be it English dissenters, Hastings and his East Indian cohorts, or Jacobins, these sinister forces all are characterized by vigor. "Activity," "energy," "confidence," these are the stuff of which the forces of destruction are made. Their "strong passions awaken the faculties." They are possessed of "a strength to heap mountains upon mountains."[40] Standing in opposition to these images of strength and vigor is property, which is "sluggish, inert, timid." The British, we are told, are "passive, . . . a dull, sluggish race." But we are not to suspect that political inaction is indicative of decay. On the contrary, "moral timidity" is the appropriate posture of the citizen. Burke's description of the English citizenry as "thousands of great cattle, reposed beneath the shadow of the British oak, chew[ing] the cud, and . . . silent" is perhaps an unsurpassed image of political lethargy; yet this is the English citizen's foremost political virtue! "Thanks . . . to the cold sluggishness of our national character, we still bear the stamp of our forefathers."[41] The deed threatens to open up the chasm between the past and the present, between fathers and sons. Action itself is revealed as the enemy.[42]

---

his *Vindication of Natural Society*) on the abstract superiority of monarchies over and against republics (*Reflections*, pp. 143-44). Fear of action and antagonism toward the republic seem here to be founded upon something other than the color of circumstance.

[40] *Reflections*, pp. 8, 10, 57, 106-7; "On the Policy of the Allies," p. 443.

[41] *Reflections*, pp. 57, 62, 97, 290. Consider also that Burke places in juxtaposition to these silent, cud-chewing cattle "half a dozen grasshoppers under a fern [making] the field ring with their importunate chink." The ancients had intimately connected acting with speaking. Burke, too, understands the relationship. His antipathy toward action extends to speaking as well, for we are told that such "insects of the hours" are "loud and troublesome" (*Reflections*, p. 97).

[42] Burke's antipathy toward action is evident in his reflections upon the epistemology of politics. If Burke's assault upon the "presumption" of philosophy was aimed, in particular, at the misplaced confidence of the Enlightenment, the more general theoretical consequences of his ideas regarding political knowledge would deny to citizens *any* bases of knowl-

Burke knew, however, that no constitution can defend itself. "Conservation," too, requires action. Fearing the people, Burke lodged his principle of action in the stability of aristocratic blood, the very embodiment of continuity, "perpetuating their benefits from generation to generation." That action which conserves and corrects is not for the citizenry, but for "those whom nature has qualified to administer in extremities this critical, ambiguous, bitter potion. . . . As it was not made for common abuses, so it is not to be agitated by common minds." The people "in a mass" are inconstant, rudderless.

> They remain what the bulk of us ever must be, when abandoned to our vulgar propensities, without guide, leader, or control: that is made too full of a blind elevation in prosperity; to despise untried dangers; to be overpowered by unexpected reverses.

Like the classical aristocratic critique, Burke's criticism of the demos rests upon their inconstancy and lack of wisdom, but with a twist—a twist informed by a Machiavellian insight. The people "despise untried dangers." Their faults are made doubly dangerous by their boldness. "Control" rather than guidance has become the watchword of aristocratic leadership.[43]

---

edge upon which to act. Burke's elevation of custom was linked to this limiting of knowledge. To be sure, custom contained political wisdom, but such knowledge was a collective possession, more akin to habit than to principle, and, in any case, beyond the comprehension of the individual citizen. It has been said of Burke that his "is the most developed and articulate of all indictments of ideology" (*Works*, Introduction, p. 7). Like Marx, Burke understood the relation of ideology and action. Fearing ideological energy, Burke sought to undercut the foundation of confidence embedded in the notion of civic knowledge. See *Reflections*, pp. 89, 114, 197; Pocock, *Ancient Constitution*, p. 34; Kirk, p. 150; McWilliams, p. 26. See also Mansfield, *Statesmanship*, p. 158. Mansfield argues that for Burke a people exhibits its virtue in "forbearance from rule."

[43] "Fourth Letter," p. 100; *Reflections*, pp. 24, 28, 34, 58; "Letter to Duke of Richmond," quoted in Kramnick [1], p. 7; "Three Letters," pp. 249-50. To allow the people an active role in the state would be a "usurpation on the prerogatives of nature" (*Reflections*, p. 56).

The republic was characterized by the union of piety and vigor, reverence and glory. Its greatness was the product of the unification of such ambivalences in the breasts of her citizens. Both piety and vigor are present in the Burkean state, but their republican unity has been severed. Each has become, as it were, the particular virtue of a class. Russell Kirk has understood the teaching of his mentor well enough: prescription, the "dead hand" of tradition, is to be the guide for "the mass of men"; statesmen, who must penetrate the veil of tradition in the name of worldly exigency, are to be guided by "expedience." They are to imitate Lord Somers and "observe with what address [the] temporary solution of continuity [that is, radical discontinuity] is kept from the eye." The most expedient of all actions is to throw "a politic, well-wrought veil over every circumstance . . . which might furnish a precedent for any future departure" from the customary.[44]

There can be no glory, even for those who save their country. The memorable deed threatens to call forth its repetition. The inheritance of the fathers is menaced by glory's claim upon the memory. And if the house of the forefathers has its "gallery of portraits," they are without faces and without names.[45] "It is our ignorance of things that causes all our admiration." Thus, the true temple of Burkean piety is Stonehenge, where "the Monuments themselves come to be venerated—and not the less because the reason for venerating them [is] no longer known." Nietzsche knew the ritual and had witnessed the sacrament: "Their path . . . is obstructed and their air darkened when one dances idolatrously and diligently round a half-

---

[44] Kirk, pp. 146-49; *Reflections*, pp. 20-21.

[45] In aristocracies founded exclusively upon blood, remembrance remains private, within the walls of ancestral castles and behind heraldic shields, the property of descendants, but denied to the nation as example. In Burke's history, only the deeds of kings are remembered; such men are beyond emulation (while Oliver Cromwell, the only man who dared supplant a king, remains a "great bad man").

understood monument of some great past . . . as though [the] motto were: let the dead bury the living."[46]

The Political Imagery of the Sublime and the Beautiful

Along with his *Vindication of Natural Society* (1756), *A Philosophical Enquiry into the Origin of Our Ideas of the Sublime and Beautiful* (1757) was the foundation upon which Burke established his literary reputation and his means of access to the bluestocking circle of English literati. Its early date and its philosophical cast have made it an infrequent source for those who have sought to understand Burke as a political thinker. This is unfortunate, for in the later, more ideological work, Burke generally is content to allow the curtain of naturalness to remain unbroken, leaving the political sentiments mysterious: "We look up with awe to kings . . . [and] it is natural to be so affected." In contrast to his overtly political work, Burke's investigations into aesthetics were decidedly psychological, so much so that one commentator has attributed the great popularity of this treatise among the Germans (as compared to the general indifference with which it was received among English empiricists) to its psychological approach. Burke himself, in a remarkable passage in the *Enquiry*, gives us warrant to rummage through his aesthetics. Our passions, terror, and love, Burke teaches, have their origin "at a time of which all sort of memory is worn out of our minds . . . [and] which we find it very hard afterwards to distinguish from natural effects." The parallel to many of Burke's political arguments is striking. This decay of memory, which be-

[46] *On the Sublime and Beautiful*, p. 245; "Abridgement of English History," p. 185; Nietzsche, p. 18. Consider also Arendt's observation regarding the power of tradition: "The end of a tradition does not necessarily mean that traditional concepts have lost their power over the minds of men. On the contrary, it sometimes seems that this power of well-worn notions and categories becomes more tyrannical as the tradition loses its living force and as the memory of its beginning recedes" (*Between Past and Future*, p. 26).

comes the necessary boundary to the work on politics, is penetrated in the work on aesthetics.[47]

Of the Beautiful, Burke writes:

Beauty is a name I shall apply to all such qualities in things as to induce in us a sense of affection and tenderness.

Of the Sublime:

I know of nothing sublime, which is not some modification of power. And this branch rises . . . from terror, the common stock of every thing that is sublime.

More generally, the Beautiful is characterized by "weakness," "softness," "smoothness;" the Sublime by "power," "strength," "violence," "pain," "terror." More revealing is the association of the Beautiful with familiarity, immanence, while the Sublime partakes of "obscurity." "How greatly night adds to our dread," observes Burke. Concluding with a commentary upon Milton's Satan, Burke writes; "All is dark, uncertain, confused, terrible, and sublime to the last degree."[48]

While the portraits are starkly drawn, neither we nor Kramnick are surprised when Burke invokes the mother and the father as the embodiment of the Beautiful and Sublime. Beauty is characterized by repetition of form, which Kramnick correctly associates with the repetitive rhythms of life and nature that characterize the female principle. The Sublime is associated with being "conversant about terrible things." This is the esoteric knowledge of the father. Such knowledge gives rise to "glorying" and to a sense of "inward greatness" which is linked to the destruction of continuity. The maternal principle, in McWilliams's phrase, is convicted of "ignorance" and "parochiality" by a knowing paternity. In Burke's view, armed with the sublime

[47] *Reflections*, p. 98; *On the Sublime and Beautiful*, p. 306.
[48] *On the Sublime and Beautiful*, pp. 237, 243, 248.

knowledge of terror, the paternal principle seeks mastery over the maternal Beautiful.[49]

In these passages, the *Enquiry* makes explicit what is only hinted at in the *Reflections*: repetitive, cyclical continuity associated with the secrets of the mother and in opposition to the knowledge of the father, a knowledge related to a sense of inward greatness and a desire for remembrance. But while there is this similarity between the teaching of the *Enquiry* and that of the *Reflections*, the two works also differ in one respect. The teaching of the *Reflections* is characterized by a taunting laughter, reminding would-be fathers of their weakness and the futility of the quest for immortality. In the *Enquiry*, the depth of Burke's own terror is underlined. The female "contempt," hidden by a mother's love, in turn hides the fear of masculine power which is associated with the knowledge of terrible things.

Surprisingly, Burke is quick to associate the knowledge of the father with the origin of political authority: The power which arises from institution in kings and commanders has the same connection with terror." Authority rests upon "dread majesty." It is this dreadful quality that is the psychological component of Burke's monarchism. Authority leaves men awestruck, taking "away the free use of their faculties." Burke quotes the Book of Job: "When I prepared my seat in the street, the young men saw me, and hid themselves." The source of Burke's secret antagonism to the republic also is suggested here. The republic rests upon the possibility of the internalization of authority—the unification of piety and action in a dialectic of reverence and glory. Burke's formulation radically dissociates the two. "Dread majesty" destroys the foundation of the republic, what Arendt has called "public space." The presence of the father "takes away the free use of . . . faculties" and causes "young men" to hide. The authority of the father

[49] *On the Sublime and Beautiful*, p. 225; Kramnick [2], pp. 95-97; McWilliams, pp. 12-13.

stands in opposition to the desire of young men to be seen and heard. Majesty vitiates "words and deeds."[50]

If Burke denies the reality of that peculiar ambivalence upon which the republic rests, he is not without his own ambivalence toward the authority of the father.

> The authority of the father, so useful to our well-being, and so justly venerable upon all accounts, hinders us from having that entire love for him that we have for our mothers where the parental authority is almost melted down into the mother's fondness and indulgence. But we generally have great love for our grandfathers, in whom this authority is removed a degree from us, and where the weakness of age mellows it into something of feminine partiality.

While the father's power is necessary, it is also, we suspect, prone to excess. Obedience is founded upon love as well as fear. Authority must be feminized, mellowed with "weakness." Burke associates custom (becoming accustomed) with this process of feminization.

> Custom reconciles us to everything. After we have been used to the sight of black objects the terror abates, and the smoothness and glossiness, or some agreeable accident of bodies so coloured (qualities of beauty), softens in some measure the horror and sternness of their original nature; yet the nature of the original impression still continues.

In the *Enquiry*, authority is given a double aspect—paternal and maternal, terror softened by familiarity. In the political works, authority is associated only with prescription—the maternal principle—which grows through time, is related to familiarity, and is manifested in custom. To the extent that the paternal priciple is revealed, it is associated with power and force only. Paternal "tyranny" is juxtaposed to

[50] *On the Sublime and Beautiful*, p. 250.

136

the maternal authority of prescription. In the *Reflections*, Burke tells us that prescription "mellows into legality governments that were violent in their commencement." Like the "feminine partiality" of a grandfather, governments "mellow," but from "violence" to "legality." Unlike the teaching of the *Enquiry*, the *Reflections* conceal the true origins of authority, terror, and ascribe to beginnings the character of violence only. The "reverence," "admiration," and "respect" associated with the father, and their relation to the knowledge of "terrible things," are hidden behind a curtain—a curtain we now see as founded upon the maternal principle. It is of this curtain and not of the true beginnings of government that Burke speaks in his "Speech on the Reform of the Representation in Commons": "A prescriptive government, such as ours, never was the work of any legislator, never was made upon any foregone theory." The truth about the origin of authority is concealed behind the natural appearance of custom and prescription. Burke knew that behind the curtain lurked a great father whose founding was, in Burke's words, "very absolute in substance and effect." William the Conqueror had molded the state "according to his own pleasure." Indeed, it was the terror of the Conquest that maternal custom had so successfully mellowed and concealed.[51]

Burke's critique of "the empire of light and reason" now takes on additional meanings. "All the decent drapery of life is to be rudely torn off." Such drapery had heretofore covered "the defects of our naked shivering nature." This

---

[51] *On the Sublime and Beautiful*, pp. 241, 290, 325; *Reflections*, p. 192; Kramnick [1], p. 35; "Abridgement of English History," p. 343. During the early days of the American Revolution, Burke spoke of the colonists as disobedient children. On one occasion, Lord Camerthen asked in debate if "the Americans are our children, . . . how can they revolt against their parent?" Burke defended "the opposition of our children" as legitimate in the face of parental "abuses of authority" and a "desire of domineering." The ministry suffered from an excess of fatherly authority. Observe also how Burke placated the potentially wrathful father with rhetorical offerings. The father was "justly venerable upon all accounts," even in his tyranny.

critique raises questions about Burke's alleged "method,"
that of "working after the pattern of nature." We begin to
suspect that Burke's teaching is to be understood not as
being in "conformity to nature," but rather as an effort to
again close the curtain of forgetfulness around a defective
nature.[52] To be sure, it is "natural" to look up to kings with
awe: "Indeed so natural is this timidity with regard to power,
and so strongly does it inhere in our constitution, that very
few are able to conquer it, but . . . by using no small violence to their natural dispositions."[53] But in a frank passage, Burke reveals another natural posture toward kings.
"Indeed, . . . the suffering of monarchs makes a delicious
repast to some sort of palates."[54] The suspicion is unavoidable. Our natural defect is somehow bound up with
this ambivalence toward paternal authority. As we have
seen, in contrast to the *Enquiry*, Burke's political writings
reveal authority only in its maternal aspect—as prescription. Nature, too, appears only in maternal form—as repetitive cycle—in the political writings. The implication of
the *Enquiry*, however, is that both the Beautiful and the
Sublime are rooted in Nature. In a letter to Dick Shackleton,
describing a flood that menaced his father's house, Burke
confirms our supposition: "It gives me great pleasure to
see nature in those great tho' terrible scenes; it fills the
mind with grand ideas."[55] Nature, we discover, also has

[52] *Reflections*, p. 87. The status of "drapery" in Burke's political theory
calls for a modification of Strauss's understanding of Burke, that the best
constitution is natural or in line with nature. Rather, the best constitution
is that which appears wholly natural or succeeds completely in hiding its
origins. See Strauss, p. 313.

[53] *On the Sublime and Beautiful*, p. 251. Compare to the *Reflections*, in
which to break with custom and habit is "to offer a sudden violence to
their minds and their feelings" (p. 180).

[54] *Reflections*, p. 83. More frank still is this outrageous slip of Burke's,
made in a conversation with Dr. Johnson and recorded by Boswell: "It
was not so necessary that there should be affection from children to
parents, as from parents to children; nay, there would be no harm in that
view though children should at a certain age eat their parents" (quoted
in Kramnick [2], pp. 64-65).

[55] Kramnick [2], p. 98.

two characters, the warm assurance of cyclical continuity and the terrifying aspect of awful power. Both the Beautiful and the Sublime are present in Nature. And as the title of the *Enquiry* suggests, the two faces of Nature have their psychological complements in *human* nature.

In this early letter, Burke also hints at the source of Nature's defect. *Seeing* terrible scenes fills the mind with grand ideas. (We are again reminded of Burke's observations regarding the Parisian terror, that men ought not to *see* such things.) In the *Enquiry*, Burke associates the paternal principle with a knowledge of terrible things, observing that such knowledge leads to a sense of "inward greatness," "glorying," and "triumph." Taken together, these descriptions point to the fundamental defect in the paternal principle. The knowledge of the father gives rise to glorying—a desire to be remembered. We recall the regicide Hugh Peters, whose "triumph" was "memorble." "Grand ideas" are manifested in the world as ambition: "It is this passion that drives men to all the ways we see in signalizing themselves, and that tends to make whatever excites in a man the idea of this distinction so very pleasant." Much later in his career, on the floor of the House of Commons, Burke returned to the topic of ambition, pointing to its darker consequences for politics and suggesting that ambition is more particularly a vice of modernity.

> That particular period of men's lives when their ambitious views had lain secretly in the corner of their hearts, almost undiscovered to themselves, were unlocked . . . ; when all their desire, their self-opinions, their vanity, their avarice and lust of power . . . were set at large and began to show themselves.[56]

The sublimity of the paternal principle is ambivalent in its very core. If the "inferior effects" of the sublime are "admiration, reverence, respect," the sublime in the high-

---

[56] *On the Sublime and Beautiful*, p. 236; Kramnick [2], p. 192.

est degree gives rise to "astonishment" and "horror." (The French Revolution is both "astonishing" and "horrible" according to Burke.) The origins of political authority spring from the same natural passion that threatens all political order. Traditional society had kept the paternal principle from the eye, cloaking it in a feminine continuity.

> But now all is to be changed. All the pleasing illusions which made power gentle and obedience liberal, which harmonized the different shades of life, and which, by a bland assimilation, incorporated into politics the sentiments which beautify and soften private society, are to be dissolved by this new conquering empire of light and reason.

The Enlightenment had pierced "the decent drapery" of custom, democratizing the esoteric knowledge of the father. Ambition had been unchained. Glory had once been the private demesne of kings. Of the Conqueror, Burke could write, "There is nothing more memorable in history than the actions, fortunes, and character of this great man." But the philosophes had taught that "a king is but a man." What had once been regal exchange was made common currency. Cromwell had shown how kings may be treated. Now each citizen, "actuated by sinister ambition and a lust for meritorious glory," sought to partake of fatherhood.[57]

Viewed through the categories of his aesthetics, modernity is revealed as the consequence of the paternal principle unleashed. Thus, Burke's politics can be seen as an effort to recast the state in maternal categories. "A nation," Burke

---

[57] *On the Sublime and Beautiful*, p. 241; *Reflections*, pp. 46, 87; "Abridgement of English History," p. 362. Burke's understanding of Nature has profound consequences for the defense of aristocracy. The ancient justification of aristocracy was founded upon natural hierarchy, with the state under the guidance of "the best." The "prerogatives of nature" enjoyed by Burkean aristocrats prove to be but "pleasing illusion," "drapery" which hides the subversive truth of egalitarianism. Order demands that the state be founded on a lie (unlike the Platonic aristocracy, in which the myth of the metals is an approximation of a more esoteric truth). Burke, however, secretly concedes Paine's point, presaging the anxiety of aristocracy without moral justification.

insists, "is an idea of continuity." His method—the feminization of politics—brings "the dispositions that are lovely in private life into the service and conduct of the Commonwealth." Against the sublimity of modern politics, Burke attempts to touch the tattered remains of the maternal curtain with a self-conscious rhetoric of sentiment and affection.

> You see, Sir, that in this enlightened age I am bold enough to confess that we are generally men of untaught feelings, that, instead of casting away all our old prejudices, we cherish them to a very considerable degree, and, to take more shame to ourselves, we cherish them because they are prejudices; and the longer they have lasted and the more generally they have prevailed, the more we cherish them.

In the *Reflections*, we find the motto for Burke's method: "To make us love our country, our country ought to be lovely."[58]

Ambition and Modernity

> The French Revolution is the most astonishing that has hitherto happened in the world. . . . Everything seems out of nature in this strange chaos of levity and ferocity, and of all sorts of crimes jumbled together with all sorts of follies. In viewing this monstrous tragicomic scene, the most opposite passions necessarily succeed and sometimes mix with each other in the mind, alternate contempt and indignation, alternate laughter and tears, alternate scorn and horror.

The French Revolution was the purest of political sublimities. Burke rightly saw the extraordinary character of the events of 1789. The Revolution was not to be compre-

---

[58] *Reflections*, pp. 88, 98-99; Kramnick [2], p. 114. In contrast, Jacobins have "unfeeling hearts" and are "cold hearted" (*Reflections*, pp. 74, 86, 197).

hended as simply the grandest of political revolutions, nor even as one of those epochal phenomena in human history in which the hand of Providence seems evident. The Revolution was these but it was more. Its power and importance could be comprehended only as a psychical revolution. It was "a vast, tremendous, unformed spectre in a far more terrific guise than any which ever yet have overpowered the imagination and subdued the fortitude of man." As Burke knew, it was this transformative quality, rather than any conscious designs that the revolutionists may have had, that made the Revolution "a great crisis, not of the affairs of France alone, but of all Europe, perhaps of more than Europe." The threat posed by 1789 was the very grandeur of the event itself. The Revolution was utterly sublime, at once terrible and delightful.[59]

In Burke's view, the most dangerous progeny of 1789 was not so much the principles of the Revolution as the modern consciousness of which "liberté, égalité, fraternité" were but an expression. The French Revolution was not the author of modern consciousness, but only the most visible consequence and the most complete revelation of the meaning of that consciousness. It was a monument to human ambition. Its power and energy made it an object of fascination, even to those who abhorred it; its memory would become a perennial source of inspiration.[60]

[59] *Reflections*, p. 11; "Three Letters," p. 237; *On the Sublime and Beautiful*, p. 225. Burke knew the delight not less than the terror, and his dread was a measure of his temptation. Burke was one of the chief publicists of the Revolution and contributed greatly to its stature as an event. The hyperbole of Burkean rhetoric, in a sense, perfected the "sublimity" of the Revolution and helped make it *the* singular spectacle of modern times.

[60] Burke probably dated the beginning of the modern period from the Reformation. While he is careful not to condemn the Reformation out of hand, he understands Protestantism as essentially antagonistic to worldly authority ("On Conciliation with America," p. 105). His antipathy toward English dissenters (the most protestant of English protestants) and his offhand observation that the call for revolution often emanates from "pulpits" (*Reflections*, p. 28) point to a secret antagonism toward the theoretical implications of Protestant theology. The Protestant Reformation, in the name of the Heavenly Father, had sought to overturn the authority of

Medieval culture had succeeded in circumscribing ambition. Religion, the chivalric code, class distinctions founded on birth, all these hid ambition from the eye or at least contained it within politically manageable limits. (If the sons of Henry II or Richard III were men with "grand ideas," blood right prevented such boundless ambition from infecting the populace.) But modern men, Burke tells us, are driven by "a lust for meritorious glory." The bourgeois principle of *merit*, in its assault upon blood, had contributed to the unchaining of ambition, elevating new men (of whom Oliver Cromwell was only the most conspicuous) to fatherhood.

Although sons most often succeed to fatherhood with the blessings of their fathers, Freud knew (as did hereditary aristocracies) that peaceful succession masked underlying antagonism. Burke linked the paternal principle to glory and triumph, and to a desire for distinction. The idea of succession hid the secret desire to supplant the father. Aristocracies shore up the father through the practical principle of primogeniture no less than through the mysteries of blood, knowing that a father's property is "no small tie" upon the obedience of a son.[61] The egalitarian ideology of

terrestrial fathers (popes and kings), and Burke saw the politics of the previous two centuries as deriving its distinctive hue from the Reformation ("Thoughts on French Affairs," p. 320). Moreover, the Reformation resembled the French Revolution in its ideological character. They were both at base revolutions of doctrine. But whatever misgivings or antagonisms Burke may have entertained toward the consequences of protestantism, the Protestant Revolution differed from the French Revolution in one important respect. The saints had sought only to reduce the *intermediate* fathers to the status of egalitarian sonhood, while the "patriarchal rebels" of 1789 were prepared "to wage war with heaven itself" (*Reflections*, p. 10).

[61] The phrase, of course, is Locke's, and it points to psychological, if not analytic, problems in his theory of authority. For ideological reasons, Locke had sought to separate paternal and political authority. Fatherhood and kingship were only arbitrarily related. Despite the brilliant rhetorical effort of the *Two Treatises*, Burke knew Locke's claim to be both anthropologically and psychologically false. Locke, himself, when confronted with the problems of obedience associated with the *fatherless* authority of the Second Treatise, had recourse to the powers and prerogatives of

modernity had freed the dark side of ambition from the psychic and social fetters of aristocratic culture, unleashing "the death-dance of democratic revolution."[62]

Long before the "impious parricide" of the Jacobins, Burke had drawn modern politics in the images of adolescent rebellion. Before the events of 1789 occupied his thoughts and time, Burke had spent the better part of a decade pursuing Warren Hastings, the chief of the East India Company in India, in an effort to punish that man's "selfish and mischievous ambition." Hastings's regime in India was accused of the most sordid offences associated with tyrannical colonial administrations. To Burke, Hastings and his cohorts were "obscure young men" who "tossed about, subverted, and tore to pieces . . . the most ancient and revered institutions of ages and nations." The rapine and destruction wrought by the agents of the East India company were the consequence, Burke thought, of an impatience to succeed to the mantle of fatherhood—"the desperate boldness of a few obscure young men" who "drink the intoxicating draught of authority and dominion before their heads are able to bear it." A decade later, in his descriptions of the Jacobins and their English adherents, the same images dominate Burke's thought. The Jacobins are "bold, presuming young persons" whose "licentious and abandoned insolence" reveal the "fresh vigor of juvenile activity." Likewise, the Reverend Richard Price, whose impious sermon at Old Jewry had called forth Burke's *Reflections*, is inspired with "a juvenile warmth."[63]

---

paternity. The enjoyment of a father's property was, indeed, "no small tie" upon a man's obedience. If Locke's analogy depicted a cynical side of the relations of sons and citizens to authority, Locke could not avoid recourse to the paternal principle. Burke knew as much. Developing the implications of the analogy of inheritance, Burke understood the political relation to be, at base, one of sonhood.

[62] Kramnick observes that, in "Three Letters on the Proposals for Peace with the Regicide Directory," Burke is preoccupied with one facet of the Jacobin inversion of hierarchy, the assault on the family, and particularly with the erosion of paternal authority.

[63] Kramnick [2], pp. 27, 130, 131; *Reflections*, pp. 74, 98, 163.

The imagery of juvenile rebellion adds a new dimension to our understanding of Burke's teaching on ideology. In "natural" communities in which the political relation of fathers and sons is intact, "awe" of paternal power keeps ambition below the surface. Doctrine, particularly egalitarian doctrine which questions the authority of fathers, creates "theoretic interests" which cut across the hierarchical unity of patriarchy. The introduction of such doctrine into patriarchal communities creates "bands of brothers" bound together in an ideological fraternity whose bonds of loyalty no less than its principles are in violent opposition to the fathers. The nature of action is generational warfare. The experimentation with authorty within such brotherhoods makes young men "conversant with terrible things." Too many and too young, they learn the esoteric knowledge of the father; the consequence: revolution.

The Reformation and social contract theory had eroded the authority of established fathers, but the Enlightenment threatened more. In its effort to light up the darkness, it destroyed the "obscurity" in which the paternal principle was concealed and which had been the source of "dread" and "reverence." The Enlightenment attempted what Rousseau claimed to have achieved: "I dared to strip man's nature naked." It was the revelations of our nakedness, Burke thought, that gave to the Enlightenment its "malignant" disposition. Its rays destroyed reverence only to free the paternal principle, giving birth to a new species of ambitious men, the intellectual. "The men of letters," writes Burke, "fond of distinguishing themselves, are rarely adverse to innovation." Having discovered the sources of paternal authority, the philosophes wanted to make it their own. Their doctrine was at once their arms and their claim to fatherhood. "Happy if learning, not debauched by ambition, had been satisfied to continue the instructor, and not aspired to be the master!" Having disposed of their natural parent (on the advice of philosophers), the French, says Burke, "erect statutes to a wild, ferocious, low-minded, hard-hearted father" (that is, Rousseau).[64]

In the name of liberty, equality, and fraternity, the Enlightenment had taken away the "ancient opinions" that had protected the father's person as they circumscribed the paternal principle. But "on this scheme of things, . . . regicide and parricide . . . are but fictions of superstition; . . . the murder of a king . . . or a father are only common homicide." The philosophes had proclaimed the end of fatherhood. Burke knew nature better.

> But power, of some kind or other, will survive the shock in which manners and opinions perish; and it will find other and worse means for its support. The usurpation which, in order to subvert ancient institutions, has destroyed ancient principles will hold power by arts similar to those by which it has acquired it.[65]

Exposing the paternal principle to the "light" had not destroyed it, only democratized it. The unity of the fraternal band forged in the struggle against the father would soon give way to the competition for the undivided authority of paternity. Ironically, the internal logic of the quest for fatherhood was patricide.[66] In the origins of modern conservatism is the fear not of the decay of authority, but of the struggle over authority. The spectre that stalks political order is not anarchy, but civil war.[67]

---

[64] McWilliams, p. 4; Kramnick [1], p. 8; *Reflections*, pp. 89, 126; Kramnick [2], p. 154.

[65] *Reflections*, pp. 87-88.

[66] "They would soon see that criminal means once tolerated are soon preferred . . . until [only] rapacity, malice, revenge, and fear more dreadful than revenge could satiate their insatiable appetites. Such must be the consequences of losing, in the splendor of these triumphs of the rights of men, all natural sense of right and wrong" (*Reflections*, pp. 92-93). The political consequences, Burke feared, would be a perennial cycle of tyranny and revolution. See also McWilliams, p. 16.

[67] This apprehension helps explain Burke's extensive investigations into the problems of inheritance, especially his peculiar interest in the modes of inheritance and his preference for the principle of per stirpes—the

Indeed, Burke's own historical experience linked together civil war, patricide, and republicanism. The regicide of Charles I had unleashed a struggle over the authority of the father (in Pocock's language, the locus of sovereignty). The patricidal unity of 1648 gave way to a struggle among the Puritan fraternity. (We are tempted, as Burke probably was, to see the Puritan Revolution as a reenactment of the historical sin of the English polity—the problem of succession.) Cromwell's assumption of political fatherhood only postponed the final disintegration of the Commonwealth. In 1660 and again in 1688, "the nation had lost its bond of union."[68]

The extent of Burke's conscious antagonism to the republic is difficult to gauge. His often-noted consideration of "circumstances" is at odds with his extreme dislike of political action. As we have seen, his treatment of the psychology of authority is not friendly to republican institutions. He may not have realized how *principled* his objections to the republic were. Nevertheless, Burke's attack on patricide is a striking, if perhaps unwitting, assault upon Machiavelli's understanding of the nature of authority in the republic.

We have consecrated the state that no man should approach to look into its defects or corruptions but with due caution, that he should never dream of beginning its reformation by its subversion, that he should approach to the faults of the state as to the wounds of a father, with pious awe and trembling solicitude. By this wise prejudice, we are taught to look with horror on those children of their country who are prompt rashly to hack that aged parent in pieces and put him

---

singular representation of the ancestor. Related, of course, was Burke's preoccupation with the fixed character of the succession (a question which, as a matter of constitutional debate, had long since been settled). While hiding behind constitutional arguments, Burke's real concern was the modern consciousness per se.

[68] *Reflections*, p. 24.

into the kettle of magicians, in hopes that by their poisonous weeds and wild incantations they may regenerate the paternal constitution and renovate their father's life.[69]

For Burke, those who sought reverence in patricidal foundations were but "pretenders." And Burke knew this much: the republican spirit had neither "feeling" nor "respect" for kings. Of the French republic, Burke would write, "The foundation of their republic is laid in moral paradoxes. Their patriotism is always prodigy." As Machiavelli knew, it could not have been otherwise.[70]

As patricide was the logical expression of modern politics, so was it also at the center of the origins of conservatism.

In those natural feelings we learn great lessons; because in events like these our passions instruct our reason; because when kings are hurled from their thrones by the Supreme Director of this great drama and become the objects of insult to the base and of pity to the good, we behold such disasters in the moral as we should behold a miracle in the physical order of things. We are alarmed into reflection; our minds (as it has long since been observed) are purified by terror and pity, our weak, unthinking pride is humbled under the dispensations of a mysterious wisdom.

The passage is revealing. Regicide is seen as the secret center, the object of contemplation, the source of conservative inspiration. The mood is introspective. "Our" minds

---

[69] *Reflections*, p. 109. Much earlier, Burke had used similar imagery in his attack on those who sought the reform of the House of Commons (many of whom were republicans): "I look with filial reverence on the constitution of my country, and never will cut it in pieces, and put it in the kettle of magicians, in order to boil it, with the puddle of their compounds, into youth and vigor. On the contrary, I will drive away such pretenders; I will nurse its venerable age, and with lenient arts extend a parent's breath" (quoted in Kramnick [2], p. 64).

[70] "Abridgement of English History," p. 194; "Three Letters," p. 311.

are purified; "our" pride is humbled. Gone is the vituper-
ation and the self-righteousness. In their place lies an inescapable sense of complicity. In the pages immediately preceding this extract, Burke's fascination with the killing of
fathers and kings (which, like the sublime, is both "terrible" and "delightful") reaches a gruesome crescendo in his
narration of the events of the 6th of October, 1789. Blood,
massacre, humilation, and terror are graphically portrayed.
Horror is heaped upon horror (many of which, Kramnick
observes, are but the imaginings of the author). The sense
is one of compulsion rather than of rhetorical intent. In the
paragraph immediately preceding the quotation under discussion, Burke, emotionally exhausted, apologizes for his
outburst.

> Excuse me, therefore, if I have dwelt too long on the
> atrocious spectacle of the 6th of October, 1789, or have
> given too much scope to the reflections which have
> arisen in my mind on occasion of the most important
> of all revolutions which may be dated from that day—
> I mean a revolution in sentiments, manners, and moral
> opinions.[71]

In venting his own terror, Burke's mind is "purified"
and "alarmed into reflection." For an instant the psychological core of conservatism is bared, revealing the depth
of the modern horror. The Revolution was no unnatural
aberration: "Its spirit lies deep in the corruptions of our
common nature." Burke shuddered—even he (especially
he!) was not free of the mark of modernity. Burke, too,
was a man of ambition. (Throughout his life, Burke was
never able to shake the characterization of his family by
contemporary gossips as "Irish adventurers.") The *Reflections* ends with a bit of self-pleading with Burke trying to
convince others of his humility. He was no philosophe!

---

[71] *Reflections*, p. 91. See also Mansfield's discussion of Burke's "unnatural deference" (*Statesmanship*, pp. 202-207).

I have little to recommend my opinions but long observation and much impartiality. They come from one
who has been no tool of power, no flatterer of greatness; and who in his last acts does not wish to belie
the tenor of his life . . . and who snatches from his
share in the endeavors which are used by good men
to discredit opulent oppression the hours he has employed on your affairs; and who in so doing persuades
himself he has not departed from his usual office; they
come from one who desires honors, distinctions, and
emoluments but little.[72]

His political theory, *his* erudition aims at no glory. Against
whom must Burke proclaim his guiltlessness? An offhand
remark of Burke's about Jacobinism is suggestive: "Those
who do not dread it, love it." Here is the psychological
center. The darkest terror is on the inside: "We feared more
from what threatened to fail within than what menaced to
oppress us from abroad." Burke's often-noted vitriol, his
propensity for overstatement and exaggeration, his rhetorical overkill, these are the marks of a man possessed by
demons. Of the Revolution, Burke observed, "We cannot
bear to look that frightful form in the face."[73] What did he
fear if not his own reflection? And, like Luther, Burke's
denial, too, is "roared": "*Ich bin's nit! Ich bin's nit!*" rever-
berates throughout his work.[74]

New meanings now suggest themselves in Burke's plea
for oblivion. In retirement, Burke writes, "I find it neces-

[72] "Three Letters," p. 343; *Reflections*, p. 291.
[73] "Three Letters," p. 233. Equally revealing is this extract from "Thoughts
and Details on Scarcity," in *Works*, vol. 5, p. 167: "That state has fallen
by the hands of the parricides of their country, called the Revolutionists
and Constitutionalists of France: a species of traitors, of whose fury and
atrocious wickedness nothing in the annals of frenzy and deprivation of
mankind had before furnished an example, and of whom I can never
think or speak without a mixed sensation of disgust, of horror, and of
detestation, not easy to be expressed."
[74] "It isn't me! It isn't me!" See Erikson, *Young Man Luther*, chapter 11,
especially p. 23.

sary to call to my aid an oblivion of most of the circumstances, pleasant and unpleasant, of my life" (see note 14).
Indeed, Burke had to forget especially the pleasant circumstances, his personal "triumphs"—those public successes
that called forth "grand ideas" and reminded Burke of his
complicity in the crime of modernity. Burkean conservatism was a plea for forgetting that was at once political and
personal. In the deepest sense, it was reaction—psychological reaction; its doctrine, a proclamation of innocence
that only the guilt-ridden could make: "Above all things,
I was resolved not to be guilty of tampering—the odious
vice of restless and unstable minds. I put my foot in the
tracks of our forefathers, where I can neither wander nor
stumble."[75]

In all its garbs, Burke's teaching is aimed at the foremost
among the ambitious, the most furious seekers after glory—
those who would begin. Custom's "method", the patrimonial analogy: these are ranged against beginners. Custom's method hides originators from view. Imposing anonymity upon human creation, custom denies remembrance
to beginners, while the myth of "immemoriality" deni-
grates the very idea of beginnings. The "idea of inheritance," too, reviles the first ones, but is more outspoken in
its opposition to glory: "This idea of a liberal descent in-
spires us with a sense of habitual native dignity which
prevents that upstart insolence almost inevitably adhering
to and disgracing those who are the first acquirers of any
distinction." The opposition of "inheritance" and "glory"
is nowhere in Burke's work more succinctly stated. The
very idea of glory becomes in Burke's hands "upstart insolence." That for which the ancients had reserved the
highest glory Burke reserves the most scathing denuncia-
tion: "The very idea of the fabrication of a new government
is enough to fill us with disgust and horror."[76]

[75] "On Conciliation with America," p. 26.
[76] *Reflections*, pp. 35, 39.

It was such "fabrication" that constituted the French error. They were fearless, even "desperate . . . aeronaughts," unafraid to begin. For Burke, the restoration of order in France was not enough. Should order alone be restored, it would be but a monument to beginners. The Bourbons must be set back upon their throne: "We have no others to govern France." Burke's insistence upon a genuine restoration in France is instructive. His restorationism was a kind of penance, a renunciation of the deed, a placation of the furies. It was at once a political solution and an offering. Only by "acting as if in the presence of canonized forefathers [can] the spirit of freedom, leading in itself to misrule and excess, [be] tempered with an awful gravity." Awe-full-ness requires the resurrection of the father (the realization of "dread possibility"). Only with "each on his patrimonial ground" will the young men hide themselves.[77]

[77] *Reflections*, p. 39; "On the Policy of the Allies," p. 426. We ought not to miss the description of these forefathers. They are "canonized"—made sacrosanct; their persons are sacred, untouchable, their presence the cause of "holy dread." In his *Theory of Moral Sentiments* (which, as editor of the *Annual Register*, Burke had reviewed very favorably), Adam Smith, with whom Burke would later become a fast friend, had written of the restoration of Charles II as a revival of "the old principles of loyalty." Speaking of the regicide, Smith observed that acts of violence against "those to whom they have been accustomed to look up to as their natural superiors" give rise to unusual psychological consequences: "Compassion soon takes the place of resentment." In *Totem and Taboo*, Freud noted the ritual paradox of a devoured and yet deified father. The deification of the father and the placating of this potentially wrathful god with offerings suggest a hedge against the dread possibility that the spirit of the father has survived. In England, the person of the father is resurrected and Burke offers his work as a lamb upon the altar, knowing that "kings will be tyrants from policy when subjects are rebels from principle" (*Reflections*, pp. 88-89), while men love what submits to them.

Burke also engages in a sort of self-conscious servility designed to humble the vestiges of pride and ambition: "You people of great families and hereditary trusts and fortunes, are not like such as I am, who, whatever we may be by the rapidity of our growth, and even by the fruit we bear, and flatter ourselves that while we creep on the ground, we belly into melons that are exquisite for size and flavor, yet still are but annual plants, that perish without season, and leave no sort of traces behind us"

Faced with the greatest revolution the world had ever known, Burke could only recommend the forms of the past. Musing in his *Reflections* over the conservative dilemma, he writes: "Who could conceive that men who are habitually meddling, daring, subtle, active, of litigious dispositions and unquiet minds would easily fall back in their old condition?" Having once tasted the authority of the father, men would not willingly give it up and return to political childhood. They would not forget. Failing oblivion, the restoration must be founded on compulsion. Yet Burke never understood the cost in public spirit of such a return. True, England had succeeded in its own restoration, but only at the price of making patriotism "the last refuge of a scoundrel." Obedience, once the fruit of affection, had become the offspring of unaided power.[78]

Burke had feared that without ancient opinion to soften and mellow authority power would appear only as a fist of mail. Ironically, this grim prophecy would become the first principle of conservative theory and practice. Only raw power could meet the challenge of the forces unleashed by modernity.

Society requires not only that the passions of individuals should be subjected, but that even in the mass and body, as well as in the individuals, the inclinations of men should be frequently thwarted, their will controlled, and their passions brought into subjection. This

(Letter to the Duke of Richmond, quoted in Kramnick [2], p. 4). See also Freud, *Totem and Taboo*, p. 150, and Adam Smith, quoted in Kramnick [2], p. 194. For Burke's familiarity with Smith's *Theory of Moral Sentiments*, see Copeland, *Our Eminent Friend Edmund Burke*, p. 120.

[78] *Reflections*, p. 48. The events of 1660 and 1688 were consolidated at a great cost to public life. Burke was painfully aware of the decline in public spirit in England since the first half of the seventeenth century ("On Conciliation with America," pp. 103-6), but never associated it with the vast demobilization that characterized English politics after 1660 (of which the disenfranchisement of all dissenters and, later, the centralization of political life under Walpole were but the tips of an iceberg). And while Burke spoke often of "love of country," it was the epigram of his good friend, Dr. Johnson, that captured the mood of the nation.

can only be done *by a power out of themselves*, and not, in the exercise of its function, subject to that will and to those passions which it is its office to bridle and subdue.

Burkean conservatism, which spoke of the political world first in the language of weakness, affection, and mellowed authority, speaks last in a different tongue. Thwart, control, bridle, subdue, these become the vocabulary of conservatism, the patrimony of Edmund Burke.[79]

[79] *Reflections*, pp. 68-69. One last word on the "prescience" of Burke is appropriate. His admirers (and others) often point, for instance, to his prediction of the rise of Napoleon. To be sure, Burke's understanding of the nature of the French Revolution, as well as his remarkable and still valuable insights into the role of ideology and doctrine in modern politics, gave him what Machiavelli would have called "foresight." But like most seers, he is best remembered for what he foretold and rarely called up on his "shortsightedness." In Burke's case, such generosity is costly, for while his theory is sprinkled with great insight, it is built upon shortsightedness. Burke was blinded by his own terror and guilt; as close as he was to America, he never understood the prophetic meaning of 1776. And if he feared for the European order and the paternity upon which it rested, he never imagined the possibility of a new discipline—that out of the tombs of murdered fathers would arise a new patriotism.

F O U R

* * * *

ALEXIS DE TOCQUEVILLE:
THE POLITICS OF AFFECTION

An Affair of the Heart

In the first paragraph of the Author's Introduction to the first part of *Democracy in America*, Alexis de Tocqueville names the "primary fact" of modern politics. This "fact" is equality of condition. Its importance rests, in part, on the scope of its influence, for it "extends far beyond the political character and the laws of the country, and it has no less effect on civil society than on government." Tocqueville thus puts the reader on notice that it is not laws or even institutions that chiefly interest him, but "opinions," "customs," and "sentiments." His is a theory which places *les moeurs publiques* at the center of political inquiry. This would be the enduring concern of his work, "that everything in politics is only a consequence and a symptom, and that it is the ideas and the sentiments prevalent among the people which are the cause of everything." The insight of his youth, it remained the foundation of his mature thought. Among the notes and fragments for the projected second volume of *The Old Regime and the French Revolution* is found this observation: "Not mechanical legal structures but the ideas and the passions of men are the motive forces of human affairs. It is always in men's souls that one may find the symptoms of forthcoming events."[1] Tocqueville was not the first to lay such emphasis on the political passions and sentiments. Two generations earlier, Burke had placed "prejudice" at the center of his political thought. But Burke, Tocqueville thought, had remained "confined within England, within the old world," and could write only of English sentiment. Tocqueville's manner was "French," however, and his would be a theory suited to the new world, to democracy. As such, it would outline the "general ideas" of political sentiment.[2] Emile Faguet once observed, and accurately, that Tocqueville attempted to "penetrate . . . beneath history to the physiology of peoples." Against the rationalism of the eighteenth century which, when it looked at political societies, saw only discreet individuals, Tocqueville insisted upon the importance of national character. Modernity had revealed the mutability of insitutions, opinions, and customs, but beneath this history lay nations. In the New World, Tocqueville had encountered French and English side by side. He pondered the vast difference of character that he found between the Americans and the French Canadians, the descendants of the two European races which had come to inhabit the

[1] Tocqueville, *The European Revolution and Correspondence with Gobineau*, p. 78; Letter to Bauchitte, September 23, 1853, quoted in Gargan, *Alexis de Tocqueville: The Critical Years 1848-1851* (hereafter cited as Gargan [1]), p. 249; Tocqueville, *Democracy in America*, vol. 1, p. 3. [Hereafter in this chapter, works by Tocqueville are cited by title, volume (where appropriate), and page number(s) only.]

[2] *European Revolution*, p. 163. A study which remains to be done and which can only be hinted at in this chapter is the democratic character of the man and his work. In his *Memoir*, Gustave de Beaumont said of his friend that while he "had imbibed democratic notions, he retained aristocratic sentiments." Tocqueville's self-assessment goes further, insisting that "I love . . . equality by instinct and reason." See *Memoir, Letters and Remains*, vol. 1, p. 45; Letter to J. S. Mill, June 1835, in Lively, p. 19. See also two letters to J. S. Mill, February 10, 1836 and November 15, 1839, in *Memoir, Letters and Remains*, vol. 2, pp. 31, 58. Hereafter, unless otherwise stated, all letters cited are from these volumes and will be identified only by correspondent, date, volume, and page number(s).

North American wilderness. These differences suggested the eighteenth century's error.

> Some philosophers believed that human nature everywhere the same only varies according to the institutions and laws of different societies. That is one of the opinions to which the history of the world seems to give the lie on every page. In history all nations, like individuals, show their own peculiar physiognomy. Their characteristic traits reproduce themselves through all the transformations that they undergo. Laws, morals, religions alter; dominion and wealth change hands; external appearances vary; the dress is different; prejudices vanish or are replaced by others. Through all these diverse changes you always recognize the same people. Something inflexible shows through in spite of all man's adaptability.[3]

The first task of Tocqueville's "new science" was to discover the nature of the locus of permanence in the flux of history—those things "inflexible."

Tocqueville's preoccupation with what he called "national physiognomy" has led some to proclaim him the first political sociologist. Had he been asked, Tocqueville might have described himself rather as a theorist of the political affections, a student of the relation of politics and the heart. An inveterate scribbler, Tocqueville records in an early fragment (*Tour in Sicily*) the circumstances surrounding the origin of his insight. While the passage is long, it has been reproduced in its entirety, for in the prose of its young author can be seen the outline of both the man and the philosopher.

> One day I was sitting on the sands, with my head on my hands, looking out on the sea, and turning over carelessly in my mind the saddest thoughts. I had long been looking at a boat coming in; it annoyed me, for

[3] *Journey to America*, p. 365.

it was full of people singing at the top of their voices as they drew near. It was a poor fisherman's family, husband, wife, and children; it comprehended at least three generations. They all rowed, and the boat soon touched the land. The father and the elder ones jumped into the water, and dragged the boat upon the beach. Just then I saw come out of one of the huts on the coast a half-naked child, about two or three years old; he hurried along, crawling on all fours, and shouting for joy.

This baby became the object of general attention. As soon as a middle-aged woman who had just stepped out of the boat caught sight of him, she ran to embrace him, and raising him in her arms, covered him with kisses, and said to him a thousand things which I could not understand. He was soon surrounded by all the party, each had something to say to him; he was passed from one to the other; the men set their fish before him, and made him touch the scales; the children all brought him some trifle from their recent expedition, and even the littlest ones of all took pains to put brace-lets of shells on his arm, and then ran away quite delighted. He was evidently the last born of the family.

Till now I had never understood the misery of banish-ment, and the reality of those instincts which, however far one may be from one's country, draw one towards it in spite of obstacles and dangers.

The recollection of France and all that is comprehended in that one word, pounced upon me as its prey. The longing I had to see her again was so vehement, as to be far beyond any wish that I had ever formed for anything, and I know not what sacrifice I would not have made to find myself instantly on her shores.

The happiness of living in one's own country, like all other happiness, is not felt while it is possessed. But let exile or misfortune come upon you, and then leave memory to do its work. You will then learn to value things aright.

In the images of family, Tocqueville recognizes his country. Bound up with nurturance and continuity, patriotism is the deepest of affections. Animated by a kind of "joy," yet it is also inseparable from "the saddest thoughts." This complex of emotions, sentiments, and affections, rooted in the earliest and most primitive of recollections, is the foundation of political life.[4]

The Sicilian insight, before which Tocqueville "had never understood . . . the reality of those instincts which . . . draw one towards . . . one's country," finds its way into the first part of the *Democracy* under the heading "instinctive patriotism."

There is one sort of patriotic attachment which principally arises from that instinctive, disinterested, and undefinable feeling which connects the affections of man with his birthplace. This natural fondness is united with a taste for ancient customs and a reverence for traditions of the past; those who cherish it love their country as they love the mansion of their fathers. They love the tranquility that it affords them; they cling to the peaceful habits that they have contracted within its bosom; they are attached to the reminiscences that it awakens; and they are even pleased by living there in a state of obedience. This patriotism is sometimes stimulated by religious enthusiasm, and then it is capable of making prodigious efforts. It is in itself a kind of religion: it does not reason but acts from the impulse of faith and sentiment.

[4] *Tour in Sicily*, in *Memoir, Letters and Remains*, vol. 1, pp. 121-22; "Reflections on English History," in *Journeys to England and Ireland*, p. 33. See also Tocqueville's request of the clergy in Letter to Madame Swetchine, October 20, 1856, vol. 2, pp. 332-33.

This passage is unmistakably autobiographical. Few have loved "the mansion of their fathers" more dearly than did Tocqueville. Tocquevillian patriotism is decidedly pacific. Citizens "love the tranquility" and "cling to the peaceful habits" of this civic life. And if these patriots are "capable of making prodigious efforts" in its defense, Tocqueville draws our attention instead to the domestic sweetness of their fathers' house, the unambiguous affections, the fond "reminiscences," and the love of ancient things which form a large part of such feelings.[5]

Like the ancients with whom he shared much, Tocqueville's primary concern was with domestic relations. Conspicuously absent in Tocqueville's portrait of republican sweetness is that well-known unity of republican thought, the citizen-soldier. Tocqueville was not unfamiliar with this unity. Indeed, he was all too familiar with the relation of *la patrie* and the Napoleonic idea of glory and conquest. And while Tocqueville never doubted that love of country and political liberty often callled for the highest sacrifices

[5] *Democracy*, vol. 1, pp. 250-51. Tocqueville's republican *sweetness* contrasts with Machiavelli's republican *vengeance*. Tocqueville's classical concern with the inside of the city may be compared with Machiavelli's more modern preoccupation with the outside: the sweetness of peace contrasted with the vengeance of war. For Machiavelli, war was a necessary and even desirable outlet for republican energy. But on a more fundamental level, Machiavelli, too, was concerned with the inside. Both theorists would root the political affections in the remembrance of first things. But for Tocqueville these affections were unambiguous, pure, without the deep psychological ambivalence with which Machiavelli had invested them. The Tocquevillian conception of these "undefinable" affections is gentle, like the man himself. In particular, there is none of Machiavelli's great ambivalence towards power and the problems of ruling and being ruled. Tocqueville's instinctive patriot is "pleased" to obey, such obedience being "natural and self-existent, without effort, like the authority of a parent" (*Democracy*, vol. 1, p. 175), what Tocqueville would later call "involuntary respect" (*European Revolution*, p. 34). As we shall see, Tocqueville knew the psychic and political forces which Machiavelli tried to harness, but he greatly feared them. For Machiavelli, the Imperial Republic remained a glorious historical image. For Tocqueville, it had been a fearful reality. Thus, he sought to separate the soft from the hard and to shield political life from its own exuberance. No one loved civic life more and military glory less than Alexis de Tocqueville.

from the patriot, he was inclined to view the war-like patriotism of the Imperial Republic as a perversion of more generous affections and a positive danger to civic vitality. If war often drew upon the affections for its requisite fury, it also undermined the foundations of such affections, destroying, as it were, the soil in which they grew. That war sustained the virtue of the ancient city (which to Machiavelli had appeared true) was, to Tocqueville's mind, a dubious proposition. In any case, the experience of the past no longer threw "light" on the problem. Among other things, war in modern large-scale societies increased the pressures for centralized authority, contributing to the breakdown of local institutions and thus relaxing "the sinews of strength." While it provided a grand stage for the exhibition of patriotic sentiment, war ultimately led to the enervation of public spirit. This teaching was particularly important in an age of youthful nationalism, but it was a lesson which the new democracies would not or could not abide.[6]

His interest in those sentiments which rule *inside* the city directed Tocqueville's investigations toward the inner structure of civic life. For while "the vague impulse of patriotism . . . never abandons the human heart, . . . it depends upon the laws to awaken and direct" it. In the good state, the affections are properly organized. Tocqueville knew what the eighteenth century had forgotten, that the affections are limited, sensuous, tactile. The legislator must act in the knowledge that men have "bodies" as well as "souls," and that the vast state can present "no definite

---

[6] Consider, for example, Tocqueville's remarks concerning "the permanence, the glory, [and] the prosperity" once enjoyed under the despotism of the Sultan, although "the Turkish tribes" were denied "an active share in the conduct of affairs" (*Democracy*, vol. 1, p. 97). Consider also Tocqueville's observation that the French peasant, after leaving the army, "will become the poor clown who we used to know, and will carry with him into the civil world none of the sentiments which he exhibited in his little military one" (Letter to Madame Swetchine, October 15, 1855, vol. 2, p. 299). See also letter to Nassau William Senior, September 16, 1855, vol. 2, p. 295, and *Democracy*, vol. 1, p. 90.

object" for the affections. Such entities must inevitably remain "remote" and can give rise only to "a vague and ill-defined sentiment." Limited in scope, the affections more readily attach themselves to what is "familiar" and "dear." American patriotism remained strong and constant because it was the sum of the patriotism of lesser and more ancient communities. The "garrulous" patriotism of the American had its secret source in this "attachment to his little republic." The strength of such civic attachment lay in its identification "with the soil, . . . the domestic affections, . . . the recollections of the past." Without such as these, Tocqueville warned, a nation may have "subjects," but it will never have "citizens." "When we recollect the traditions, the customs, the prejudices of local and familiar attachment with which it is connected, we cannot doubt the superiority of a power that rests on the instinct of patriotism, so natural to the human heart."[7]

---

[7] *Democracy*, vol. 1, pp. 69, 97, 170, 175, 402; Letter to Louis de Kergorlay, August 15, 1836, vol. 1, p. 304. This is, perhaps, the place to address Tocqueville's doctrine of "self-interest rightly understood." It is standard fare among Tocqueville's commentators to regard Tocqueville as a theorist of interest. Tocqueville himself lends much support to this view. While he prefers the unity that derives from common and ancient affections, he often seems to despair of the possibility of such politics under modern conditions. Thus, he appears to replace a patriotism of the heart with a patriotism of reason which, while less generous, is more lasting (see, for example, *Democracy*, vol. 1, pp. 250-51). Tocqueville, it is true, places considerable emphasis on the role of interest in democratic societies, but liberals have been too quick to claim him as their own. While interest is forever hovering before the eyes of democratic man, Tocqueville always thought interest unaided an insufficient bond (*Democracy*, vol. 1, p. 408). And while Tocqueville insists upon the importance in democracies of the covenant of "reciprocal aid," France's political difficulties are in part the result of the disappearance of common opinion and the effort of the middle class to found politics solely upon interest (*Democracy*, vol. 2, pp. 7, 186). In contrast to such schemes, Tocqueville praises the patriotism of the lower classes, which, though untrained, is more pure (*Democracy*, vol. 1, p. 208). In a thoroughly Tocquevillian vein, McWilliams observes that while the American individualist justified his collective institutions in the utilitarian language of "mutual assistance," collective life created "joy in its own right." The American, Tocqueville observes, would gratify his egalitarian instincts with the vocal insistence upon the unity of private

It was upon these reflections on the nature of the political affections that Tocqueville based his praise of American municipal government and his more general critique of "centralized administration." For despite the sweetness of the familiar, "so natural to the human heart," the affections of men also "turn towards power," so that provinces and towns, "having lost their immunities, their customs, their prejudices, their traditions, and even their names . . . [are] not more difficult to oppress . . . all together than it was formerly difficult to oppress one . . . separately." Tocqueville's most fundamental teaching regarding political memory is this: to live in the present alone is to be made ready for servitude. The vessel of all that is cherished, remembrance is also the foundation of political liberty. For as Tocqueville knew, only a lover is "capable of making prodigious efforts."[8]

---

and public interest, but Tocqueville nonetheless insists that this public life is the "only pleasure an American knows" and, should he be denied this political activity, he "would be robbed of one half of his existence" (*Democracy*, vol. 1, p. 259; vol. 2, p. 131; McWilliams, pp. 389-90). Finally, it might be added that any theory which places national character at the center of its argument, as Tocqueville's does, appears on its face to be more than a theory of interest. The notion of cultural cohesion and the attendant notion of peoplehood stand in sharp contrast to the liberal conception of discrete individuals who are the building blocks of a politics of interest.

[8] *Democracy*, vol. 1, pp. 339-40. In the last chapter of the first part of the *Democracy*, Tocqueville gives two poignant examples of this teaching: "The Negro of the United States has lost even the remembrance of his country; the language which his forefathers spoke is never heard around him; he abjured their religion and forgot their customs when he ceased to belong to Africa, without acquiring any claim to European privileges. But he remains half-way between the two communities, isolated between two races; sold by the one, repulsed by the other; finding not a spot in the universe to call by the name of country, except the faint image of a home which the shelter of his master's roof affords. . . . Violence made him a slave, and the habit of servitude gives him the thoughts and desires of a slave; he admires his tyrants more than he hates them, and finds his joy and his pride in the servile imitation of those who oppress him. His understanding is degraded to the level of his soul" (vol. 1, pp. 344-45). While the fate of the American Indian is different from that of the American Negro, the causes are strikingly similiar: "When the North American Indians had lost the sentiment of attachment to their country; when their

The relation of the affections to remembrance is suggestive, for it is through recollection that the affections achieve
permanence, becoming "true and lasting passions." For
Tocqueville, memory is a tableau, not of events but of emotions. Men are often less certain of events than of the aura
which surrounds them. In any case, Tocqueville insists, it
is not the "importance" or the "greatness" of events, but
the character of the emotions attending them that engrave
events upon the memory: "Every recollection of past emo-
tion is a sort of landmark, like the objects which measure
the road to the traveller."[9]

Tocqueville was well situated to appreciate the subtle
emotional nuances of remembrance. He possessed what
George Pierson has called "a sense of time and sadness."
In a confession to a friend, Tocqueville writes:

> Well, here I am at Tocqueville, in my old family ruin.
> A league away is the harbour from which William set
> out to conquer England. I am surrounded by Normans
> whose names figure in the lists of the conquerors. All
> that, I must admit, "flatters the proud weakness of my
> heart," and sometimes stirs a childish enthusiasm of
> which afterwards I am ashamed.[10]

---

families were dispersed, their traditions obscured, and the chain of their
recollections broken; when all their habits were changed, and their wants
increased beyond measure, European tyranny rendered them more dis-
orderly and less civilized than they were before. The moral and physical
condition of these tribes continually grew worse, and they became more
barbarous as they became more wretched" (vol. 1, p. 346).

[9] Letter to Eugene Stoffels, April 3, 1844, vol. 1, p. 349; Letter to Ampere,
August 10, 1841, vol. 2, p. 74. In this regard, consider also Tocqueville's
description of the impact which the recollection of the events of July 30,
1830 had upon him (Letter to Eugene Stoffels, October 18, 1831, vol. 1,
pp. 371-72).

[10] "Reflections on English History," p. 21. In an arrangement with his
brothers, Tocqueville took possession of the rundown ancestral chateau,
a "little spot [which] is for me full of recollections of the best years in my
life, and the invisible portion of my being which is connected with all
around me, lends to every object a charm which exists only for me. The
trees, the fields, the sea, all seem to wear a different aspect here than
elsewhere" (Letter to Madame Swetchine, July 20, 1855, vol. 2, p. 289).

Indeed, Tocqueville's own name, Clérel, was among those lists. The sweetness of such recollections was, for Tocqueville, always accompanied by an admixture of sadness, imparting to remembrance the bittersweet quality often associated with the memories of old men: a strange combination of "joy" and "sorrow" that comes from the contemplation of "times that will never return." The complexity and depth of Tocqueville's attitude toward the past is suggested further in a passage from his *Recollections*.

> It is wonderful how much brighter and more vivid than reality are the colours of a man's imagination. I had just seen the Monarchy fall; since then I have witnessed the most terrible scenes of bloodshed. All the same I declare that neither at the time nor now in recollection do I feel such deep and poignant emotion about any of those disasters as I felt that day at the sight of the ancient home of my ancestors and at the memory of the quiet, happy days I passed there without realizing how precious they were. Believe me, it was then and there that I most fully understood the utter bitterness of revolutions.

It is in such recollections that we find the origin of that often-noted melancholia which colored Tocqueville's thought and which (as he would say late in his life) was so "interwoven with my best feelings . . . [that] I do not wish to even shake it off."[11]

An anecdote about this "family ruin" tells much of its proprietor. Among the dilapidated buildings at Tocqueville stood a roofless tower. The tower had once housed the family pigeons, the keeping of which, during "the old days," had been a privilege of the aristocracy. While the Clérels (Tocqueville's family name) had enjoyed generally amiable relations with their peasants, the pigeon house had been razed during the Revolution. Its burnt-out shell remained as a grim reminder of the hatred of privilege which lay in the heart of the French peasantry. After taking possession of the chateau, Tocqueville refurbished the ancestral seat but left the charred stones of the pigeon house untouched.

[11] *Recollections*, pp. 94-95; Letter to Ampere, January 27, 1857, vol. 2, p. 345.

This "sadness of remembrance" is of some interest. As evident in the musings of the young man on a Sicilian beach as it is in the *Recollections* of the statesman and scholar, this melancholia must be considered Tocqueville's primary emotional response to the act of remembrance. To be sure, memory's other emotions also were known to him—the exaltation that accompanies the consummation of an ancient yearning or the hatred that springs from the contemplation of an ancient injury. But these, Tocqueville thought, were derivative, rooted in distortions of original affections. While such emotions were often natural, and sometimes useful or even saving, the exuberance of ancient loves and hates, the excesses of a fevered memory, threatened the well-being of one's country, the very object of sweet remembrance. The consequences of such fevered recollections may be even "heroic" or "brilliant" and yet "most unhappy." Tocqueville knew well the weaknesses to which political memory was prone, for he was a man of deep, even violent, political passions, passions to which Beaumont was privy.

> Such, dear friend, was the first history book which fell into my hands, and I cannot convey the impression it made on me; every event is engraved on my memory, and thence derives that often unreflecting instinct of hate which rouses me against the English. Time and time again when I came to those disastrous battles in which valour was always crushed by superior discipline, I have skipped the pages and left out whole passages to which nonetheless irresistible curiosity would later drive me intermittently back. But forgive me, I am running off talking about myself.[12]

While the Frenchman's hatred of the English was natural, having all the marks of a political instinct, Tocqueville

[12] "Reflections on English History," p. 33. See also Letter to Eugene Stoffels, October 18, 1831, vol. 1, p. 373.

also knew that *la haine de l'Anglais* could serve equally the tyrant and the patriot. The foundation of all that was good in political life, the affections were also "the fabric on which the innovators drew such monstrous and grotesque patterns." Hence, Tocqueville would insist, "nothing merits the serious study of philosophers and statesmen more than the background on which they are working."[13]

The Limits of Novelty

In an early letter, a young and as yet unknown Alexis de Tocqueville sketches the parameters of a historical study.

> There is something in the broad picture [of the barbarian invasions of Britain] which strikes the imagination; revolution after revolution compared to which those of our own times are trifles. . . . I am sure that deep research into those times would enable us to explain many things . . . , as for instance certain maxims of legal procedure which have become laws throughout Europe, but of which we can neither trace the origin, nor account for the reason why people are so obstinately attached to them.

While Tocqueville's book on England was never written, the question which animated this proposal continued to haunt the mind of its author. "Much can be learnt," Tocqueville thought, from a consideration of these early revolutions and the obstinate attachment which everywhere succeeded the terrible "march" of the peoples of the north. Indeed, it was the radical *impermanence* of men's affections that had characterized Europe's most recent rev-

[13] Senior, *Correspondence and Conversations of Alexis de Tocqueville with Nassau William Senior, 1834-1859*, vol. 2, p. 106; *Recollections*, p. 76. Commenting on the genius of the New England town, Tocqueville attests to the common origin of all political passions: "The passions that commonly embroil society change their character when they find a vent so near the domestic hearth and the family circle" (*Democracy*, vol. 1, p. 70). France's political problem results in part from the destruction of such vents.

olutionary period. Tocqueville had "lived in a country which for forty years had tried everything, and settled nothing." Where is the locus of permanence in human societies and what degree of permanence is possible in democratic societies? The first questions are also the most abiding in Tocqueville's work. It was in America that he first sought the answers.[14]

Tocquevillian scholars are fortunate in one respect. No political theorist has left a more extensive record, in notebooks and letters, of the development of his ideas than Tocqueville. This is particularly true in regard to *Democracy in America*. We are witnesses to the concerns Tocqueville brings with him from France, the impact of the panorama of American life upon those concerns, and the maturing vision that results from the confrontation of European sentiment and American fact.

The first of these impressions is of the newness of the New World, of a nation without a past. In the first letter from American soil, Tocqueville writes to de Chabrol:

> Picture to yourself my dear friend, if you can, a society which comprises all the nations of the world—English, French, German: people differing from one another in language, in beliefs, in opinions; in a word, a society possessing no roots, no memories, no prejudices, no routine, no common ideas, no national character.

These are the impressions of May, those of a young aristocrat with that sense of human antiquity that only Europe can foster, who is confronted with the spectacle of America's novelty. Three weeks later, however, Tocqueville confesses his confusion to his friend and cousin, Louis de Kergorlay.

[14] "Reflections on English History," pp. 22-23; Letter to Henry Reeve, March 22, 1837, vol. 2, p. 40. In the second part of the *Democracy*, Tocqueville calls attention to the great permanence the Americans had achieved within a democratic society: "They arrived on the soil they occupy in nearly the condition in which we see them in the present day; and this is of considerable importance" (vol. 2, p. 7).

Every foreign nation has a peculiar physiognomy, seen at the first glance and easily described. When afterwards you try to penetrate deeper, you are met by real and unexpected difficulties; you advance with a slowness that drives you to despair, and the farther you go the more you doubt. I feel that at this moment my head is a chaos of contradictory notions. I tire myself in seeking for some clear and decisive results; I find none.

Tocqueville envies the great commonality of opinion among all ranks in America, but the source of these national "convictions" remains as yet a mystery.

As for what we generally consider as making up the convictions of a nation, such as the moral standard, old traditions, recollections, of these I see as yet no traces.

But the impressions of spring and New York would soon give way to those of autumn and New England.[15]

It was not until late September that Tocqueville had his now famous conversations with Jared Sparks (which were faithfully recorded in the American notebooks).

I think our origin is the fact that best explains our government and our manners. When we arrived here we were enthusiastic republicans and men of religion. We found ourselves left to our own devices, forgotten

[15] Letter to de Chabrol, in Mayer, *Alexis de Tocqueville, A Biographical Study*, p. 22; Letter to Louis de Kergorlay, June 20, 1831, vol. 1, pp. 291-93. See also *Journey to America*, p. 211. The impact of New England upon Tocqueville is certain. For Tocqueville, New England was truly "like a beacon lit upon a hill" which diffused its "warmth" to the American continent. It is to this conviction that both his insight and his errors are attributed. Bryce criticized Tocqueville for minimizing the relation of American and English principles and institutions. More recently, Mayer has insisted that Tocqueville's enterprise was in fact to refute such a relation (p. 28). In fact, Tocqueville saw this relation as problematic. What *are* the implications of a "new country peopled by an old people"? (*Journey to America*, p. 129).

in this corner of the world. Almost all societies, even in America, have begun in one place where the government was concentrated, and have then spread out around that central point. Our forefathers on the contrary founded *the locality before the State*. Plymouth, Salem, Charleston existed before one could speak of a government of Massachusetts; they only became united later and by an act of deliberate will. You can see what strength such a point of departure must have given to the *spirit of locality* which so eminently distinguishes us even among other Americans, and to republican principles. Those who would like to imitate us should remember that there are no precedents for our history.

These conversations were the seedbeds of many interconnected ideas that are now recognized as *Tocquevillian*. Mr. Sparks's insight was confirmed by many others with whom Tocqueville spoke. If such observations were standard patriotic New English fare, they became in Tocqueville's hands a matter for profound reflection. In particular, what was the meaning of this "point de départ?"[16]

Chapter 2 of the first part of the *Democracy* (a chapter described by Tocqueville as "the germ of all that is to follow and the key to almost the whole work") begins thus:

A man has come into the world; his early years are spent without notice in the pleasures and activities of childhood. As he grows up, the world receives him when his manhood begins, and he enters into contact with his fellows. He is then studied for the first time,

---

[16] *Journey to America*, p. 59. For similar observations, see Tocqueville's conversations with Mr. Gray (p. 59), Mr. Everett (p. 58), and Mr. Adams (p. 120). During the previous May, while traveling through New York State, Tocqueville had been shown the home of a descendant of Oliver Cromwell. His notation of this fact is unaccompanied by comment. It was not until his visit to New England that Tocqueville realized the significance of such religio-political sentiment (p. 208).

and it is imagined that the germ of the vices and the virtues of his maturer years is then formed.

This, if I am not mistaken, is a great error. We must begin higher up; we must watch the infant in his mother's arms; we must see the first images which the external world casts upon the dark mirror of his mind, the first occurrences that he witnesses; we must hear the first words which awaken the sleeping powers of thought, and stand by his earliest efforts if we would understand the prejudices, the habits, and the passions which will rule his life. The entire man is, so to speak, to be seen in the cradle of the child.

The growth of nations presents something analogous to this; they all bear some marks of their origin. The circumstances that accompanied their birth and contributed to their development affected the whole term of their being.

If we were able to go back to the elements of states and to examine the oldest monuments of their history, I doubt not that we should discover in them the primal cause of the prejudices, the habits, the ruling passions, and, in short, all that constitutes what is called the national character.

Tocqueville's practical American experience had convinced him of the truth of an ancient teaching: that the beginnings of nations have a profound effect upon their destiny. The Sicilian insight finds its experiential foundation in America, where the beginnings of a nation are still discernible. The first images that are cast "upon the dark mirror of [the] mind" shape and mold the affections, identifying their objects. While subsequent experience alters and bends these original attachments, few affections rival the tenacity of those rooted in the earliest memories.[17]

[17] *Democracy*, vol. 1, pp. 27-28; see also p. 300. Tocqueville also quotes

This first principle of understanding the character or spirit of nations, that one must search for first causes in the cradle and that nations bear the marks of their birth, is to be found in the structure no less than in the teaching of the *Democracy*. In his discussion of American institutions, Tocqueville begins with the townships ("that fruitful germ"). The title of chapter 5—"The Necessity of Examining the Condition of the States Before that of the Union at Large"—suggests the self-conscious character of the book's structure. The development of the book from township through state to national government is indicative of precedence in both time and importance.

While the principle of origins is the first principle of Tocqueville's teaching regarding national character, it is the beginning and not the end of that teaching—its preliminary foundation rather than its conclusion. It is just this: the germ of what is to follow. What interests Tocqueville more are the implications of a "new country peopled by an old people." In other words, what are the consequences of emigration? What is the significance of the "sea" which stands between aristocracy and democracy, between the ancient regime and the more recent past?[18]

In August of 1831 (that is, between the impressions of New York and those of New England), Tocqueville visited the maritime provinces of Canada. He was struck by the character of the French Canadians: "This people is prodi-

---

from Nathaniel Morton's *New England's Memorial*: "What we have seen, and what our fathers have told us, we may not hide from our children, showing to the generations to come the praises of the Lord; that especially the seed of Abraham his servant, and the children of Jacob his chosen, may remember his marvelous works in the beginning" (pp. 33-34). Several years later, in the second part of the *Democracy*, Tocqueville reiterates this judgment of America, that the "opinions of the first fathers of the colonies have left very deep traces on the minds of their descendants" (vol. 2, p. 88).

[18] The notion of traversing a sea, a fact for North Americans, became also a metaphor for the political history of post-revolutionary France. To some extent, Tocqueville considered such *crossings* analogous in his reflections upon American and French experience.

giously like the French people. Or rather these still are the French people." Three months later Tocqueville would write: "We see in Canada Frenchmen who have been living for seventy years under English rule, and remain exactly like their former compatriots in France. In the midst of them lives an English population which has lost nothing of its national character." Still fond of his village, his ancient mode of cultivation, and his church spire, the affections of the French-Canadian peasant are those of the French peasant. And yet Tocqueville would observe in January of 1832 that the Americans could be "understood" because they had built "from a clean start."[19]

But how is it possible for a mature people to make "a clean start?" Do crossings always cleanse a people, or is the American starting point a singular one? The notion of a point of departure appears more complex than we had originally imagined. These questions and others draw us back to Tocqueville's notes, where we find this observation

> Here [are] all the elements of a great people. The French of America are to the French of France as the Americans are to the English. They have preserved the greater part of the original traits of the national character, and have added more morality and more simplicity. They, like them, have broken free from a crowd of prejudices and false points of departure which cause and will cause all the miseries of Europe. In a word, they have in them all that is needed to create a great memory of France in the New World.[20]

Although unnamed, the sea is the background against which the comparison takes place. Tocqueville suggests

---

[19] *Journey to America*, pp. 161, 177; see also pp. 39, 190-93.

[20] *Journey to America*, pp. 189-90. Elsewhere we find this observation: "The Americans in coming over brought what was most democratic in Europe. They arrived having left on the other side of the Atlantic most of the national prejudices in which they had been raised. They became a new nation, developed habits, new customs, something of a national character" (quoted in Drescher, *Tocqueville and England*, p. 32).

that those who came to the New World crossed psychic as
well as geographical waters. This "coming over" had subjected the affections to certain shocks and strains. It involved a leaving and a bringing, a breaking free and a
carrying over. In the *Democracy,* we are reminded that the
Puritans were "called . . . from the comforts of their homes
. . . [by] a purely intellectual craving." As Sparks had suggested, it was political and religious principles which became the objects of great attachment. For reasons Tocqueville considers almost impenetrable, the crossing of the
Atlantic had divested certain "prejudices" and "false points
of departure" of emotional content while heightening the
content of others. In the second and most important chapter of the *Democracy,* Tocqueville emphasizes the passions
associated with this leaving and coming, the implications
of being "snatched away" from what one loves. To this
end, Tocqueville reproduces lengthy extracts from William
Bradford's *Of Plymouth Plantation,* divided by a paragraph
of commentary and a footnote. As the careful reader of the
Democracy will observe, few philosophers are less inclined
to cite others in support of their opinions than is Tocqueville. This infrequency of citation in general, the location
of the Bradford citation, and its extraordinary length all
point to its importance. The first part of this citation describes the scene at the docks of Amsterdam as the Pilgrims
prepared to set sail, and it concludes with a portrait of
sorrow.

> They went on board, and their friends, where truly
> doleful was the sight of that sad and mournful parting,
> to hear what sighs and sobs and prayers did sound
> amongst them; what tears did gush from every eye,
> and pithy speeches pierced each other's heart, . . . and
> then with mutual embraces and many tears they took
> their leave one of another, which proved to be the last
> leave to many of them.

The passage records the emotional trauma associated with
this great leaving; the affections are submitted to a violence

which rends the soul. As the first part of the citation discusses the leaving, the second discusses the coming.

> Being now past the vast ocean, and a sea of troubles before them in expectation, they had now no friends to welcome them, no inns to entertain or refresh them, no houses, or much less towns, to repair unto to seek for succour, . . . Which way soever they turned their eyes . . . they could have but little solace or content in respect of any outward object, . . . If they looked behind them, there was the mighty ocean which they had passed, and which was now as a main bar or gulph to separate them from all the civil parts of the world.

With approval, Tocqueville cites Bradford's description of the Atlantic as a "bar" or "gulph." Bradford contrasts the familiar and dear of Amsterdam with the "wild and savage hew" of wintery Massachusetts, the friend-filled shores of the Dutch harbor with the friendlessness of "unknown coasts," the human face of Europe with the "hideous and desolate wilderness" of North America. In the face of these wrenching contrasts, the Pilgrims could find "little solace or content in respect of any outward object." Indeed, they had left the original objects of their affections behind. As the narrative suggests, the founding of Plymouth Plantation was accompanied by emotional disarray and heightened affective intensity.[21]

---

[21] *Democracy*, vol. 1, pp. 34-36. Tocqueville identifies the author of these observations as Nathaniel Morton and their source a history entitled *New England's Memorial*. We recognize the source of the citations as William Bradford's *Of Plymouth Plantation*. At the time of the writing of the *Democracy*, however, Bradford's history was known only by reputation and through those fragments which later historians had included in their own works (the original manuscript disappeared during the eighteenth century and was only rediscovered in 1858 in the possession of the London Episcopate). Among the earliest and most important of these later histories is Morton's *Memorial*, first published in 1669. The *Memorial* is a compilation of early sources, but is drawn principally from the manuscripts of William Bradford (Morton's uncle), as well as from the journals of Edward Winslow. I am indebted to Professor Norman Jacobson for calling this peculiarity to my attention.

Between these poignant descriptions of leaving and coming is a short paragraph of Tocqueville's in which certain specifics of the voyage are detailed (the number of emigrants, their original destination) and which concludes, "They were forced to land on the arid coast of New England, at the spot which is now the town of Plymouth. The rock is still shown on which the Pilgrims disembarked." But what a change had overtaken these pilgrims! The emigrants had lived in Leyden for "above eleven years," but that city had been only their "resting place" for "they knew that they were pilgrims and strangers here below, and looked not much on these things." Yet these people who cared so little for place, now having crossed a vast ocean, invested the first place of their arrival with great meaning. Lest we fail to see the significance of this new attachment, Tocqueville adds this remarkable footnote.

This rock has become an object of veneration in the United States. I have seen bits of it carefully preserved in several towns of the Union. Does not this sufficiently show how all human power and greatness are entirely in the soul? Here is a stone which the feet of a few poor fugitives pressed for an instant, and this stone becomes famous; it is treasured by a great nation, a fragment is prized as a relic. But what has become of the doorsteps of a thousand palaces? Who troubles himself about them?[22]

Tocqueville has offered Bradford's testimony as evidence of great emotional content and affective upheaval associated with the American point of departure. Here is the source of the ambiguity about "the link" which connects "the emigrants with the land of their forefathers." Deprived of their original objects, the affections attach themselves violently to new objects while repressing those old objects, the remembrance of which is filled with the pain

[22] *Democracy*, vol. 1, pp. 35-36.

and suffering of separation. Hence, "once they set foot on American soil, it could be said that they became strangers to England."[23]

But the forgetting of the old in the attachment to the new is not complete. The emigrants bring "democracy" from England. While its feudal antecedents fall away, the attachment to republican principles becomes extreme. Tocqueville marvels at the uniformity of republican belief in America. The crossing over had obliterated some affections while intensifying others. Still others are both preserved but obscured. This peculiar and incomplete form of remembrance is quite evident in language. Language is the primary vehicle of a nation's character, and, while it often hides as much as it reveals, it is uniquely suited to preserve the affections of a people. Tocqueville finds a telling example of simultaneous preserving and obscuring of affections during his tour of Canada. In pre-revolutionary France, the most hated tax among the peasantry was the *taille*. The French Canadians, who had "broken free" of the structures of administration and privilege which had given rise to this odious tax, had forgotten the origin of the word, but the word itself remained part of common parlance. For these French Canadians, the word *taille* had become synonymous with "misery" and "evil." The language of these peasants had retained, even generalized, the affective content of the original *taille* obscuring its origins yet preserving its meaning as an ancient remembrance of tyranny—"something not to be tolerated"—and shaping their political proclivities in the face of English oppression.[24]

The "tenacious" character of the affective content of language is paralleled closely by a people's strength of attachment to certain institutions and habits of mind. The place that trial by jury and the common law continued to enjoy among the Anglo-Americans suggested that this was

[23] *Democracy,* vol. 1, p. 38; Drescher, p. 29.
[24] *Journey to America,* p. 45; *European Revolution,* p. 133; *Democracy,* vol. 1, p. 37.

especially true of legal customs and institutions. Tocqueville is struck particularly by the phenomenon of Ohio, which is the quintessence of impermanence. Its residents "have come without knowing one another." Having "arrived only yesterday," they will leave again tomorrow. Thus, "no common tie binds them together." In Ohio, democracy is "carried to extreme limits," and the minds of men are free from even the most "feeble influences" of "historical memory." And yet, Tocqueville observes, "society prospers. But does it prosper because of democracy or in spite of it? That is the point." To "explain" his meaning, Tocqueville speaks of the nature of emigration and its impact upon a people's law. While successive emigrations obliterate conventional "ties" and "habits," obscuring "the trace" of the law's origin, one can still follow "the progress of this intellectual and physical movement." In the face of democracy's impatience with the past, ancient habits persist. Tocqueville concludes that "when one bears in mind that this law was probably given to the English by the Saxons, one cannot but be astonished at the influence which the point of departure has upon the good or ill destiny of peoples."[25]

It is such tenacity which particularly interests and disturbs Tocqueville. Lest his treatment of America's new beginning obscure the tenacious character of the affections, the last section of chapter 2 of the *Democracy* begins with a warning.

> The reader is cautioned not to draw too general or too absolute an inference from what has been said. The social condition, the religion, and the customs of the first immigrants undoubtedly exercised an immense influence on the destiny of their new country. Nevertheless, they could not found a state of things originating solely in themselves . . . and the settlers, in-

[25] *Journey to America*, pp. 262-63. See also *Democracy*, vol. 1, p. 287. For a discussion of "tenacious peculiarity," see Letter to Beaumont, November 3, 1853, vol. 2, p. 237.

tentionally or not, mingled habits and notions derived from their education and the traditions of their country with those habits and notions which were exclusively their own.

Whatever the truth of the American experience, "the shot heard round the world" had fueled revolutionary enthusiasm on the continent, suggesting, especially to the French, the possibility of pure novelty in politics. Tocqueville's American "monomania" can only be understood alongside the revolutionary mania of the French. The lesson of chapter 2 is conservative: "No man can entirely shake off the influence of the past." While praising the extraordinary wisdom and virtue of America's founders, Tocqueville insists also that her beginning owes much to chance or, perhaps, to an inscrutable destiny. In any case, intention could not thoroughly master the unintentional, and that which was brought over as well as that which was left behind seemed out of the hands of men. Tocqueville takes seriously the claims of New England's "historian": "In our eyes as well as in his own," these first settlers were indeed "blessed," for this "germ of a great nation" was "wafted by Providence to a predestined shore."[26]

"Astonished" at the interplay of the forces of recollection, the theorist is humbled. The incompleteness of remembrance and oblivion, the relation of that which is remembered and that which is forgotten, the tenacity of obscure memories and the presence of vivid recollection, all these conspire to convince Tocqueville of the limitations imposed on the legislator. While his reflections on national character reveal the central characteristic of political life to be the affections, the complexity of their relations to their objects and to one another imposes severe restrictions on the political art. Consider in this regard Tocqueville's admission of ignorance after a life spent studying the political affections: "I do not know how national character is formed,

---

[26] *Democracy*, vol. 1, p. 46.

but I do know that when once formed, it draws such broad distinctions between nations, that to discover what is passing in the minds of foreigners, one must give up one's nationality, almost one's identity." The complexity of the affections magnifies the influence of fortune in human affairs. The play of chance looms so large that the legislator must confine his activities to the modification and manipulation of existent affections, not to the creation of new ones. If the Americans could begin "from a clean start," they were also the most fortunate of nations. Indeed, the Americans appeared the beneficiaries of a most fortuitous remembering and forgetting. Jared Sparks's caution had sunk deep into his young auditor: "Those who would like to imitate us should remember that there are no precedents for our history." Tocqueville's is the practiced humility of dark knowledge, the understanding of modernity's limitations: "I do not possess the parent of all illusions—enthusiasm." Gone is that sense of bold endeavor that one finds at the beginning of the epoch. Machiavelli had painted with bold and daring strokes, challenging fortuna and speaking confidently of new beginnings. But Machiavellian confidence had given way to Tocquevillian melancholy: "What good can one hope will come out of the ideas and feelings of France, which are the result of a long and pernicious education? To tell the truth I do not know."[27]

For forty years and more, France had been torn by "two great parties," neither of whom understood her national physiognomy, the legacy of her past. The eighteenth century's elevation of Reason had captured those who loved the past no less than those who hated it. As one sought to make France what she once was, the other sought to make her what she should be. But Reason's empire had obscured the affective foundations of political order. Exhausted from the struggle between those with "too good

[27] Letter to Mrs. Grote, January 31, 1857, vol. 2, p. 347; *Recollections*, p. 62; Letter to Bauchitte, September 23, 1853, in Gargan [1], p. 249. For a discussion of the Americans' good fortune, see *Journey to America*, p. 51.

a memory" and those with none, France became an easy prey for despotism. Against the illusions of youth and decrepitude, Tocqueville would teach that wisdom which an "old people" must acquire.

> In a people, time gives birth to many different interests and consecrates many rights. In the establishment of a general constitution, all these interests and rights form natural obstacles, hindering the application of any single political principle. It is, therefore, only at the birth of societies that laws can be completely logical. A people enjoys this advantage, not because it is wise, but because it is young.[28]

Aristocratic Pedagogy

With the publication of the first part of *Democracy in America* its young and as yet unknown author was catapulted to a position of international prominence and heralded as the greatest political thinker since Montesquieu. But while it was widely acclaimed, Tocqueville nonetheless complained that his *Democracy* was no less widely misunderstood: "I please many persons of opposite opinions, not because they penetrate my meaning, but because, looking at only one side of my work, they think that they find in it arguments in favor of their own convictions." Ironically, the *Democracy*, a book for and about democracy, was of such a character that, as Royer-Collard cautioned, not "ten persons" would "thoroughly enter into the spirit of [the] book."[29]

---

[28] Quoted in Lively, p. 47.

[29] Letter to Henry Reeve, March 22, 1837, vol. 2, p. 39. Royer-Collard's observation is quoted by Tocqueville himself in a letter to Ampere (August 27, 1840, vol. 2, p. 64). For an example of the misunderstanding of even his dearest friends, see the letter to Eugene Stoffels, February 21, 1835, vol. 1, pp. 377-78. Royer-Collard's warning is confirmed in a glance at the variety of teachings and allegiances attributed to Tocqueville by friends and enemies alike. Despite Tocqueville's protestations, commentators persisted in "looking at only one side" of his work. Subsequent intellectual history has confirmed Royer-Collard's caution. We stand forewarned; Tocqueville's is a difficult teaching.

The difficulty in discerning Tocqueville's meaning is in part the result of his attempt "to produce a double effect on the men of [his] day." Tocqueville wrote to both "those who fancied an ideal democracy" and "those for whom the word democracy is synonymous with destruction, anarchy, spoilation, and murder." The *Democracy* attempts to speak to both democratic and aristocratic spirits. As the democratic party was animated by a hatred of the past, so the aristocratic party hated the present. And while democrats thought that men could simply discard the past, aristocrats conceived the present as easily forgotten. Democrats and aristocrats alike, in their attempts at creation or recreation, overestimated the possibilities of oblivion. They foolishly thought "that by tearing a page out of history, they [would] be able to take it up where they left off."[30]

Wishing to "diminish the ardor of the Republican party," the *Democracy* teaches that "no man can entirely shake off the influence of the past." But Tocqueville's teaching has a second aspect. If the education of Democracy is the most exalted aim of the *Democracy*, it is not its most immediate. Ironically, the education of democracy waits upon the education of the aristocracy. Tocqueville addresses both democrats and aristocrats, but he addresses especially aristocrats. Thus, the *Democracy* is a book about democracy whose most urgent teachings are addressed to the French noblesse.

I have endeavored to abate the claims of the Aristocrats, and to make them bend to an irresistible future; so that the impulse in one quarter and the resistance in the other being less violent, society may march on peaceably towards the fulfilment of its destiny. This

[30] The citation, from a letter to G. Grote (February 2, 1849, vol. 2, pp. 99, 103), refers in particular to those republicans who fancied themselves "back in '91." But in more general terms, it reflects Tocqueville's long-standing criticism of the French inclination toward naive historical reminiscence which, by then, had plagued France for sixty years.

is the dominant idea in the book—an idea which embraces all the others.

To democrats and aristocrats alike, Tocqueville would teach the nature of the democratic spirit, what men and nations might "hope" and "fear." But the gravest dangers resulted not from democracy itself but from a democracy opposed. It was the consequences of such opposition that drove men "beyond the natural limits of [their] opinions" and threatened a violent future. Hence the most immediate aim of the *Democracy* was "to abate the claims of the Aristocrats."[31]

These facts call into question Tocqueville's supposed neutrality. On at least three occasions, Tocqueville insists upon the impartiality of his judgment. Two instances occur in letters to his English friend and translator, Henry Reeve. The first letter to Reeve is the earliest and most important of these instances.

> Myself belonging to the ancient aristocracy of my country, I had no natural hatred or jealousy of the aristocracy; nor could I have any natural affection for it, since that aristocracy had ceased to exist, and one can be strongly attached only to the living. I was near enough to know it thoroughly, and far enough to judge dispassionately. I may say as much for the democratic element. It had done me, as an individual, neither good nor harm. I had no personal motive, apart from my public convictions, to love or to hate it. Balanced between the past and the future, with no natural instinctive attraction towards either, I could without an effort look quietly on each side of the question.

As a philosopher and even as an aristocrat, Tocqueville gives us no cause to doubt his claims. However, we have good reason to doubt the neutrality of this author's book, which endeavors above all else to "abate the claims of the

---

[31] Letter to Eugene Stoffels, February 21, 1835, vol. 1, p. 378; *Democracy*, vol. 1, p. 12; *Recollections*, p. 28.

Aristocrats" and to bend them "to an irresistible future."
The second letter to Reeve says as much. While "the spirit
of my book . . . is one of true impartiality in the theoretical
judgment of the two societies, the old and the new," it
exhibits "also a sincere desire to see the new establish itself." Any understanding of the *Democracy* must begin with
an understanding of Tocqueville's "political object."[32]

We return to the first Reeve letter. Essentially autobiographical, Tocqueville's self-explanation is called forth by
the failure of his critics to understand his meaning and his
felt need to explain the origin of his vision. The letter tells
us that those who make Tocqueville out "a party-man"
ascribe to him "alternately aristocratic and democratic prejudices." Tocqueville pleads his innocence—he had no
"passions" in this regard, only "opinions." We discover
that those who do have such passions are also committed
to certain "forms of government," but that Tocqueville is
not. Tocqueville attributes the clarity of his vision to his
being free of such prejudices. Indeed, it is the political
consequences of such prejudices that puts Tocqueville "on
guard . . . against political illusions." The suggestion is that
allegiance to form is at the center of the dangerous illusions
which mystify Tocqueville's contemporaries. Tocqueville,
on the other hand, "balanced" as he is "between the past
and the future," has neither "natural hatred" nor "natural
affection" for *any* form of government. The political illusions of the French, it is hinted, are rooted in a passionate
remembrance of the past, a remembrance characterized by
"love" and "hate."[33]

Embedded in Tocqueville's discussion is a conception of

[32] Letter to Henry Reeve, March 22, 1837, vol. 2, p. 40; Letter to Henry
Reeve, November 15, 1839, in Gargan [1], p. 39.
[33] Letter to Henry Reeve, March 22, 1837, vol. 2, pp. 39-40. This letter
is quite remarkable: it is both autobiography and political history. It is
also a discussion of Tocqueville's relation to that history. As such, it is a
door which opens upon the foundations of Tocqueville's thought and to
which one must return again and again in any consideration of Tocqueville's teaching.

the political psychology that attends the violent transformation of traditional societies. The event that had given rise to the partisanship over "form" was the collapse of the ancient regime. Memory, Tocqueville insists, is properly the home not of knowledge, but of affection (that which "feels" but doesn't "reason"). Memory identifies and preserves that which is "familiar" and "dear," that which is deserving of affection. Memory is thus bound up with "passion," not "judgment." To look for knowledge in historical example is to risk deception. Because "all historical events differ, . . . the past teaches one little about the present." This distinction is obscured, however, in traditional societies. In such societies, human beings love custom and custom *is* knowledge. Thus, traditional societies are in the habit of looking to the past for knowledge. The breakdown of traditional societies is accompanied not only by the detachment of the affections from their customary objects, but also by a great uncertainty as to what men know. This is especially true of political knowledge, which in all societies, but particularly in traditional ones, is concealed behind political forms.

During such times, the fear of wandering "in obscurity" is so great that human beings seize upon form as the only political firmament. The certain comforts of their fathers' house give way to anxieties over the nature of their inheritance. Possessed by uncertainty, they enlist memory in their search for knowledge, finding in remembrance sometimes an "example," sometimes a "warning." Thus "newborn ideas [come to be] enclosed and swathed in [the] swaddles of antiquity." Unlike the "tranquility and moderation" that are characteristic of the patriot's natural affection for "the mansion of his fathers," the fevered remembrance which attends the breakdown of traditional society is characterized by excess. "Inflated sentimentalism, . . . exaggerated expressions, . . . incoherence, . . . ungainly images," all these haunt human memories, which now "overflow" beyond their "original idea or sentiment."

185

Thus, ironically, at that point when "the past no longer throws light on the future," love, hatred, and fear attach men to the most reified forms of "historical resemblance."[34]

While this allegiance to form is the aim of French politics in general, it is the particular sin of the French aristocracy, and it must be addressed if Tocqueville is "to abate the claims of the Aristocrats." It is significant that this sin receives varying treatment by Tocqueville. His harshest criticism of the French aristocracy is found in his article for Mill's *Westminster Review*, Tocqueville's only publication not intended for French consumption. Its title and subject matter, "The Political and Social Condition of France Before the Revolution," invite comparison with Tocqueville's later history of the same period, *The Old Régime and the French Revolution*. (We, too, will make such a comparison in its proper place.) But it is perhaps even more appropriate to compare this work to the *Democracy*. Written in 1836, this piece is closest in time to the first part and lies in between the first and second parts of the *Democracy*. But whereas the *Democracy* is written for a country in which "the fight is finished," the article written for the *Westminster Review* is penned for a country in which the aristocracy remains

---

[34] Tocqueville's work abounds with references to this inclination and his impatience with it. "Nothing is more deceitful than historical resemblance," Tocqueville would write less than one year before his death (Letter to Freslon, September 11, 1857, vol. 2, p. 384). His *Recollections* decry "the learned daydreams" of the historians (pp. 64-66). But the most interesting and extensive treatment of man's inclination to drag examples "from the attic of the past" is to be found in the unfinished second volume of his history (*European Revolution*, pp. 46-52). Here, Tocqueville recounts the phenomenon of 1787—the calling of the Estates-General: "What happened in 1787 was that these ancient precedents were suddenly put into action again. The old governmental machine was again set in motion; yet it soon became apparent that the machine was propelled by some new and unknown power which, instead of making it run well, was going to destroy it." But this is only the most extraordinary case of the French taste for "reminiscence historique." See also *Democracy*, vol. 2, p. 349; *Recollections*, pp. 37, 97, 98; "Address to Académie des Sciences Morales et Politiques," in Mayer, p. 89; *Journeys to England and Ireland*, p. 80; Gargan [1], p. 61.

healthy and predominant in public affairs. In the *Democracy*, a book written for a democracy, Tocqueville tells "hard truths" about democracies. In "The Political and Social Condition of France Before the Revolution," an article written for the last surviving aristocracy, Tocqueville tells equally hard truths about aristocracies—truths the English aristocracy must learn if England is to be saved from revolution. Political salvation is beyond the French noblesse. If Tocqueville does not hide the truth from the French aristocracy, neither does he prepare them for self-defense against the democratic onslaught. While the English aristocracy must be taught how to defend the present, its French counterpart must be taught how to give up the past ("the only honourable task" for democratic France). Hence, while the pedagogy of "France Before the Revolution" is often severe and sometimes scathing, that of the *Democracy* is gentle, persuasive, consoling. We begin with the former.[35]

In "France Before the Revolution," the French noblesse's love of form is shown in all its stupidity as the mortal sin of an aristocracy become a caste. While the form of aristocratic rule is founded upon blood, a virile aristocracy also must unite this form with the substance of power, that is, with wealth and knowledge. In such an aristocracy, blood is simply the principle around which power is organized. In France, as power became more fluid or less easily contained within this principle, the aristocracy showed an increasing affection for the ancient forms of their fathers. As Tocqueville wryly observes, "They were more attached to the semblance of power than to power itself." While these "modern nobles . . . abandoned most of the ideas of their ancestors," they nonetheless clung ever more tenaciously to those "privileges of their fathers . . . which make aris-

---

[35] "The Political and Social Condition of France Before the Revolution," in *Memoir, Letters and Remains*, vol. 1, pp. 210-11. Tocqueville reveals how an aristocracy can be destroyed, and thus how it also might save itself. For the hardness of Tocqueville's truth, see Letter to J. S. Mill, November 15, 1839, vol. 2, p. 58.

tocracies hated." This adherence is not to be attributed to their simple conservatism or to their inability to "move with the times." Rather, the aristocracy's attachment to ancient *form* grew in proportion to the loss of their ancient *power*. Tocqueville concludes simply:

> In isolating themselves from the aristocracy of wealth, and from that of intellect, the nobles believed they were remaining faithful to the example of their fathers. They did not remark, that in imitating the conduct they were missing the aim of their ancestors.[36]

This is the "hard truth" about the French aristocracy. We suspect it is the truth regarding all declining classes, a study in the weaknesses to which political memory is prone. In any case, it is a lesson which Tocqueville hopes will not be lost on the English. Such tough talk, however, would only further enrage the aristocratic party in France, the anger of weakness attaching the nobility more strongly to the semblance of their ancient strength. The political health of France depends first upon freeing these opponents of democracy from their attachment to ancient form. The Author's Introduction to the *Democracy* outlines the problem:

> The first of the duties that are at this time imposed upon those who direct our affairs is to educate democracy. . . . This, however, is what we think of least; placed in the middle of a rapid stream, we obstinately fix our eyes on the ruins that may still be descried upon the shore we have left, while the current hurries us away and drags us backward towards the abyss.

If the new is to "establish itself," the aristocracy must be wooed from their obstinate attachment to dead form. While the English aristocracy can bear hard truths because they

[36] "France Before the Revolution," pp. 210, 211, 214, 220. See also *European Revolution*, pp. 72-73; *The Old Régime and the French Revolution*, p. 143.

are strong, Tocqueville must exercise greater care with tender French sensibilities.[37]

Tocqueville was well equipped to engage in such an enterprise for, as Beaumont tells us, his democratic "notions" had not obliterated his aristocratic "sentiments." He understood the distemper of the aristocratic affections, that its origin lay in a great sense of loss. He, too, had drunk from the bitter cup of revolution.[38] But he also knew the futility of aristocratic anger and the dangers of that peculiar kind of necrophilia which attends the rage of the once great.[39] Tocqueville knew more. He knew that which lay at the center of the aristocrats' sense of loss, the hidden core of aristocratic anger: "In aristocratic communities, where a small number of persons manage everything, the outward intercourse of men is subject to settled conventional rules." In such communities, the "marks of respect" and "condescension" are known and practiced by everyone. Democracy, "which destroys or obscures almost all the old conventional rules of society," has only "contempt" for tradition and form. Equality brings confusion to "distinctions of rank," and democratic man neither expects nor gives those "attentions" to which aristocracies grow so attached.[40]

At the core of aristocratic anger is wounded pride. It is the stubborness of the proud that Tocqueville must overcome.

For the real question is no longer how to retain the peculiar advantages offered by inequality of condition

[37] *Democracy*, vol. 1, p. 7.

[38] *Recollections*, p. 95. Indeed, despite his democratic notions, Tocqueville retained even extreme aristocratic sensibilities. Consider in this regard Tocqueville's disgust with the spectacle of lower-class democracy in England (*Journeys to England and Ireland*, p. 45).

[39] The first letter to Reeve (above) argues that one cannot love dead things, but its context suggests rather that to love dead things is to become the victim of illusions.

[40] *Democracy*, vol. 2, pp. 181-82, 207. For some interesting reflections on aristocratic pride and democratic anxiety (and their relation to "ranks being no longer defined"), see *Journeys to England and Ireland*, p. 75.

but to grasp the new advantages offered by equality.
We must try not to model ourselves on our fathers,
but to achieve the grandeur and happiness which is
possible for us.

Before the French aristocracy would give up their "peculiar
advantages" for "new advantages," however, they had to
be made to see the futility of their rage.[41]

Ironically, the spectacle of the Terror had infected all
political parties in France with the revolutionary illusion:
that a single act of violence could transform the political
landscape. This lesson joined with the fevered recollection
of the aristocrats to give their politics a revolutionary edge,
leading to what Tocqueville called "rash projects." (Indeed,
Tocqueville's oldest friend, Louis de Kergorlay, was heavily involved in Legitimist intrigues against Louis Philippe
and, on one occasion, probably would have been convicted
and executed for treason had not Tocqueville defended him
brilliantly.) "Pre-occupied with their remembrance," these
aristocrats were "ill acquainted with the haven towards
which they [were] bound." The first task of the *Democracy*
was to convince the aristocracy that all such attempts to
restore ancient form are a species of "blindness."

If the men of our time should be convinced, by atten-
tive observation and sincere reflection, that the gradual
and progressive development of social equality is at
once the past and future of their history, this discovery
alone would confer upon the change the sacred character of a divine decree. To attempt to check democracy
would be in that case to resist the will of God; and the
nations would then be constrained to make the best
of the social lot awarded to them by Providence.[42]

Presented as revelation in the Author's Introduction, the
providential character of equality is rehearsed throughout

[41] Quoted in Lively, p. 41.
[42] *Democracy*, vol. 1, pp. 7, 338, 341.

the *Democracy*. Tocqueville's favorite image of democracy is of a great flood against which "dikes" are useless and whose irresistible power destroys all that stands against it. The rage from which the aristocracy suffers is that which accompanies the loss of something cherished. The recognition of democracy's irresistible character is the beginning of the transformation of that rage into the melancholy of renunciation, as the anger lodged in memory gives way to "the sadness of remembrance." Tocqueville would lead others through the same process of renunciation that had been his own. (In keeping with the need to give up those "peculiar advantages," Tocqueville never adopted the title of "Count" which was properly his.) He confesses that the *Democracy* (a token of his own reconciliation) was written "under a kind of religious awe produced on the author's mind by the view of that irresistible revolution." Only after the French noblesse are in "awe" of democracy's power will they become receptive to its "new advantages."[43]

As aristocratic pedagogy, the *Democracy* moves deftly back and forth between persuasion and commiseration, sharing the aristocrat's distaste for democratic things while softening his pride. When it comes time to teach the truth about the adherence to empty form, that truth is presented softly. Tocqueville turns not to France, but to China, where "aim" also had been sacrificed to "example."

> The Chinese, in following the track of their forefathers, had forgotten the reasons by which the latter had been guided. They still used the formula without asking for its meaning; they retained the instrument, but they no longer possessed the art of altering or renewing it. The Chinese, then, had lost the power of change; for them improvement was impossible. They were compelled at all times and in all points to imitate their predecessors lest they should stray into utter darkness by de-

[43] For an example of democracy's flood-like character, see *Recollections*, p. 77.

viating for an instant from the path already laid down for them. The source of human knowledge was all but dry; and though the stream still ran on, it could neither swell its waters nor alter its course.

Tocqueville concludes this teaching with a recognition of the value of even empty form in China, where "physical prosperity was everywhere discernible, revolutions were rare, and war was, so to speak, unknown"; the aristocrat is left to consider for himself the meaning of this teaching for France.[44]

Likewise, in his treatment of "family" (that institution at the center of aristocratic form and the chief object of aristocratic affection), Tocqueville's method is gentle, combining a generous understanding of the place "family" enjoys in aristocratic affections with an attempt to take the aristocrat beyond such affections. In a self-knowing passage, Tocqueville links the love of family with its physical embodiment—the ancestral domain.

> Among nations whose law of descent is founded upon the right of primogeniture, landed estates often pass from generation to generation without undergoing division; the consequence of this is that family feeling is to a certain degree incorporated with the estate. The family represents the estate, the estate the family, whose name, together with its origin, its glory, its power, and its virtues, is thus perpetuated in an imperishable memorial of the past and as a sure pledge of the future.[45]

But equality had brought about the partition of property, destroying "the intimate connection . . . between family

---

[44] *Democracy*, vol. 2, pp. 48-49. What Max Lerner and others see as Tocqueville's ambivalence towards aristocratic societies, his alternating praise and criticism, can best be explained as pedagogical technique. As Tocqueville was known for his mania for literary precision, the gentle oscillation noted in his work, its two-sided quality, must be considered, at the least, to be by design.

[45] *Democracy*, vol. 1, p. 51.

feeling and the preservation of the paternal estate." Underneath the wounded pride of the aristocracy lay a deep fear that democracy would bring an end to the permanence of human things. Indeed, Tocqueville himself suspected that the loss of enduring objects for the affections threatened a new kind of selfishness, a democratic narcissism which "makes the passion for physical gratification and the exclusive love of the present predominate in the human heart." (As we shall later see, Tocqueville's attempt to substitute a "living" and permanent object for the "dead" shell of the ancient regime extended beyond his interest in an aristocratic pedagogy.) This insight is itself aristocratic, originating in the deep knowledge of permanence which that class still remembered. But pride and fear had blinded the French noblesse to that "which is possible for us." In the third chapter of the first part of the *Democracy*, the place in the text where the aristocratic family first makes its appearance, Tocqueville speaks of the virtues of this institution, but not of its vices. Yet, in a matter-of-fact manner, he reveals the first lesson the aristocrat must learn in his accommodation to democracy: "to perpetuate and immortalize himself, as it were, in his great-grandchildren" is no longer possible. This is the most difficult lesson of the *Democracy*'s aristocratic pedagogy—that "what is called family pride is often founded upon an illusion of self-love."[46]

As Tocqueville knew, the origin of the aristocrat's antipathy to democracy was self-referential, the product of "self-love." Like most people, the aristocrat equated personal evil with evil generally. The revolution that had legitimated the principle of equality was necessarily hostile to the hereditary principle. Democratic novelty appeared nowhere more radical than in its rejection of what had been the foundation of permanence in the ancient regime. Threatened with personal impermanence (the decline of the aristocratic family as an institution) and witness to that

[46] *Democracy*, vol. 1, pp. 51-52; vol. 2, pp. 260-61.

extreme love of novelty so characteristic of "the revolutionary spirit," the aristocrat conceived anarchy and disorder to be the very spirit of democracy. Privately, Tocqueville admitted that the "absence of coherence and
permanence" in democracy made it something less than
"the best form of government"; however, an important
part of the "political object" of the Democracy was to qualify
such opinions in an effort to foreclose reaction.[47]

The first teaching of the Democracy, it is also the last.
Having completed his "task," Tocqueville speaks of his
purpose. He begins by warning that the example of America ought not to be the object of slavish "imitation." The
import of the book is not its "form," but its "substance":
"My aim has been to show, by the example of America,
that laws, and especially customs, may allow a democratic
people to remain free." The Democracy is framed, as it were,
by the association of democracy with reverence and permanence. Consoling the aristocrat in his loss while con-
vincing him of its irretrievability, Tocqueville mitigates the
aristocrat's deepest fears while denying to him the foundation for a righteous opposition.[48]

The Democracy's pedagogy had been, in a sense,
Tocqueville's own. Calling himself an "advisor" to democracy, Tocqueville's insight was rooted in a sensibility
toward time that was essentially aristocratic. The rhythm

[47] Letter to Louis de Kergorlay, June 20, 1831, vol. 1, p. 297.
[48] Letter to de Chabrol, in Mayer, p. 22; Democracy, vol. 1, pp. 48, 341-
42. The careful reader will note that the two chapters of part one cited
here are chapters 2 and 17 (the first and last chapters are, obviously, 1
and 18). The importance of chapter 2 has already been attested to, and
we would add only that chapter 1 deals with the "Exterior Form of North
America"; it is only with chapter 2 that Tocqueville begins his discussion
of American democracy. Chapter 17 is not the last but, in fact, the next-
to-last chapter, placing towards the middle that which we insist is the
important end. That chapter 17 is indeed the end (it is followed by one
chapter of prophecy outside the scope of the book's more important
purpose) is made clear by the first sentence of chapter 18: "The principle
task that I have imposed upon myself is now performed: I have shown
as far as I was able the laws and customs of the American democracy"
(vol. 1, p. 343).

of the *Democracy*, especially of the second part, is the result of this movement from the past to the present, from the dead to the living. The first part of the *Democracy* is the first part of the aristocrat's democratic education. It aims at softening aristocratic anger and mitigating aristocratic fear. The second part of the *Democracy* attempts more. If the first part aims at making the aristocrat a less dangerous citizen, the second would make of him a patriot. The second part is more daring and honest than the first part. It tells a more complete truth about aristocracy and democracy, hiding less behind the "singular" example of America. It is, in Beaumont's words, "reflections upon reflections," and it presupposes the pedagogical preliminaries of part one.[49]

It is only in the second part that Tocqueville reveals what we have called the hidden core of the aristocrat's hatred of equality. The aristocratic love of form is bound up with "distinctions of rank" and with those marks of deference which confirm the aristocrat's sense of self-worth. Democracy denies the aristocrat the "satisfaction" of "condescension." Therefore, it is especially the "manners" of democracy to which the aristocrat must become accustomed. It is in the third book of the second part that Tocqueville treats the "influence of democracy on manners properly so called." He begins this book with an observation on the character of aristocracies.

> Among an aristocratic people each caste has its own opinions, feelings, rights, customs, and modes of living. Thus the men who compose it do not resemble the mass of their fellow citizens; they do not think or feel in the same manner, and they scarcely believe that they belong to the same race. They cannot, therefore, thoroughly understand what others feel nor judge of others by themselves.

[49] Gustave de Beaumont, *Memoir*, in *Memoir, Letters and Remains*, vol. 1, p. 50; Letter to J. S. Mill, November 15, 1839, vol. 2, p. 58.

While Tocqueville also emphasizes the "mutual obliga-
tions" and "generosity" that characterized "the old times,"
he does not shrink from identifying the political limitiations
of a society of rigid hereditary rank. These limitations orig-
inate in the very source of aristocratic strength. For "although [the old obligations] prompted men to great acts
of self-devotion, they created no real sympathies, for real
sympathies can exist only between those who are alike,
and in aristocratic ages men acknowledge none but their
own caste to be like themselves." In chapter 2 of Book
Three, we are shown the beneficial consequences of such
sympathy. Unlike the aristocratic English who remain
preoccupied with rank, two Americans "in a foreign country . . . are at once friends simply because they are Americans." "Repulsed by no prejudice," these fellow-citizens
are "attracted by their common country." First among
equality's "new advantages," then, is the unity of the community, as *nation* is elevated above *family* or *caste* in the
hierarchy of membership. The first part of the *Democracy*
had juxtaposed family and self, duty and pleasure. In the
second part, Tocqueville reveals a third pole which we
suspect is the proper object of democratic "self-devotion"
and the only real alternative to democratic self-indulgence.[50]

With this new groundwork of patriotism laid, chapter 3
quite properly addresses the issue of democratic "pride":
"The temper of the Americans is vindictive, like that of all
serious and reflecting nations. They hardly ever forget an
offense, but it is not easy to offend them, and their resentment is as slow to kindle as it is to abate." Thus, the
chapter begins with an assertion of the existence of a democratic pride and "manly confidence" which, in many respects, bears a striking resemblance to the aristocrat's self-
conception. Having first witnessed the rule of excess and
the mob, followed by the narrow greed of the middle class,

[50] *Democracy*, vol. 2, p. 173.

the aristocrat had supposed the sentiments of democracy
to be a strange amalgam of arrogance and servility. But
Tocqueville insists that democracy is not inimical to a life
of honor. Only after Tocqueville has insisted upon the existence of a kind of democratic honor is the unseemly foundation of aristocratic honor revealed to be a preoccupation
with "respect" and "condescension." Thus, the aristocrat
is led gently from the "dead" to the "living." Although
unconcerned with the distinctions among men, the Americans remain a proud people (indeed, they are "swollen"
with pride), and Tocqueville repeats the political lesson of
chapters 1 and 2, that the Americans "are too strongly
interested in living harmoniously" to allow "rank" to in-
terpose.[51]

Confronted with the manners of democracy, the aristocrat is immediately conscious of the great differences in
civility between the "old" and the "new" societies, but
Tocqueville calls attention as well to certain underlying
similarities. If aristocratic institutions gave the French noblesse a lofty notion of its families and itself, "democratic
institutions give men a lofty notion of their country and
themselves." So presented, the chief difference between
aristocratic and democratic pride and affection is the object
to which these are attached. Whereas the aristocrat looks
into the past and future and sees his family, the democrat
sees his country. If elsewhere in the *Democracy* the long
memory of aristocracies is favorably compared to democracies' love of the present, the Americans, at least, are said
to "hardly ever forget an offense." Impressed with the
upright and masculine virtue of the Americans, Tocqueville
hopes his aristocratic audience will likewise be taken by
the spirit of this first of the new democracies. But lest this
audience miss the point, chapters 1 through 3 are summarized in chapter 4 (entitled simply "Consequences Of
The Three Preceding Chapters"). In chapter 4, Tocqueville

[51] *Democracy*, vol. 2, pp. 181-83.

demonstrates the relation of the Americans' fellow feeling to the weakness of equality, comparing their "cooperation" to that found within the several classes of Europe. In the last paragraph of chapter 4, the teaching of the preceding three chapters is reduced to aphorism: "Extend to a people the remark here applied to a class and you will understand my meaning." It is precisely the extension of aristocratic affections from a class to a people that Tocqueville intends.[52]

Tocqueville leaves off the discussion of honor and democracy only to return to it again in chapter 18. As before, the text moves from the "dead" to the "living." "In feudal society," Tocqueville observes, "the whole system of the commonwealth rested upon the sentiment of the fidelity to the person of the lord. To destroy that sentiment was to fall into anarchy." This point of view remained the basis of the aristocratic reaction and the theoretical foundation for identifying democracy with disorder. But fealty was dead, and Tocqueville sought in democracy a living principle of allegiance and a new object of affection.

Few traces are to be found in the Middle Ages of the passion that constituted the life of the nations of antiquity; I mean patriotism. The word itself is not of very ancient date in the language. Feudal institutions concealed the country at large from men's sight and rendered the love of it less necessary. The nation was forgotten in the passions that attached men to persons. Hence it was no part of the strict law of feudal honor to remain faithful to one's country. Not indeed that the love of their country did not exist in the hearts of our forefathers, but it constituted a dim and feeble instinct, which has grown more clear and strong in proportion as aristocratic classes have been abolished and the supreme power of the nation centralized.[53]

[52] *Democracy*, vol. 2, pp. 181-86.
[53] *Democracy*, vol. 2, pp. 245-46; Letter to Henry Reeve, March 22, 1837, vol. 2, p. 40.

This account of the rebirth of patriotism against the back-drop of a decaying feudalism is presented as a historical description. But if this instinct "has grown more clear and strong," the aristocratic allegiance to the "ruins" of the past suggests that it is neither as visible nor as strong as is "necessary." (The "modern noble," despite his pretensions, is no less susceptible than other democratic men to the isolation and self-indulgence characteristic of equality of condition.) In Tocqueville's account, patriotism appears to grow out of the remains of fealty; the new living object of affection succeeds naturally, as it were, to those ancient but now barren allegiances. Once "concealed" by aristocratic institutions and "forgotten" in aristocratic passions, *la patrie* has now come into view. This history of patriotism is also the pedagogy of a patriot as the aristocrat is brought face-to-face with his "country."[54]

For Tocqueville, America remained the first example of the successful establishment of democratic affections. In America, where "all families disappear after the second or third genertion," there is hardly a person "to be met with who does not claim some remote kindred with the first founders of the colonies." The American experience suggested the place of the *nation* in the imagination of democratic men. Indeed, Tocqueville had come to believe that patriotism remained the only living force capable of making "the whole body of citizens go persistently forward toward the same goal."[55]

Having himself made the journey from aristocrat to pa-

[54] Consider, for example, the "dishonor" of the Constable de Bourbon, branded by "our forefathers" for bearing arms "against the King" and "in our eyes" for making war "against his country" (*Democracy*, vol. 2, p. 246).

[55] *Democracy*, vol. 2, p. 184; *Journey to America*, p. 20; Lerner, p. 88. Tocqueville suggests that religion and patriotism are both capable of generating such exertions. Yet he was painfully aware of the weakness of religion, particularly in France. Love of country seemed to him that single affection that might yet save her. In a letter to J. S. Mill, December 18, 1840, Tocqueville remarks, "The most elevated feeling now left to us is national pride" (vol. 2, p. 68).

triot, Tocqueville knew that concealed behind "aristocratic extravagances" was the potential for "love of one's country and enthusiasm for bold and brilliant actions." He knew also that only the action of lovers could save France from the tepid politics of the middle class and the master who lay beyond. At the end of aristocratic pedagogy is an oath. The democratic oath of Tocqueville's youth, it is an oath to the living: "The deed done, I continue to believe what I have always believed, that my most strict duty is not to a man nor to a family but to my country."[56]

The Theorist as Historian

Alexis de Tocqueville is the author of two books. Tocqueville's output, of course, is not exhausted in the enumeration of *Democracy in America* and *The Old Régime and the French Revolution* (as Machiavelli's is not in citing *The Prince* and the *Discourses*). But just as Machiavelli's work is framed by these two books, the *Democracy* and *The Old Régime* frame Tocqueville's political reflections. Moreover, unlike Machiavelli's, Tocqueville's two books form the parameter of his life as well as of his ideas. Like Marx's work, Tocqueville's is open to the dichotomy of "young" and "old." To this dichotomy may be added another, that of theorist and historian. Those who carve up the Frenchman, however, generally do so less in terms of ideas than in terms of mood.

---

[56] Letter to Louis de Kergorlay, October 17, 1830, in Gargan [1], pp. 8-9. The statement is in fact Tocqueville's justification to his cousin Louis (a Legitimist conspirator) of his oath of allegiance to the July Monarchy. While the other members of Tocqueville's family lacked Louis's taste for intrigue, their political allegiances (at least since the Revolution) were ultramontane, and they were strong supporters of the Bourbon. With the ascendance of Louis Philippe, Tocqueville's father left government service, and there is good reason to believe that he was quite put out at young Alexis's refusal to follow his lead. Thus, while addressed to Louis, his oldest friend, and referring on its surface to the older branch of the monarchy and its representative, Tocqueville's justification is also, less obviously, directed to his father in its attempts to explain Tocqueville's nonpartisan patriotism.

A dark pessimism, alien to the young Tocqueville, is ascribed to the seasoned statesman. The intentions of the historian are imagined to differ from those of the youthful scholar who visited America a quarter of a century earlier. If the *Democracy* was written by a young man whose "soul" yearned for the "freedom" and "renown" of France, *The Old Régime* is the work of a tired and beleaguered old man who can only narrate the inescapable servitude of his country. The hope of the theorist has been replaced by the dismal prognostications of the historian. This Tocqueville has become a "retrospective prophet" (Mayer); "somber and less balanced" (Lerner); a scholar of despair whose sole surviving motive for writing is personal immortality (Herr). This view of Tocqueville's history has at least two origins. The first is Tocqueville's observation that his history does not teach a lesson. The second is the despairing mood discernible in the *Recollections*, written in the period immediately following the coup of Louis Napoleon and Tocqueville's retirement from public life. Those who find in Tocqueville's despair the clue to the meaning of the history (Herr perhaps being the most extreme is his linkages of mood and intention) project the sentiments of his private *Recollections* into the subsequent (and public) *Old Régime*.[57]

Against the "two Tocquevilles" interpretation (which contrasts the patriot/theorist of the *Democracy* with the prophet/historian of *The Old Régime*) stands Tocqueville's own characterization of his two books: "To explain to men how to escape tyranny, that is the idea of both my books." Unified in theme, the *Democracy* and *The Old Régime* also

---

[57] Mayer, pp. 6, 76; Lerner, p. 19; Herr, *Tocqueville and the Old Regime*, p. 90. Herr, in particular, is forced into an extreme position in this regard, dismissing Tocqueville's protestations and the radical shifts in mood to which he was increasingly prone with what amounts to a claim to know Tocqueville better than Tocqueville knew himself: that the aging scholar/ statesman was endowed with a "considerable capacity for self-deception" (p. 90).

share a practical intent.[58] Still, the theorist turned historian is a matter which deserves additional comment. We know, for example, that Tocqueville was extremely critical of what he considered the naive use of history (a criticism which reaches a scathing summit in the pages of the *Recollections*). It is noteworthy that contemporary French political practice had witnessed the emergence of a peculiar hybrid—the historian/statesman, of which Guizot, Thiers, and Lamartine were the most notable examples. Tocqueville criticized the latter two for what he considered a nostalgia which had assumed a literary and historical mode. Furthermore, we have Tocqueville's famous outburst against history as recorded in Nassau William Senior's journal.

> The constitution, with all its defects, might be endurable, if we could only believe in its permanence. But we read History. We see that republican institutions have never lasted in France, and we infer that these which we have now must be short-lived. This reading of History is our bane. If we could forget the past, we might apply a calm impartial judgement to the present. But we are always thinking of precedents. Sometimes we draw them from our own history; sometimes from yours. Sometimes we use the precedent as an example, sometimes as warning. But as the circumstances under which we apply it differ materially from those under which it originally took place, it almost always misleads us.

In addition to these more general criticisms of historical science and its relation to politics, we have Tocqueville's paradoxical and, on its face, false claim regarding his own

[58] Consider also Tocqueville's insistence on this point in a letter to Ampere (August 1856): "The unity of my life and thought is the most important thing which I need to maintain before the public eye; the man is as involved in that as is the author" (quoted in Drescher, p. 1). We should not overlook the ambiguity of the idea of escaping, which can mean either to avoid certain circumstances or to free oneself from them. Such ambiguity haunts both books.

work: "I am not writing a history of the Revolution." All this leads us to ask, what, in fact, Tocqueville was doing in *The Old Régime and the French Revolution*.[59]

We turn first to Tocqueville's critique of historicism found in his correspondence with Gobineau, which takes place in the period between the writing of the *Recollections* and that of *The Old Régime*. Chiding Gobineau for being "captivated" by the "novelty" or even the "philosophical merit" of the German school, Tocqueville insists upon the importance of an idea's "moral or political effects." Responding to Gobineau's racial doctrines, Tocqueville observes, "I believe that they are probably quite false; I know that they are certainly very pernicious." These and other citations point to a continuing interest on Tocqueville's part in the practical character of ideas. But most interesting in this regard is a letter dated January 8, 1856 (when Tocqueville was in the midst of his work on *The Old Régime*), in which he responds again to the younger Gobineau's insistent demands for praise and criticism from his benefactor and would-be mentor.

What I disapprove of in the book I told you before: it is less the work itself than its tendency, which I consider dangerous. If we were to suffer from excessive enthusiasm and self-confidence, as did our ancestors of 1789, I would consider your book a salutary *cold shower*. But we have disgracefully come to the opposite extreme. We have no regard for anything, beginning with ourselves; we have no faith in anything, including ourselves. A book which tries to prove that men in this world are merely obeying their physical *constitutions* and that their will power can do almost nothing to influence their destinies is like opium given to a patient whose blood has already weakened. So much for the book.[60]

[59] Senior, vol. 1, p. 255.
[60] *European Revolution*, p. 270; see also pp. 227-232.

For our purposes, this citation is important in two respects. First, it tells us Tocqueville's general attitude towards books and what they are for. A book cannot be separated from its "moral and political effects." Every book has a "tendency" with respect to the actions of men. Second, it reveals what tendency Tocqueville regards as presently "dangerous," thus suggesting what in fact would be salutary. The French are without "faith," without "will power." They have lost control of their destiny. In short, they are without the resources to act. Gobineau's book is "pernicious" because it is like "opium." Tocqueville's book, we suspect, aims at an opposite effect; that is, it will concern itself with "faith."

What Tocqueville insists upon in the Gobineau correspondence is present elsewhere in his work during this late period. In an address to the Academy of Moral and Political Sciences, Tocqueville emphasized the power of "general concepts" which "form a kind of atmosphere surrounding each society in which both rulers and governed . . . draw intellectual breath and . . . the principles of action." In letters to Barrot and Kergorlay, Tocqueville rehearses the theme of the transformation of "abstract ideas" into "passions and facts." Indeed, the theme is so prevalent in Tocqueville's thoughts and writings during the period of the composition of *The Old Régime* as to appear his central preoccupation.[61]

Let us return momentarily to the two origins of the dichotomized Tocqueville—the despairing mood of the *Recollections* and Tocqueville's reluctance to teach in his history. Both of these require significant qualification. First, while the *Recollections* testifies to Tocqueville's despair in the face of France's never-ending revolution after the events of 1848, that despair is accompanied by a new clarity of choice. For now "there [is] no room left for moral hesita-

[61] Gargan [1], p. 236; Letter to Louis de Kergorlay, July 29, 1856, vol. 1, p. 356.

tion." If the condition of France had become objectively worse, the new situation was superior to that of the July Monarchy in at least one important respect—there was no longer any question about what to *do*. Second, while *The Old Régime* lacks the explicit intention of the *Democracy* (to "educate" democracy), it is not "lessonless" without purpose. The clearest statement of its purposefulness is to be found in a letter to Corcelle.

> It [is] not my intention to suggest a remedy for the state into which the Ancient Regime, the Republic, and the Empire, have thrown our country. This is true: my fixed resolution is to stop before I set foot on this ground, to consider it only from afar, and not to try and write a book of temporary interest. But it by no means follows that no clear results are to be drawn from the historical study on which I am at work, that it is to give only a vague notion of the opinions and sentiments of the author, and to leave the reader uncertain as to the judgments which he ought to form upon facts, and upon men; on the events themselves, on their causes, and as to the lessons which they teach us. It would be strange, considering that I enter upon this work with decided and often enthusiastic preferences, fixed opinions, and a clear and certain object, if I should leave the reader to float rudderless on the sea of my ideas and of his own.
>
> I think that the books which have most roused men to reflection, and have had most influence upon their opinions and their actions, are those in which the author does not tell them dogmatically what they are to think, but puts them into the way of finding the truth for themselves. If God grants me time and strength enough to finish my task, you may be sure that no one will have any doubts as to my object.[62]

[62] *Recollections*, p. 85; Letter to Corcelle, September 17, 1853, vol. 2, p. 229.

Tocqueville never did complete his "task"; he finished the first volume of his history, but left only notes and fragments of what was to be the second volume. Thus, "doubt" remains as to the "object" of Tocquevillian history. But the letter to Corcelle is suggestive. While France (in the language of the *Recollections*) continues to "rove the seas" without any immediate hope of reaching "solid land," Tocqueville vows not to leave his audience "rudderless." If the history does not attempt to point out a safe harbor ("suggest a remedy"), it would provide that which is necessary for the French to find their own way. The history is akin to a navigator's instruments, seeking to identify those landmarks in the past which may yet put the French "into the way" of the truth. In another sense, it is especially in democracies (as Tocqueville well knew) that men must find the truth out "for themselves." Thus, while Tocqueville is silent about the purpose of his history, its truth is salutary and presumably accessible to democratic men. It remains for us, then, to discover the substance of this salutary truth.

As we have already seen, the historian's dictum, that history teaches simply, is not Tocqueville's. A decade earlier, in a letter to Kergorlay, Tocqueville had summarized his historical attitude in regard to France: "The prejudices arising from . . . what our history tells us stand in our way more than our ignorance." It is this dictum, that of the theorist rather than the historian, that finds its way into the pages of *The Old Régime* and helps explain Tocqueville's refusal to write "a history" of the Revolution. Of Tocqueville's intention, Beaumont writes that he endeavored "to awaken ideas which may be dormant in the public mind, but can never perish." He adds that *The Old Régime* was written for a generation that was about to be excluded from public life. The history, Beaumont suggests, is a kind of civic education for those denied the practical political education which free institutions provide. Tocqueville sets history or a remembrance of the past against the "martial force" of tyranny that has driven men out of the public realm. As Gargan observes, Tocqueville was forced to write *like* an historian. His was a "paradoxical and ironic mode of reflection on the past designed to stir the conscience of his own age."[63]

But what could Tocqueville's civic education masquerading as history hope to accomplish? As a vehicle for knowledge, history was wholly inadequate, more often the companion of deceit than of truth. And even if history might assist in the creation of lasting institutions, these, Tocqueville thought, exert "only a secondary influence over the destinies of men." Beaumont's phraseology, that *The Old Régime* attempted to "awaken" that which was "dormant" but imperishable, is reminiscent of the *Democracy's* description of the patriotic instinct, "which never abandons the human heart." Again, Gargan is helpful, suggesting that Tocqueville's history attempts to guide France toward a "spiritual" solution to her problems. We return to the Corcelle letter.

I am convinced that the excellence of political societies does not depend upon their laws, but upon what they are prepared to become by the sentiments, principles, and opinions, the moral and intellectual qualities given by nature and education to the men of whom they consist. If this truth does not appear in every part of my book; if it does not induce the reader to apply this lesson continually to himself; if it does not, without pretending to teach, show to him in every page what are the sentiments, opinions, and morals which lead to prosperity and freedom, and what are the vices and errors infallibly opposed to these blessings, I shall not have attained the chief, and I may say the only, object that I have in view.[64]

---

[63] Letter to Louis de Kergorlay, October 19, 1843, vol. 1, p. 341; *Memoir, Letters and Remains*, vol. 1, pp. 21, 71-72; Gargan, *De Tocqueville* (hereafter cited as Gargan [2], pp. 61-62.

[64] Letter to Corcelle, September 17, 1853, vol. 2, p. 230; Gargan [1], p. 243.

Tocqueville is more explicit, more bold, in the foreword to *The Old Régime*; rewritten one month before publication, the foreword must be considered a studied introduction to Tocqueville's history. In this introduction, the sentiments which lead to freedom and those which lead to despotism are named. The despot is no longer the simple consequence of democratic isolation, but its active promulgator: "Their feelings toward each other already growing cold; despotism freezes them." It is against this destruction of "solidarity" and "good neighborly feelings" that Tocqueville erects his history, a history which aims to make his readers "aware at every moment that they belong each and all to a vaster entity, above and around them—their native land."[65] The foreword thus suggests that the intent of Tocqueville's history is to touch in some way a dormant patriotic instinct; that this involves a clarification of the political sentiments of the nation; that such clarification necessarily requires a historical perspective; and that such a perspective will assist France in overcoming the twin problems of fragmentation and frigidity.[66] Explicitly, Tocqueville says he will

[65] *The Old Régime*, pp. xiii-xiv; Herr, pp. 84-85. While boldly speaking of despotism in a despotic France, Tocqueville is not rash. The foreword conveys the impression that what follows is simply history, a narration of the loss of freedom rather than an "action" aimed at its recovery (see Letter to Henry Reeve, May 20, 1857, vol. 2, p. 371). Thus, Tocqueville writes in the foreward, "I have tried not merely to diagnose the malady of which the sick man died but also to discover how he might have been saved. In fact, my method has been that of the anatomist who dissects each defunct organ with a view to eliciting the laws of life, and my aim has been to supply a picture that while scientifically accurate, may also be instructive" (p. xii). Commentators such as Mayer and Herr are deceived by the same device with which Tocqueville sought to deceive the censors: speaking of the "dormant" as if it were dead, that is, in the past tense. Tocqueville's *instruction*, however, aims at more than the anatomist's—it aims to bring the cadaver back to life.

[66] Any attempt to fully understand Tocqueville's history requires that *The Old Régime* be considered alongside the proposed "sequel" to which Tocqueville alludes in the foreword and of which we have but notes and fragments. We shall also continue to draw upon Tocqueville's correspondence, always a rich source in the effort to penetrate the author's meaning.

accomplish this by distinguishing the political sentiments according to virtue and vice.

> Whenever I found in our forefathers any of those virtues so vital to a nation but now well-nigh extinct—a spirit of healthy independence, high ambitions, faith in oneself and in a cause—I have thrown them into relief. Similarly, whenever I found traces of any of those vices which after destroying the old order still affect the body politic, I have emphasized them; for it is in the light of the evils to which they formerly gave rise that we can gauge the harm they yet may do.[67]

In keeping with Tocqueville's method, we will examine the "virtues" and "vices" of French remembrance.

Ancient Vice

The substance of *The Old Régime* is rendered difficult for, like the *Democracy*, the history attempts to speak to multiple audiences and to accomplish multiple purposes. These several audiences are divided by ancient "hatreds and mutual jealousies" ("old sores") whose beginnings are shrouded by the curtain of the Revolution. Originating with "the old kings," these divisions are the most pernicious legacy of the ancient regime and the foundation upon which a democratic despotism has twice been erected.[68]

Tocqueville begins with a history of the present affections, for an understanding of their origin is a necessary prelude to any effort to modify or redirect them. The failures of the ancient regime, the seething hatreds which festered under the surface of French society, the disappointments, dissatisfactions, fears, and jealousies, all these

[67] *The Old Régime*, p. xii.
[68] *The Old Régime*, pp. vii, xii, 26; Letter to Comte de Circourt, June 24, 1854, vol. 2, p. 258; Gargan [2], p. 75; *European Revolution*, pp. 76-77. See also the discussion in the *Recollections* of the need to discover "new virtues" and discard "old vices" (p. 68).

crystalized, as it were, into a general hatred of the old regime. While blame for the original divisions and hatreds within French society could be laid to the "old kings," the peculiar antipathy which characterized France at the close of the eighteenth century is described in terms of sickness, a strange "malady." The philosophes ("for whom it was enough that a thing was old for it to be bad") bore some responsibility for this antipathy; in another sense, however; they merely gave voice to the diseased sentiments from which the entire nation suffered. (Rather, they are to be blamed for leading the nation into revolution without first trying to unite it.) The disease which attacked French society was "a new and unknown virus." Tocqueville points beyond the Enlightenment's critique of ancient institutions to a "mood" which permeated even the most commonplace affairs. He quotes a contemporary German observer: "This sudden aversion for everything that is old is indeed a strange phenomenon. The 'new ideas' are bandied about the family circle, creating an atmosphere of restlessness, and we find our modern German housewives clamoring to get rid of furniture that has been in the family for generations." This "uncertain agitation of minds" reached its height among the educated classes, for whom "that instinctive attachment and involuntary respect which men of all ages and nations are wont to feel for their own institutions, for their traditional customs, and for the wisdom or the virtues of their forefathers had almost ceased to exist." Burke had called it "the French disease," but Tocqueville suspected that his countrymen suffered rather from a particularly virulent strain of that peculiar malady to which egalitarian societies are susceptible—the "exclusive love of the present."[69]

Of significance for Tocqueville is not simply the love of

[69] Letter to Nassau William Senior, July 2, 1853, vol. 2, p. 217. See also Letter to Comte de Circourt, June 14, 1852, vol. 2, p. 200; Gargan [2], p. 75; Letter to Louis de Kergorlay, May 16, 1858, in Herr, p. 102; *The Old Régime*, pp. 17-18; *European Revolution*, pp. 33-34.

novelty, but also the hatred of the ancient: "But—and this is a point upon which I would lay stress—all that was vital, most active in the life of the day, was a new order; indeed not merely new but frankly hostile to the past." The "new and unknown virus" which attacked the French body politic at the end of the eighteenth century was at its center a disease of the French memory. The antipathies so long nurtured had at last infected the most fundamental affections of the nation. What was familiar and once dear was "now detested." Ancient affections had not simply weakened but had somehow become inverted; the objects of love had become the objects of hate. The promulgation of political hatred was the "great crime" of the monarchy. Tocqueville can forgive the kings their errors, their vices, even their ambition, but not this. For in "dividing men so as to better rule them," the monarchy destroyed those ancient affections which held the nation together. In so doing, the French kings called down upon the ancient regime what Tocqueville had come to believe was a just sentence, attested to by the fact that the depth and permanence of the hatred it inspired had become a "national instinct."[70]

The Old Régime and its sequel are preoccupied with the theme of hatred. Hatred is the most lasting of political sentiments. It is in the Irish notebooks that we first find the peculiar longevity of hatred discussed. In Ireland, Tocqueville discovered that the recollection of the "dispossessed" had lasted for centuries, and that their testimony regarding "the great persecutions" exhibited "a terrifying exactitude of local memory." While the objects of affection are enjoyed for the most part, unconsciously, with an ease and naturalness which almost conceal their pres-

---

[70] *The Old Régime*, pp. 18, 136-37; *European Revolution*, pp. 22-23, 109, 136. "And when the last king sought to repair the error of his predecessors, he allowed to grow out of ignorance what they had nurtured by design (*European Revolution*, p. 79). See also Letter to Corcelle, July 2, 1857, vol. 2, p. 376, in which Tocqueville reveals his envy of England, "undisturbed" by "hatreds" and "jealousies."

ence, the objects of antipathy thrust themselves into the consciousness in a violent fashion. The "aftermath" of injury and fear, antipathy burns itself into the recollections of men. Hatreds are thus restive and "vivid."[71]

The last chapter of Book Three of the sequel "completes" Tocqueville's discussion of political hatred; its topic: "how much easier it is for men to remain constant in their antipathies than in their affections." This chapter is a study in political hatred, and culminates in the revelation of the relation of hatred to despotism.

> The parties themselves, decimated, apathetic, and weary, longed to rest for a time during a dictatorship of any kind, provided only that it was exercised by an outsider and that it weighed upon their rivals as much as on themselves. This feature completes the picture. When great political parties begin to cool in their attachments without softening their hatreds, and at last reach the point of wishing less to succeed than to prevent the success of their opponents, one should prepare for servitude—the master is near.

We have at last arrived at the core of the problem of political hatred. If passionate hatred may keep a nation divided, its most serious consequence is, ironically, spiritual exhaustion. While hatred is itself a great passion, the "vivid" recollection of injury consumes the spirit. (This fact alone justifies the proscription of private vengeance, a commandment of God and the political community alike.) Literary examples such as Edmond Dantes and Roger Chillingsworth come to mind. Hatred is thus the most destructive

---

[71] *Journeys to England and Ireland*, pp. 174-75; see also pp. 122, 141, 155-56, 168. Consider as well this extract from Senior's journal (August 17, 1850): "The remembrance of the Marian persecutions is still vivid in England after 300 years. Our fears of the revival of the tour et colombier are as fantastic as your dread of the fagot and the rack; but why should they not last as long?" (Senior, vol. 1, p. 103).

of passions, for it debilitates the soul, threatening passion itself.[72]

"Weary" and longing to "rest," the nation welcomed a "master." Paradoxically, the affective vacuum left by weakened attachments was filled by the despot. Devoured by hatred and without love, the nation focused attention on the master amidst affective disarray. At the center of the "enigma" of the Revolution was the imposing figure of Napoleon. Again we draw upon the intimate knowledge of Beaumont: "His aim was not to paint the ancient state of society. He used it only as a background to throw into relief the new state of things; the year 1789; the revolution, its consequences; the empire; and, above all, the Emperor." Despite the general and permanent hatred of the old state of things, shared antipathy had not been translated into mutual affection. The Revolution was the central and imposing event in all memories, but its education had been "pernicious." It had failed to unite the nation around a common object of affection. Love of the Revolution was a great but ambiguous, even contradictory, legacy. The Revolution was the parent of twin sentiments—those which lead to freedom and those which lead to despotsim.[73]

Tocqueville's history investigates the nature of this legacy—its twin images of Republic and Empire. *The Old Régime* is often praised as a sociology of revolution; it is more. It is a study of the revolutionary imagination, of the evocative power of images in the memory of a nation. Tocqueville's is a history of "spiritual currents," an entering into the "vibrations" of the "minds" and "hearts" of France. "Like the flow of the Rhone," such currents appear "lost," only to "reappear" later. These images often lie dormant, hidden beneath the exterior of the present, latent and yet with the power to "surprise" and "frighten." It was the "merit" or "luck" of Louis Napoleon to discover this fact.

---

[72] *European Revolution*, pp. 138-39. The study of political hatred spans pp. 131-39.

[73] *Memoir, Letters and Remains*, vol. 1, p. 78.

The Uncle had acquired a "super-human power" over the minds of his contemporaries (a measure of their mutual hatred and exhaustion). The rise of the Nephew revealed "the power of a memory": "The 10th of December showed that the memory of the Emperor, vague and ill-defined, but therefore the more imposing, still dwelt like an heroic legend in the imaginations of the peasantry."[74] Tocqueville is less interested in the "facts" of the Revolution than in the men and the shadows they cast, and especially in that one man "who alone filled the immense stage which the Revolution had opened." Among his notes for the history is found this one, entitled "Original concept; general approach to the subject," which begins:

> My aim is:
> 1. The true portrait of a man, extraordinary rather than great, who as yet has not, I believe, been drawn with adequate fidelity or depth. Novel side of my aim.

Book Four of the sequel addresses the Consulate and the Empire. Tocqueville's intentions are detailed in chapter 1, of which the first section is overarching. It begins:

> What I want to paint is not so much the events themselves, however surprising or important they may have been, as the spirit of these events; less the different acts in the life of Napoleon than Napoleon himself, that singular, incomplete, but really *marvelous* person.

Likewise, it ends:

> I should, finally, like to propose through what course of excesses and errors he himself precipitated his fall. And despite these errors and excesses I must pursue the immense traces he left behind him in this world,

---

[74] *European Revolution*, pp. 32, 152; *The Old Régime*, p. 211; Letter to W. R. Greg, May 23, 1853, vol. 2, p. 214; Senior, vol. 2, p. 11; *Tour in Sicily*, p. 111; *Recollections*, p. 205. The idea that the power of a memory extended to the leader as well as to his adherents can be found in Senior, vol. 1, pp. 192-95, and *Recollections*, p. 86.

not only memories, but lasting influences and deeds: I want to describe what it is that died with him and what it is that endures. . . . The memories; silence.[75]

For Tocqueville, the figure of Napoleon lay at the center of what one commentator has called the "deficient inheritance" of the Revolution. Founded on hatred and weakness, the imperial memory was the "tragic burden" of the French nation. In the *Recollections*, Tocqueville indicates that his fears for the republic and the constitution are grounded upon the "wider dominion [of the executive] in the memories and habits of the people."[76]

Exhausted by the events of 1848, the imagination of the nation was again filled with the image of the Emperor. Yet Tocqueville had long suspected the difficulty. As early as 1842, in his "Discours de réception à l'Académie Française," Tocqueville had cried out against what he called "la légende napoléonienne." Less than two years earlier, the ashes of the Emperor had been transferred from St. Helena to the Invalides and Tocqueville sensed the danger. The historians had participated in the construction of the legend (particularly Thiers, whose history was an adulation of the Empire), and Tocqueville condemned them for it. "The historians of antiquity taught how to command, those of our day teach only how to obey."[77]

Having just read the most recent volume of Grote's extensive history of Greece, Tocqueville wrote the author's wife in August of 1856:

Mr. Grote, while he removes Alexander from legend to history, effaces the brilliant colors with which the conqueror was gilded by imagination. After all, it is a service to humanity to strip its enemies of their ill-gained brilliancy, and to reduce them to what they generally have really been—great birds of prey.

[75] *European Revolution*, pp. 31, 143-46.
[76] *Recollections*, pp. 177, 200; Gargan [1], pp. 44, 230.
[77] Herr, p. 68; Lively, p. 39.

Had Tocqueville begun a similar "service" in *The Old Régime*? Did he contemplate its completion in the sequel? We begin with the sequel, for it is here that Tocqueville intended to address the problem of Napoleon explicitly. While the text bears directly on the issue at hand, it is fragmentary and incomplete. After Tocqueville describes his "aim" at the beginning of Book Four, there are ten planned chapters, followed by a last group of notes entitled "Another chapter"; we may at least presume that these were intended to complete the picture of the Emperor. This final portrait, the notes insist, must include "the comic charlatan, petty, even vulgar side of this great man. His characteristics of someone newly rich, of a parvenu. His taste for tinsel, for false grandeur, for the inflated, the gigantic." Here, it seems, is an attempt to remove Napoleon from "legend" to "history," to transform the revolutionary hero into the crude predator, to strip the gilding from an imagined memory.[78]

All this, of course, is from only a section of an unwritten sequel. And while the shadow of Napoleon hangs over *The Old Régime*, our elevation of Tocqueville's fear of a memory appears open to the charge of making a minor theme into a major preoccupation, and thereby distorting, if not completely misunderstanding, the book. Still, we have Beaumont's assertion that the presentation of the "ancient state of society" was "only as a backdrop" to "above all, the Emperor." As almost every commentator has observed, the principal teaching of *The Old Régime* is that the origin of centralized administration is not to be attributed to the Revolution, but was, in fact, an important and well-established feature of the ancient regime. As Tocqueville observes in the foreword to *The Old Régime*, "No nation had ever before embarked on so resolute an attempt as that of

[78] Letter to Mrs. Grote, August 10, 1856, vol. 2, p. 321; *European Revolution*, p. 145. Tocqueville attacks Napoleon's character, then follows this with suggestions which proceed to attack his genius, imparting to his policy a "fickleness" and "incoherence" which led to his own and his country's destruction (*European Revolution*, pp. 145-46).

the French of 1789 to break with the past, to make, as it were, a scission in their life line and to create an unbridgeable gulf between all they had hitherto been and all they now aspired to be." He adds, "I have always felt that they were far less successful in this curious attempt than is generally supposed in other countries and that they themselves at first believed." Tocqueville emphasizes the "family likeness" between the administration of the ancient regime and that of modern France. Indeed, they "join hands across the abyss." *The Old Régime* is peppered with repetitions and examples of this insight, but Tocqueville's intention is suggested most clearly in the following passage.

That ancient institution, the French monarchy, after being swept away by the tidal wave of the Revolution, was restored in 1800. It was not, as is often supposed, the principles of 1789 that triumphed at that time . . . ; on the contrary, it was the principles of the old order that were revived.[79]

In approaching *The Old Régime*, we must not lose sight of the significance of Tocqueville's historical revisionism. As Beaumont tells us, these revelations were "surprising" to Tocqueville's contemporaries. Before the publication of *The Old Régime*, it was historical commonplace to view the modernization of French political institutions as the handiwork of Napoleon. The consequence of this attribution was twofold. While the centralized administrative apparatus traded, so to speak, on the reputation of Napoleon and the Revolution, the very predominance of the bureaucracy at the same time enhanced the glory of the Emperor, conferring upon him the ancient title of lawgiver.

It is thus significant that the first volume of Tocqueville's history attempts above all to destroy the link between political creation and the name of Napoleon. While denying the Emperor the mantle of Solon, Tocqueville reveals cen-

[79] *The Old Régime*, pp. vii, 32, 57, 60, 61, 72, 209.

tralization to be the inheritance of the "detested" past. Writing *like* a historian, Tocqueville paints "la légende napoléonienne" with the brush of the ancient regime.

In any attempt to penetrate the meaning of *The Old Régime*, we must keep in mind Tocqueville's effort to teach "from afar" and his insistence that his readers discover the truth "for themselves." As we have demonstrated, it is the memory of Napoleon which Tocqueville most deeply fears. Whatever the historical merit of Tocqueville's revisionism, what better way to soil that memory, to transform "legend" into "history," than to link the Emperor to that which is permanently hated. Indeed, *The Old Régime* suggests that in the rise of Napoleon is not to be seen, "as is often supposed," the triumph of "the principles of 1789," but those of "the old order." The revolutionary hero is unmasked.

At the very end of *The Old Régime*, Tocqueville again returns to the problem of the Emperor. He describes Napoleon's enterprise and the circumstances surrounding it in these terms: "Rash though this venture may have been, it was carried through with entire success for the good reason that the people took into account only what was under their eyes and forgot what they had seen before." In this sense, *The Old Régime* is salutary recollection.[80]

Forgotten Virtue

Many commentators have called attention to the twin peaks of Tocqueville's history. In his foreword to *The Old Régime*, Tocqueville focuses attention on these peaks: "The Revolution had, indeed, two distinct phases: one in which the sole aim of the French nation seemed to be to make a clean sweep of the past; the second, in which attempts were made to salvage fragments from the wreckage of the old order." "The vices which we have inherited" are, however, but one side of the French problem. If "servile traditions" remain lodged in the memory of the nation, certain "vir-

[80] *The Old Régime*, p. 209.

tues" are now almost "extinct." The difficulty lies not only
in what men remember, but also in what they have forgotten. The French of today, Tocqueville writes Gobineau,
are unlike their "ancestors of 1789." They have "no regard
for anything, beginning with themselves, no faith in anything, including themselves."[81]

Tocqueville not only delineates the Revolution's phases,
but, in fact, juxtaposes them. Against the monarchical/
Napoleonic tradition are set "the principles of 1789." Again,
from the note entitled "Original concept," Tocqueville insists that it is "because" of Napoleon that he must "paint
. . . the Revolution." Finally, in a passage which is truly
"the foreward" of Tocqueville's history, the first phase is
eulogized; its purpose is revealed.

> Youth was at the helm in that age of fervid enthusiasm,
> of proud and generous aspirations, whose memory,
> despite its extravagances, men will forever cherish: a
> phase of history that for many years to come will trou-
> ble the sleep of all who seek to demoralize the nation
> and reduce it to a servile state.[82]

We begin our consideration of Tocqueville's eulogy of
1789 by noting its curiosity. By his own admission, no man
loved the revolutionary spirit less than he. No lover of the
Revolution as a young man, there is little to suggest a
reassessment during his later years. If anything, the events
of 1848 had only deepened Tocqueville's concern with what
had become a "habit of iconoclasm." We are reminded that
the *Recollections* in which Tocqueville speaks most bitterly
of France's "revolutionary education," is written in that
period immediately preceding his historical work.[83]

---

[81] Letter to Gobineau, January 8, 1856, in *European Revolution*, p. 270;
see also p. 31 (all of the Gobineau correspondence is from this volume)
and *The Old Régime*, p. x.

[82] *The Old Régime*, pp. x-xi.

[83] Letters to Eugene Stoffels, October 5, 1836 and July 21, 1848, vol. 1,
pp. 383, 397-400; Letter to Nassau William Senior, July 24, 1851, vol. 2,
pp. 163-67; *Recollections*, pp. 63, 65.

We are still intrigued, however, by Tocqueville's insistence that "instead of sleeping away our acquired ideas, we should seek fresh ones, make the new opinions fight with the old ones, and those of youth with an altered state of thought and society." In an earlier letter to Kergorlay, reflecting on his otherwise sterile ten years in public life, he remarks that this experience has "shed a truer light upon human affairs. . . . I believe, therefore, that I am in a better position than I was when I wrote the *Democracy* to deal well with a great subject of political literature." While his years in public life undoubtedly taught Tocqueville a variety of lessons, the *Recollections* records one which is portrayed as a startling discovery. The events of February 1848 brought new men to the Assembly. In the manner, customs, even the very language of these men of the people, Tocqueville discovered "a new nation," the existence of which he had hardly been aware.[84]

In his early work, Tocqueville addressed in particular the remnants of the aristocracy. Writing to Kergorlay in 1837 of his contempt for the middle class's narrow politics of interest, Tocqueville had described "love of country" as an aristocratic sentiment. Writing to Senior in April of 1848, Tocqueville admits to being "astonished" at the patriotism of the people, and he now confesses that his "chief hope is in the lower orders." It was, of course, among the lower orders that the memory of the Revolution, "vague and ill-defined," had taken on mythical proportions. In his *Democracy*, Tocqueville had observed that democracies do not reason, but "feel." If this was true of democratic men generally, it was especially true of the French, who were creatures of "the heart." Discussing his history with Duvergier

[84] Letters to Louis de Kergorlay, February 2, 1857, vol. 1, pp. 356-57, and December 15, 1850, in Gargan [1], pp. 185-86; *Recollections*, pp. 100-104. Tocqueville was not particularly impressed with the leadership of the popular element and of some, such as Blanqui, he was both contemptuous and afraid. Yet the presence of these men taught Tocqueville something about the democratic culture of which, until then, he had been ignorant.

de Hauranne, Tocqueville observes that while the ancient regime is "dead" and "the feelings associated with it are weak," the Revolution is "alive," its feelings vital; to the Comtesse de Circourt, he writes, "The echo of the ideas and feelings of the men [of 1789] . . . is not yet silent in our own hearts." Explaining his choice of a topic to Gobineau, Tocqueville writes, "I took the only subject which even now is capable of electrifying public opinion." Finally, there is Tocqueville's insistence that "the manner in which this part of the past is appreciated may considerably influence the future." If Tocqueville remained ambivalent, even bitter, toward the Revolution, the grandeur and singularity of the spectacle of 1789 towered over the historical landscape and alone rivaled that other historical peak in the imaginations of democratic France—the imposing figure of the Emperor.[85]

The *Recollections* is useful for understanding Tocqueville's historical enterprise, not only because of the close proximity in time of the two works, but also because the *Recollections* is the *most private* of reflections, written, as the first page reveals, for the author "alone." In the pages that follow are the unguarded impressions of the theorist and statesman, the political knowledge that informs Tocqueville's history.

If Tocqueville speaks privately with disgust of "the literary spirit" of the French which judges by "impressions" rather than "reasons," he also acknowledges in the *Recollections* the importance of this fact for the theorist: "One must . . . never forget that the effect of events depends less on themselves than on the impression they give." As

[85] Letters to Louis de Kergorlay, December 15, 1850, in Gargan [1], pp. 185-86, and July 5, 1837, vol. 1, p. 319; Letter to Duvergier de Hauranne, September 1, 1856, vol. 2, p. 322; Letter to Comtesse de Circourt, September 18, 1852, vol. 2, p. 207; Letter to Gobineau, July 30, 1856, p. 294; Letter to Henry Reeve, May 20, 1857, vol. 2, p. 371; *Journey to America*, p. 188; *Democracy*, vol. 1, p. 237. For a discussion of middle-class politics and that class's inability to generate political passion, see *Recollections*, p. 5.

Tocqueville himself knew, the "colours" of "imagination" and "memory" are often "brighter" and more "vivid" than "reality." These almost *Machiavellian* reflections on the relation of politics and illusion are inseparable, however, from Tocqueville's sense of limitation ("for the great masses of men move for reasons almost as unknown to mortal men as the reasons that regulate the movements of the sea"). Whatever the limitations of the image of 1789 as an alternative to the Napoleonic legend, the legislator was powerless, in any case, to prevent the nation from remembering and loving the Revolution. But "as men ever love to feed on agreeable fantasies," Tocqueville might yet alter the "effect" of the event through the "impression" it conveyed. More directly to the point, however, is the observation that one should "cling" to "the smallest simulacrum of tradition" or "broken fragment of authority" not only if one would "preserve what remains of a half-destroyed constitution," but also if one would "clear it away completely."[86]

The rhetoric of Tocqueville's history constructs three related impressions of the past which correspond to three related problems of the present: disunity, exhaustion, and centralization (and which together are the foundation upon which "the master" erects his despotism). We shall examine these in turn.

There can be no "common action" unless the minds of the citizens are "rallied" and "held together" by certain predominant ideas, and each citizen draws his opinions from this "common source." Nations united around "a single principle or a single feeling" (even if such "symbols" are "fictions") are the strongest and most durable. Such is the teaching of the *Democracy*. We have already touched on Tocqueville's concern with those hatreds which divided French citizens one against another and which provided

---

[86] *Recollections*, pp. 47, 67, 94, 101, 188-89. Indeed, these "agreeable fantasies" are shown to be the illusions of historical resemblance.

despotism with its opportunity. While the Revolution was singular and omnipotent in its presentment to the French mind, it gave rise to multiple principles and feelings. These were rooted in the mutual hatreds which the revolutionary process rekindled and fostered after 1789. But Tocqueville also knew that, for a time, the Revolution had "lulled all private passions." Against the divisive memories of 1791 Tocqueville holds up the example of 1788, "when the *entire* nation moved against . . . despotism."

The theorist's intention in *The Old Régime* and its sequel is suggested by a comparison with Tocqueville's earlier history, "France Before the Revolution." Unlike this earlier history, in which the aristocracy is severely blamed for cultivating hateful privileges and distinctions, *The Old Régime* singles out "royal despotism" as the culprit in dividing the classes, asserting rather that "these ancestors of ours were *all* for unity." In the sequel, as the emphasis on despotism is more pronounced, so, too, is the emphasis on unity, particularly the actions of the parliament of Dauphine, "where class grievances were perhaps more intense than in any other place." And yet "no where did the cause which it defended find more unanimous support or more passionate champions." In Dauphine, nobility, clergy, and commons stood shoulder to shoulder in defense of their local institutions. If Tocqueville faults the violence and immoderate language of these enthusiastic citizens, he cites with admiration the minutes of the parliament which reveal a patriotic "zeal," adding that "nowhere as yet had there been so signal an example of the union of all classes." The unity of 1788, Tocqueville insists, was itself "truly a very great revolution," overcoming, if only momentarily, the hatred of centuries. If the revolution of 1788 was "destined to be obscured by history, lost in the immensity of the revolution about to follow," Tocqueville would restore it to the memories of his contemporaries. The account of the parliament of Dauphine concludes with a veiled teaching applicable to the present but stated in the language of the past.

The unchecked power of the King had prevailed only by dividing the classes, by hedging them round with the prejudices, the jealousies, the hatreds of each so as never to have to do with more than one class at a time, and to bring the weight of all the others to bear against it.

It was enough that these different classes should lower, if only for a moment, the barriers by which they had been divided; that they should be in accord but for a single day. The absolute power of the government was defeated on the day they thus met.[87]

Despite the destruction it would soon wreak (as "union" gave way to "hatred"), Tocqueville refuses to criticize the "zeal" and "enthusiasm" of the Revolution, distinguishing carefully between political passion and its excesses. Indeed, paradoxically, in a period during which revolutions succeed one another, only to be themselves succeeded by coup d'état, it is not the excess but the disappearance of passion that Tocqueville complains of. The ascendancy of Napoleon III seemed to empty out the public world. Tocqueville writes to Beaumont:

Did the passions, the hopes, the fears, the sympathies and antipathies, which once so strongly moved us, really exist in our own time, or are they mere recollections of what we have read in history? In truth, I am tempted to believe it; for what has really existed leaves some trace, and I see none of all we imagined that we saw and felt.

[87] *The Old Régime*, pp. 96, 107; *European Revolution*, pp. 60, 61, 62, 68, 107. See also *Journey to America*, p. 20, where Mr. Livingston emphasizes for Tocqueville's benefit the importance of the unity of all classes in the American Revolution.

But this dearth of passion was only the culmination of an exhaustion which Tocqueville had long feared and struggled against "in vain" as a member of the Assembly. Indeed, while the theme of exhaustion had been an important one for the young Tocqueville, particularly in the second part of the *Democracy*, it took on a new prominence and immediacy during the years of Tocqueville's active involvement in national politics. Again from the correspondence with Beaumont:

> What good can you expect on this Dead Sea of politics? The great parts in politics need great passions to fill them. No man can battle with éclat against apathy, indifference, and an entire nation's discouragement. In vain I pile up a great fire in my imagination; I feel all about me a chill that penetrates every part of me; do what I will, it extinguishes the word in me.[88]

In the *Democracy*, revolution, civil war, and despotism were tied together in a dialectic of "servitude and licence." While this remained the substance of Tocqueville's teaching, the reappearance of the Empire added a *Machiavellian* edge to his reflections. The problem of action had become central and the need for passion immediate, so much so that "it seems as if tyranny were worse than civil war." Strangely, however, the apparent enthusiasm of 1848 only completed the exhaustion and discouragement of the nation, while the "memories" of disorder discredited Socialists, Montagnards, Republicans, and Liberals alike: "We have come out of this revolution like laborers, who leave the field hanging their heads, worn out by the day's work, thinking of nothing but to get home, get their supper, and get to bed."[89]

Tocqueville's attempt to "awaken" that which is "dor-

[88] Letters to Beaumont, February 21, 1855, vol. 2, p. 284, and November 22, 1842, in Mayer, p. 45.
[89] *Democracy*, vol. 1, p. 96 (see also p. 10); Senior, vol. 2, p. 77; *Recollections*, p. 166; Letter to Freslon, November 5, 1857, vol. 2, p. 390.

mant" must be understood against this background of despotism and lethargy. In opposition to the imperial imagery
of the action of one, Tocqueville holds up the revolutionary
imagery of the action of all; against the passionless discouragement of the July monarchy, he holds up the passionate confidence of 1789. The men of 1789, in the language of *The Old Régime*, "had that arrogant self-confidence
that often points the way to disaster, yet, lacking which a
nation can but relapse into a servile state." As a young
man, he had written Beaumont, "It is scarcely necessary
to say that it is the political man whom we must create in
ourselves: and for this we must study the history of men,
especially those who have immediately preceded us in the
world." Now, as a historian, Tocqueville wrote a similar
prescription for the nation. In *The Old Régime*, it is the
revolutionary generation which is displayed, its virtues exemplary and inspirational.

Much of my life has been devoted to the study of
history and I have no hesitation in affirming that never
in the course of my studies have I discovered a revolution in which, anyhow to begin with, so many men
displayed a patriotism so intense, such unselfishness,
such real greatness of mind. In those days of hope the
French nation manifested the chief defect but, likewise, the chief virtue of youth: inexperience, but generous enthusiasm.

Patriotism, unselfishness, greatness of mind, these were
the necessary virtues of the time, and Tocqueville would
risk the rashness of youth for its generosity.[90]

[90] *The Old Régime*, p. 156; Letter to Beaumont, October 29, 1829, vol. 1,
p. 433. The comparison of the Revolution with the Empire is interesting,
for Tocqueville's earlier comparison of Napoleon and the Republic was
between "the tyranny of one man" and "the tyranny of factions." On its
surface, at least, *The Old Régime* involves a rehabilitation of the revolutionary generation. See also *Journey to America*, p. 176.

Consider also this passage from a letter to Gobineau (August 8, 1843),
which points to the timely quality of Tocqueville's analysis: "The older I

In the sequel, this praise is heightened. Eulogy becomes panegyric as "the imagination" is "gripped" and "enraptured" at "this great sight."

I think that no epoch of history has ever witnessed so large a number so passionately devoted to the public good, so honestly forgetful of themselves, so absorbed in the contemplation of the common interest, so resolved to risk everything they cherished in their private lives, so willing to overcome the small sentiments of their hearts. This was the general source of that passion, courage, and patriotism from which all the great deeds of the French Revolution were to issue.

The spectacle was short, but it was one of incomparable grandeur. It will never be effaced from the memory of mankind.[91]

It is at this point that the edge of irony to which Gargan refers enters Tocqueville's historical ruminations. Louis Philippe had tried unsuccessfully to "drown" the political passions of the nation in bourgeois comfort. Curiously, the Revolution of 1848 accomplished what its enemies could not, for it succeeded in submerging the national spirit. And if the French, as Tocqueville would have liked to believe, were as yet only temporarily "exhausted" and not permanently "worn out," still *The Old Régime*'s appeal to "this part of the past" raises several questions. For us, who are privy to the *Recollections'* scathing but private critique of *réminiscences historiques*, the appeal to the memory of 1789 appears at the least incongruous. Gobineau, who was not privy, was nonetheless puzzled, even dismayed, at such

---

grow, the more I like the young. Were I to live in another age and another country, this might not be so. But this atmosphere chills me. Warmth and vitality seem to lessen each day, and one hardly finds any fire in the minds and hearts of the men of my own generation. I can still see a few sparks in the souls of those twenty-five years old and in those of sixty; the former still have their hopes, and the latter their memories" (*European Revolution*, p. 189).

[91] *European Revolution*, pp. 85, 86.

eulogizing. "Allow me to ask you," he responded, "what it is that you find so admirable in the Constituent Assembly of 1789? . . . I do not see the sense of showing any interest in them." Indeed, if the Revolution of 1848 had been a "parody" of its predecessor, as Tocqueville insisted it had, and if this last in a long succession of revolutions had succeeded only in further exhausting the nation, as Tocqueville insisted it did, then Gobineau's query would seem to cut to the quick. In fact, it points to Tocqueville's deepest teaching regarding political memory. In the *Recollections* we find hints to the problematic answer to Gobineau's question.[92]

The Old Régime is an attempt to sort out the nation's memory and rekindle a political passion now dormant. In the *Recollections*, Tocqueville enters the "confused . . . labyrinth" of his own "memory" and speaks first of "a marked lull . . . in every political passion." We discover that the risk of "inexperience" which Tocqueville names in *The Old Régime* is neither the only nor the greatest risk in the appeal to the past. Men in general and the French in particular are prone to "mingle literary and theatrical reminiscences with [the] most serious demonstrations." The Revolution of 1848 is, in fact, a classic example of historical parody, in which the "bloody" is replaced by the "ridiculous"; it is a study in the problems of action and remembrance. In 1848, the French had only "staged a play" about the French Revolution. The problem of parody is at once the problem of memory and passion.

> We tried without success to warm ourselves at the hearth of our fathers' passions; their gestures and attitudes as seen on the stage were imitated, but their enthusiasm could not be copied, nor their fury felt again. A tradition of violent action was being followed, without real understanding, by frigid souls.

[92] Letter to Freslon, September 11, 1857, vol. 2, p. 387; Letter to Gobineau, November 29, 1856, pp. 300-301; *Recollections*, pp. 64, 123.

A marginal note emphasizes that this "frigidity" is, in fact, the *result* of "imitation."[93]

Throughout the *Recollections* is the intimation of weakness and its relation to memory. Even Ledru-Rollin, the Robespierre of 1848, is "incapable of cutting an enemy's throat, except perhaps as an historical reminiscence." This theme is repeated in the frenzied impotence of the new Assembly, where "boldness of language" is substituted for "staunchness of heart." In short, the "passions of the past" had become "traditions," devoid of "feelings."

The transformation of "passion" into "tradition" involves a forgetting, the loss of emotional content. While the *events* of the Revolution remained vivid, the *sentiments* surrounding them seemed "buried in the night of ages." "So vast was the revolution that has intervened that its shadow falls on all that it did not destroy, and it is as if the centuries lay between the times we live in and the revolutionary epoch." In particular, the Revolution had obscured or confused those "feelings" associated with political life. The French had "forgotten . . . [the] sentiments and ideas of a free people."[94]

We are reminded again of Tocqueville's description of his contemporaries: "We have no regard for anything, beginning with ourselves, no faith in anything, including ourselves." The routinization of the once passionate is not simply the erosion of feeling, but also the substitution of "deep lethargic somnolence" for "arrogant self-confidence." Tocqueville suggests that the most immediate cause of this lethargy is fear: "When one goes to the source of all that takes place with us, that is said and done by us, one reaches always the one passion which is the origin of all—fear." And "in politics, fear is a passion that frequently grows at the expense of all others."[95]

---

[93] *Recollections*, pp. 4-5, 53, 127. Note the great similarity in Tocqueville's and Marx's characterizations of the men and events of 1848.

[94] *The Old Régime* p. 26; "France Before the Revolution," p. 245; *Recollections*, p. 127.

[95] *Recollections*, pp. 107, 110, 138-40, 191-92 (see also pp. 74, 89); *European*

Especially in their fearfulness, the French no longer resembled their forefathers. Once "firmly convinced of the
perfectibility of man," the French were now "terrified by
the uncertainty of the future." That fear which secretly
gripped the nation, "weighing down the French spirit" and
emptying recollection of passion, a fear unknown to "those
who preceded us," was the knowledge of failure: "Now-
adays . . . the perils of revolutions have made us so humble
that we scarcely believe ourselves worthy of the freedom
enjoyed by other nations." Underneath the glorious remembrance of 1789 was a legacy of impotence. Again, the
sequel describes the psychology brilliantly.

Although the dangers of 1799 were, on the whole,
infinitely less than those at the beginning of the Revolution, they inspired terror that was more intense and
more general because the nation now had less energy,
feebler passions, and more experience. All the evils
that had overpowered the people for ten years had
assembled in their fancy to form a picture of the future;
after having contributed to the most terrible catastrophes, they now trembled at their own shadows.

The revolutionary generation ended "demoralized." "Contempt" for politics translated into self-contempt as "patriots" became "idiots."

But in long revolutions men are demoralized less by
the faults and by the crimes that they commit in the
heat of their convictions and passions than by the contempt that they finally acquire for these very convictions and passions. When tired, disenchanted, and
deceived, they turn against themselves and consider
their former hopes as having been childish—their enthusiasm and, above all, their devotion absurd. No

---

Revolution, pp. 84, 101, 124, 127, 231-32, 293; *Tour in Sicily*, p. 119; Letter
to Corcelle, July 2, 1854, vol. 2, p. 262; *The Old Régime*, pp. 119, 156. See
also Senior, vol. 2, p. 68, in which Tocqueville observers that the French
remember their past only to "dislike" it.

one can conceive how often the resistance of even the strongest souls is broken during such a decline. Men thus crushed cannot only no longer attain great virtues, but they seem to have become almost incapable of great crimes.[96]

The "experience" of the revolutionary generation became the inheritance of those who followed. The action of "these forefathers" having failed, the French had little "faith" in their own. Tocqueville knew that the "contempt" and "self-pity" of the French were rooted in memory. He suspected that underneath the "frigid" parodies of the present lay a secret resentment of these revolutionary "ancestors." The incapacity of the French to "believe in anything" was rooted in their inability to believe in their "fathers." For the French, left weak by their predecessors, *imitation* masked *deprecation*. Indeed, both the *The Old Régime* and the sequel condemn the inclination of the French to "deprecate" and "belittle" their ancestors, suggesting the unwholesome origin of French political mimetics.

Remembering, yet they did not "understand." The French could not "conceive" of their "forefathers." Tocqueville hopes to reestablish sympathy between his contemporaries and their predecessors; thus, *The Old Régime* and the sequel are replete with the language of affection, expressed always in terms of relation. (Tocqueville speaks endlessly, for example, of "fathers," "our forefathers," and "our ancestors"). In this way, he hopes to "awaken" that which has been "lulled" by fear and resentment.

The French remember the deeds of their fathers, but cannot penetrate their sentiments. As Tocqueville tells Kergorlay, he has attempted to overcome this problem by *living over* certain "moments," such as the magnificent triumph of the parliaments. His narration (unlike the "crude pigments" of Lamartine's *Girondins*) is not visual, but emotive and evocative; his is a history not of "the acts themselves,"

[96] *European Revolution*, pp. 125, 129.

but of "the spirit of the acts." Better described as "impressions" than as "images," Tocqueville's history tells less of the way things *looked* and more of the way things *felt* than does almost any other history. Hiding what is "surprising" and "grandiose"—the *spectacle* of the Revolution—Tocquevillian history restores "attention to certain virtuous traits of our fathers (above all, to their civic virtues)."[97]

Men of "tepid" passions and attenuated sentiments, Tocqueville's contemporaries remembered at once too much and too little. In his history, Tocqueville attempts that for which he would later praise Royer-Collard—"as far as is possible and desirable, to connect the past and the present." We have traced these efforts through the themes of unity and passion, yet a third remains. It is also the most curious of the three, more closely resembling those "agreeable fantasies" to which Tocqueville refers in the *Recollections*. The last of Tocqueville's memories of virtue, this final theme may be called an institutional reminiscence—the recollection of a once-decentralized France. Its curiousness is immediately apparent in the focus of discussion. Passing over the role of "a territorial aristocracy" in the creation and maintenance of local institutions (a prominent argument in "France Before the Revolution"), Tocqueville concentrates on the autonomy of villages and towns. Strangely, feudalism is now praised not for its *aristocratic* virtues, but for its *republican* virtues. In *The Old Régime*, Tocqueville describes at length the destruction of this local autonomy. It is at the center of his enduring concerns, and the discussion invites comparison with the treatment of localism found in the *Democracy*. Indeed, the invitation is Tocqueville's own.[98]

---

[97] Letter to Mrs. Grote, January 31, 1857, vol. 2, p. 347; Letter to Louis de Kergorlay, May 16, 1858, vol. 1, pp. 359-61; Letter to Beaumont, January 10, 1851, in Herr, p. 19; *Recollections*, pp. 53, 74; *The Old Régime*, pp. 28-29; *European Revolution*, pp. 84, 162. It is noteworthy that Tocqueville hardly mentions the Terror or the other events which still "surprise" and "frighten."

[98] *Recollections*, p. 74; Letter to Freslon, July 8, 1858, vol. 2, p. 413

I well remember my surprise when I was for the first
time examining the records of an intendancy with a
view to finding out how a parish was administered
under the old order. For in the organization of this
small community, despite its poverty and servile state,
I discovered some of the features which had struck me
so much in the rural townships of North America:
features which I then had—wrongly—thought peculiar to the New World. Neither had permanent repre-
sentatives, that is to say a town council in the strict
sense of the term, and both were administered by officials acting separately, under instructions from the
whole community. General assemblies were convened
from time to time in both and at these the townsfolk,
acting in concert, elected their own officials and passed
orders on matters affecting the interests of the community. In short, the French and the American systems resembled each other—in so far as a dead creature
can be said to resemble one that is very much alive.

Tocqueville evinces "surprise" at his discovery of "the
democratic spirit of our forefathers." That which is the
foundation of the American democracy, "parochial self-
government," is now discovered to be the past of France
also. Tocqueville's "surprise," however, is itself curious,
for as early as 1828 Tocqueville had described feudalism in
similar terms.

The capital was of little importance in feudal days, so
it was possible that, at the same time as a baron, safe
in his corner, struck money, held court and made war
with his serfs and his liegemen, a bowshot away there
might be a town, appointing its magistrates, managing
its finances, and having its armed band under its own
flag, in a word a real republic. And in such republics
there were often heroes worthy to have lived in Rome
or Sparta. Such was the state of Europe in the twelfth
and more especially the thirteenth century. An odd

233

mixture of oppression and liberty, one can see no unity in its variegated confusion, but everywhere centers of active life.

We suspect that this surprise is not Tocqueville's own, but is meant to call attention to the *surprising fact* of France's democratic past. Some of these "democratic qualities" existed up to the Revolution, if only as "an empty show of freedom." Still, the majority of the French remained deeply attached to local self-government.

> Nonetheless, the peasants clung to these last vestiges of the old order and local self-government; indeed, even today it is the only form of freedom which, by and large, means much to them. A French peasant may be willing enough to leave the government of the nation as a whole in the hands of an autocratic central power, but he bitterly resents the idea of not having a say in the local administration of his village. Thus even the hollowest of forms has retained an "old-world" glamour.[99]

While the text's discussion of ancient self-government traces its decay, the appendix turns from what has in fact happened to what "might have happened." Curious in its location, Tocqueville's treatment of provincial autonomy also has the appearance of a wish. One of only two provinces where "true self-government" continued to exist, Languedoc is the principle topic of the appendix. Although it was subject to the same interference from the central regime as the rest of France, Languedoc nonetheless maintained a great measure of autonomy by keeping the "administration" of its affairs in its own hands. In particular, it kept its assembly autonomous, free of the "King's men"; it developed through its own initiative a program of public works which was the envy of France; and it re-

[99] *The Old Régime*, pp. 48, 50-51; "Reflections on English History," p. 27. See also "France Before the Revolution," p. 243.

tained the right of levying and administering its own taxes. After discussing these privileges, Tocqueville simply adds, "The way in which the province of Languedoc turned these privileges to account is rich in interest for every student of French history." While the history of parochial self-government might lead readers to conclude that the golden age of French democracy was perhaps admirable but had become an anachronism (the perennial position of nearly all advocates of centralization), the appendix concludes with an insistence upon the adaptability of such institutions "to the needs of modern civilization": "Owing to the special characteristics of the constitution of Languedoc, as described above, it could adjust itself without any difficulty to the new spirit of the age, which, while modifying everything, destroyed nothing in that ancient institution."[100]

These reminiscences of ancient democracy all have an ironic air about them. Tocqueville does not deny that despotism has made "hollow" and "empty" these democratic forms. In *The Old Régime*, the reader is left to ponder the relation of what has been and what might have been. Earlier, however, Tocqueville had praised the regenerative power of such ancient form and pointed to a more intimate connection between form and spirit. In his "Reflections on English History," after having described the Tudor "despotism," Tocqueville writes:

> But what was able to raise the English people from that state of degradation? The same thing as had thrown them down. The spirit of the constitution had been broken, but the forms remained: it was like the corpse of a free government. When spirits stupefied by the disasters of the civil wars began little by little to revive, when numbed hearts beat again, when the passage of time had given the Commons the strength they lacked or thought they lacked, in a word, when the nation

[100] *The Old Régime*, pp. 214-15, 220, 221.

awoke, it found the tools for regeneration at hand, and with the spirit of its ancestors all the means to be like them. Attention was naturally drawn to and fixed on something which had happened before, a circumstance which is a wonderful help to popular movements.

A description of sixteenth-century England, it is also a description of nineteenth-century France. And here again we encounter what would become the language of Beaumont in his *Memoir*, that of awaking what has been dormant. Having regained "the spirit of its ancestors and all the means to be like them," the English nation overcame "a yoke ten times more humiliating than any other." Finally, the passage calls attention to the particular utility of such ancient democratic forms to "popular movements." It would seem that Tocqueville's history attempts precisely this—to draw and fix attention on that "which has happened before." After having spoken to the French of "the spirit of their ancestors," Tocqueville (in his discussion of Languedoc) reminds them of "the means to be like them." Is *The Old Régime* too "a wonderful help?"[101]

Of the three recollections of virtue, Tocqueville's treatment of ancient decentralization is the most halting and perhaps the least forthright. This is puzzling in what is otherwise a bold book, which, written for a despotic France, dares to name those memories that lead to despotism and those that lead to freedom. This reserve has led some to dub this discussion a mere "exercise in hindsight," but this assessment is too simple and ignores what Tocqueville suggested was the practical intent of his book. Tocqueville's presentation of "what might have been" is both the knowledge that might yet save France and a recognition of the dangers and limitations confronting the legislator.

In an age of novelty, one principle alone had survived "unaltered and undissolved" the vicissitudes of successive

---

[101] "Reflections on English History," p. 39.

revolutions. That was the principle of centralization. Monarchist, imperial, republican, all parties claimed it as their own. Above all things, centralization was at the root of France's servility, having "gnawed away every ancient authority." While the ancient institutions of "parochial self-rule" were the only ones to which the French looked back "without repugnance," these appeared also as the least feasible. As early as 1836, Tocqueville had asked Kergorlay to find for him examples of Prussian decentralization, for those taken from republican nations could not hope "to produce a real impression on the ordinary crowd of illiberals." The difficulty remained: how "to attack with advantage French centralization." In the *Democracy*, Tocqueville had insisted upon the greater importance of those institutions which are close and familiar. In *The Old Régime*, the existence of such institutions in the French past is brought back to memory. But as the sequel to *The Old Régime* intimates, this lesson is the limit of the historical enterprise, the intersection of hope and despair.[102]

> Revolutions and misery might teach even the greediest and the most cowardly of people that despotism is wrong. But where will people get their real taste for liberty if they do not know it or if they have lost it? Who will teach them these noble pleasures? Who can make them love liberty if that love has not been originally planted in their hearts? Who will even pretend to make them understand those pleasures of liberty which men can no longer even imagine once they have lost their habitual experience?[103]

[102] *Recollections*, pp. 33, 170, 201; *The Old Régime*, p. 165; Herr, p. 82; Letter to Louis de Kergorlay, October 10, 1836, vol. 1, p. 312; *Democracy*, vol. 1, pp. 90, 99. Consider also Mr. Ingersol's remarks in the American notebooks: "Speaking generally, I am firmly persuaded that as long as you do not grant a strong individuality to your provinces, you will never be sure of *remaining* free" (*Journey to America*, p. 216). Consider as well the letter to Louis de Kergorlay of June 21, 1831, in which Tocqueville discusses what the Bourbons should have done (and thus what remains to be done) to reform France (vol. 1, p. 297).

[103] *European Revolution*, p. 167.

If Tocquevillan history would teach the French to "hate despotism," it could not teach them to love "liberty." If it would replace the legend of Napoleon with the myth of 1789, there remained passions that could not be "imagined." Hence, while the "spirit" of the nation was such that it could "never be broken so completely as to prevent it from shaking off the yoke of an oppressive government," it was yet "never so free that the possibility of enslaving it [was] ruled out." The fundamental problem of the *Democracy*, it remained the fundamental problem of *The Old Régime* and cast a dark shadow upon the future.[104]

Democracy and the Future

I go back from age to age up to the remotest antiquity, but I find no parallel to what is occurring before my eyes; as the past has ceased to throw its light upon the future, the mind of man wanders in obscurity.

Unlike all previous revolutions, the crisis of modernity was also a theoretical crisis. Confronted with the spectacle of utter novelty, Tocqueville called for "a new science of politics." Tocqueville's demand for a new science can be understood only in light of the old science—the tradition of political thought whose origins were to be found particularly in the concerns of Plato and Aristotle. The old science too had begun with the contemplation of democracy. Confronted with the wild passions of democracy in decay with the revolutionary cycle of tyranny and license ending only in foreign conquest, the old science was preoccupied with the problems of order and self-control—a concern which belied a deep distrust of the political passions. But whatever the virtues of the old science might have been, the "providential" character of modern democracy, Tocqueville insisted, had vitiated its point of view.[105]

---

[104] *The Old Régime*, p. 211.
[105] *Democracy*, vol. 1, p. 7; vol. 2, p. 349.

It is precisely around the problem of passion that Tocqueville would erect the new science. The new science would "penetrate deeply into the passions" in ways that the old science had not. While the tradition had been preoccupied with the excesses of passion, Tocqueville warned that it was not the excess but the dearth of passion (despite its often revolutionary appearance) which in the end threatened modern politics. Democracy had less to fear from "boldness than from paltriness of aim." Tocqueville's is a discussion of the spiritual debility of modern man, and it anticipated the themes of "strength" and "weakness" that would come to occupy a central place in the work of thinkers such as Nietzsche.

> The farther my youth is removed from me, the more indulgence,—I might almost say, respect—I feel for human passions. I love those that are good, and I am not quite sure that I hate the bad. They always show strength, and strength, wherever you meet with it, appears to advantage by the side of the weakness which surrounds us.[106]

[106] *European Revolution*, p. 91; Lerner, p. 93; Letter to Ampere, August 10, 1841, vol. 2, p. 73. It is this concern with the problem of passion or, rather, with the disappearance of passion that separates Tocqueville from the old liberals and confounds those who would make him over into a mere defender of individual rights against the state (see, for example, Lerner, pp. 37, 47). The old liberalism, with its mechanistic psychology, had never found action to be a problem. While it feared the energy of the state, it never doubted the energy of the individual. A self-proclaimed "liberal of a new kind," Tocqueville insisted that "such mechanical rules do not apply to the human spirit." Classical tyranny and bourgeois liberalism had at least one thing in common; they both banished passion to the "private realm" of civil society or "the interior realm of the family." Taking his bearings from Hobbes rather than from Locke, Tocqueville knew that, under conditions of equality, men were likely to choose peace over public liberty. What I have in mind here is Hobbes's insight that, under conditions of equality, men incline toward extremes of pride and fear. Locke succeeded in his account of the epistemological solitude in which egalitarian man judges,but concealed the excesses to which, according to Tocqueville, such epistemological assumptions are prone— namely, the exaggerated independence which conceals deep self-doubt. But in appropriating Hobbes's insight, Tocqueville inverted his teaching,

If, as Arendt suggests, the tradition of political philosophy came to an end in the nineteenth century, Tocqueville may be said to halt at its edge, not willing to cast aside the principle of the *political* for the more *aesthetic* solutions of those who followed him. Tocqueville's "science" remained the science of legislation.

The whole art of the legislator consists in discerning clearly beforehand the natural tendencies of human society in order to know where he should *help the efforts of citizens* and where it is necessary to restrain them. For these duties vary according to time.[107]

The "natural tendencies" of modern societies were rooted in their equality of condition, and it was this knowledge

for while Hobbes supposed that masterless men especially stood in need of the pedagogy of fear that teaches the love of peace, Tocqueville thought that lesson already too well taught. To say the same thing differently, Hobbes and Tocqueville differed in their opinions as to the requisites of civilization under egalitarian conditions. Tocqueville suspected that the greatest danger to freedom was not a state which prevented men from exercising their liberty, but one which encouraged them to refuse the burdens of action. Beaumont tells us that Tocqueville was fascinated by the great energy of the American republic; the truth of this claim is attested to by this entry in the American notebooks: "The wonderful effect of republican governments . . . is not in presenting a picture of *regularity* and *methodical order* in a people's administration, but in the *way of life*. Liberty does not carry out each of its undertakings with the same perfection as an intelligent despotism, but in the long run it produces more than the latter. It does not always and in all circumstances give the peoples a more skilful and faultless government; but it infuses throughout the body social an activity, a force and an energy which never exist without it, . . . which bring forth wonders (and which throughout all time have made the greatest nations). It is there that one must look for its advantages" (*Journey to America*, p. 155). Indeed, Tocqueville's praise of American institutions such as trial by jury and strong municipal government is directed not to their ability to *restrict* the power of a centralized regime, but to their serving as educative institutions which interest men in public affairs and thus forestall political lethargy. Never calling himself a republican (an uncertain term in the language of French politics), Tocqueville was concerned with passion and activity, placing him in that tradition of political discourse of which Machiavelli is the most outspoken. See also Letter to Eugene Stoffels, July 24, 1836, vol. 1., p. 381; *European Revolution*, p. 168; Letter to Comtesse de Circourt, November 26, 1853, vol. 2, p. 239; Letter to Louis de Kergorlay, October 25, 1842, vol. 1, p. 338.

[107] Quoted in Lively, p. 66.

that Tocqueville sought above all else. Not since Hobbes had anyone seen as "deeply" into the dynamics of equality as Tocqueville did. It was only with Tocqueville that Hobbes's suggestion of the relation between equality, weakness, and solitude, heretofore hidden behind Locke's "community of nature," would be thoroughly examined. The possession (and even more the *acquiring*) of equality gives rise most noticeably to feelings of individual autonomy and the sufficiency of the self. Locke's "community of nature" displays these most visible aspects of egalitarianism, but it can be said that his error (an error against which Tocqueville warns) lay in considering the *independence* of equality apart from its *powerlessness*. It is also the error of democratic man, for equality is accompanied by certain illusions. Tocqueville's description of the illusions to which democratic men are prone is striking.

> As social conditions become more equal, the number of persons increases who, although they are neither rich nor powerful enough to exercise any great influence over their fellows, have nevertheless acquired or retained sufficient education and fortune to satisfy their own wants. They owe nothing to any man, they expect nothing from any man; they acquire the habit of always considering themselves as standing alone, and they are apt to imagine that their whole destiny is in their own hands.[108]

This psychology of equality has certain intellectual consequences, "the principle characteristic" of which is that democratic man "appeals only to the individual effort of his own understanding." This inclination to "judge for oneself" is necessarily accompanied by a "contempt" for tradition and form and their implicit claim to authority and knowledge. Tradition is denied all claims to superior knowledge and is seen as but a means of information which,

[108] *Democracy*, vol. 2, pp. 105, 311.

because of its origin, is (as fathers learn) itself suspect and, at worst, seen as "a debasing yoke."

Moreover, in the geographical and social mobility associated with democratic relations, "the woof of time is every instant broken and the trace of the generations effaced. Those who went before are soon forgotten; of those who will come after, no one has any idea." Lovers of novelty and innovation, democratic communities are in "continual movement." In the midst of such circumstances, "man there readily loses all traces of the ideas of his forefathers or takes no care about them."[109]

Loosed from the "prejudice" of his fathers, democratic man sees before him a boundless landscape whose apparent opportunities beget "inordinate ambition" in the breast of each in this community of equals. In fact, democratic society is often so full of activity that on its face men would seem better advised to fear its strength than its weakness. But Tocqueville knew this to be the appearance of the surface only, for he had penetrated the deeper layers of the democratic soul. He knew that ambition masked fear, that the love of innovation concealed the terror of impotence.[110]

Released from the "debasing" (that is, unequal) relations of ancient authority, democratic man imagines a new relation of *fraternity*, but this Tocqueville fears is only the "popular exaggeration" of revolutionary passion. Behind the apparent strength of the sufficient self lies the weakness of the solitary man. Adding an ironic twist to this Hobbesian analysis, Tocqueville locates the origin of democratic weakness in the very source of democratic exuberance— the liberation from the yoke of the past.

> Thus not only does democracy make every man forget his ancestors, but it hides his descendants and separates his contemporaries from him; it throws him back forever upon himself alone and threatens in the end

[109] *Democracy*, vol. 1, p. 252; vol. 2, pp. 3, 4, 42, 105-6.
[110] *Democracy*, vol. 1, p. 252; vol. 2, pp. 43-44.

to confine him entirely within the solitude of his own heart.[111]

In the second part of the *Democracy*, Tocqueville "transports" the reader "into the midst of a democracy," thereby demonstrating the political implications of the peculiar "solitude" fostered by equality. Knowledge and power are "infinitely sub-divided" and "scattered on every side," and that which might have united men, common ideas rooted in common memories, has eroded in the face of democratic "agitation."

> They do not resemble their fathers; nay they perpetually differ from themselves, for they live in a state of incessant change of place, feelings, and fortunes. The mind of each is therefore unattached to that of his fellows by tradition or common habits; and they have never had the power, the inclination, or the time to act together.

Democratic man has forgotten the past and is content to remain ignorant of the future, and his "cowardly" and "exclusive love of the present" is Tocqueville's "dread."[112]

A creature of "present enjoyment," democratic man is preoccupied with the "comfortable" and the "convenient." While such men are moved by "a tenacious, exclusive, universal passion," that passion is attached to "small objects." "But the soul clings to them; it dwells upon them closely and day by day, till they at last shut out the rest of the world and sometimes intervene between itself and heaven." To these men, political life is a waste of "precious hours," a "useless engagement" for which they have "no time."[113]

The illusions of democratic man are costly.

> These people think they are following the principle of self-interest, but the idea they entertain of that prin-

---

[111] *European Revolution*, p. 65; *Democracy*, vol. 2, p. 106.
[112] *Democracy*, vol. 2, pp. 61, 261, 277.
[113] *Democracy*, vol. 2, p. 140.

ciple is a very crude one; and the better to look after what they call their own business, they neglect their chief business, which is to remain their own masters.

"Shut closely" within a "narrow circle," the political sentiments dry up as "great irregularities of passion" are replaced by "perpetual though useless excitement." Such men "become inaccessible to those great and powerful public emotions which perturb nations, but which develop them and recruit them."[114]

No longer a people, deprived of its "primitive energy and national character," the nation becomes a "motley multitude." As both Tocqueville and Hobbes knew, such a society is inclined to seek despotic solutions to its problems, and its chief problem (as Hobbes also knew) becomes the relations among men. Political life, at first "a troublesome impediment," now becomes "a dread" as all action appears to threaten the "private fortune of each." This passion for "tranquility" becomes more powerful "in proportion as all other passions droop and die." Having thus become "cowardly," the nation rushes toward "a master."[115]

The aim of the first part of the *Democracy*, through the example of America, had been to show men "in a democracy" how they might avoid "tyranny" and "imbecility." This "theme" is continued in the "reflections upon reflections" of the second part. Here, the image of America fades as the contrast between democracy and aristocracy comes sharply into focus. The American *exemplar* (a democratic people who have overcome "the exclusive love of the present") misunderstood, Tocqueville's method becomes *comparative*, attempting yet again to "educate" democracy.[116]

[114] *Democracy*, vol. 2, pp. 149, 261, 267, 277; Letter to Nassau William Senior, November 28, 1851, vol. 2, p. 173.

[115] *Democracy*, vol. 2, pp. 23, 61, 149; *Tour in Sicily*, p. 127; *Recollections*, p. 165; Lerner, p. 97.

[116] Letter to Louis de Kergorlay, December 26, 1836, vol. 1, p. 315. In regard to the success of the American experiment, see particularly the American's "deference to the opinions of his forefathers," so characteristic of the American legal system (*Democracy*, vol. 1, pp. 286-87).

Whatever their faults, aristocracies "naturally" overcome the love of "present convenience" in a knowledge of the past and a care for the future. In other words, they have much to teach democracies. The center of aristocratic memory and foresight is the family.

As families remain for centuries in the same condition, often on the same spot, all generations become, as it were, contemporaneous. A man almost always knows his forefathers and respects them; he thinks he already sees his remote descendants and he loves them. He willingly imposes duties on himself towards the former and the latter, and he will frequently sacrifice his personal gratifications to those who went before and to those who will come after him.

Even when standing alone, aristocratic man feels "himself sustained by his ancestors and animated by his posterity." While it is no longer possible (indeed, *because* it is no longer possible) for men to "perpetuate" and "immortalize" themselves through their families, "philosophers and those in power" must place "the objects of human action" beyond the present; for "no sooner do [men] despair of living forever, than they are disposed to act as if they were to exist but for a single day."[117]

---

[117] *Democracy*, vol. 1, pp. 52, 340; vol. 2, pp. 76, 104-5, 158-59. Tocqueville's observations regarding what "philosophers . . . ought" to do adds a new dimension to the discussion of Tocqueville as prophet. Many of those who emphasize Tocqueville's despair also call attention to his gloomy prognostications (see, for example, Mayer, p. 76). Tocqueville's understanding of the tendencies of democracy is not at issue, but rather whether these constitute prophecies of doom. In fact, on several occasions, Tocqueville denies his ability to "see into the future" and, on at least one occasion, he berates those "philosophers" who "uselessly" frighten and discourage (Lettter to Gobineau, July 30, 1856, p. 292; Letter to Eugene Stoffels, April 28, 1850, vol. 1, pp. 100-101; Letter to Comtesse de Circourt, June 19, 1850, vol. 2, pp. 100-101; *Recollections*, p. 66). Lively has noted that in Tocqueville there is the absence of that "exultant anticipation" which so often characterizes "prophets of doom," but Gargan is more to the point. Tocqueville's prognostications, while in keeping with the tendencies of democracy, were meant rather to combat this "future." Subjecting his

Tocqueville's advice regarding the proper reading of the first part of the *Democracy*—to pay more attention to the "substance" than to the "form"—is equally applicable to the second part. The substance of this deceased aristocracy's perspective (like that of a "singular" America) clarifies the nature of democracy's weaknesses, at the center of which is the isolation of democratic man. Tocqueville's investigations into possible means for coping with democratic isolation are best seen less as concrete recommendations than as tentative speculations about those principles which any solution must embody. Tocqueville's critique of democracy differs from all others in at least one important respect—his insistence that spatial remedies (the organization of political space, that is, institutional solutions) cannot be considered apart from the peculiar temporal problems associated with democracy (that is, democratic man's "exclusive love of the present"). This is to say that the problem of political sentiment, or the creation of "true and lasting passions," is the first problem of the new science of politics.[118]

In the most general terms, these speculations concern themselves with "religion" and "patriotism," for it is only these "which will make the whole body of citizens go *persistently* forward toward the same goal." There is, in fact, a "family likeness" between religious and political passions. Both faith and patriotism may be said to "tear" democratic man out of the present, to place his "chief hopes upon remote events." As the religious sentiments are rooted in God's promise, so the political sentiments are bound up with the transmission of a legacy. Both thus entail burdens and responsibilities which compel men to concern themselves with "futurity." Together, these kindred sentiments

readers to an "unrelieved series of shocks and dire prophecies," Tocqueville was attempting that which philosophers "ought" to do in democratic times—through an understanding of democracy, to drive men out of the present (Gargan [1], p. 16).

[118] Letter to Ampere, August 10, 1841, vol. 2, p. 74.

have produced "heroic passions" and "glorious deeds."
But as religion is shaken, "chance under all its forms haunts
the mind" and "the present looms large." In such circumstances,

> the moralist . . . must constantly endeavor to show his
> contemporaries that even in the midst of the perpetual
> commotion around them it is easier than they think to
> conceive and to execute protracted undertakings. He
> must teach them that although the aspect of mankind
> may have changed, the methods by which men may
> provide for their prosperity in this world are still the
> same.

In particular, it is "a wonderful help" to democratic men
if they can fix their attention "on something which has
happened before."[119]

The isolation fostered by equality is both spatial and temporal. If democratic man is "close" to his fellows, he fails
to "see" them; if he "touches" them, he does not "feel"
them. Yet isolation in space is not unique to modern democracy. If such isolation in space is made extreme under
modern conditions, it is also part of the classical description
of political corruption, that of a community whose fellow-
citizens are unattached to one another. The true novelty
of modern isolation is isolation in time, a "complacency"
with the present. And should it happen that the men of
"one period" are united, this proves "nothing," for under
modern conditions "each new generation is a new people."

[119] *Democracy*, vol. 2, pp. 158-59, 310 (see also pp. 22-23); Letter to Louis
de Kergorlay, October 19, 1843, vol. 1, p. 343; Letter to Corcelle, October
23, 1854, vol. 2, p. 273. Mayer's contention, that Tocqueville's philosophy
does not conceive of a society devoid of religious belief and thus halts at
the frontier of the twentieth century, is simply untrue (Mayer, p. 73). If
Tocqueville, in emphasizing the accidental nature of disbelief and man's
perennial need for hope, underestimated the atheistical implications of
modern society, he nonetheless sought political substitutes for the erosion
of religion.

What Gargan has called the "nightmare of modern muteness" is foremost a disease of the memory of peoples.[120]

If modern peoples see themselves in these images, such
images were for Tocqueville warnings, the destination of
democratic tendencies, neither descriptions of fact nor
prophecy. But if Tocqueville was "the last man to contend
these propensities [were] unconquerable," he also knew
that "a secret power" was fostering them "in the human
heart," and that if they were not checked they would "wholly
overgrow it."[121]

Not the least of ironies is that democratic man, sensing
the danger, has often responded with revolutionary action.
In particular, revolutionary action promises an escape from
isolation to commitment, from "apoplectic torpor" to "enthusiasm," from complacency to utopia. And while the
persistence of revolutionary passion suggests that the political sentiments are not yet "dead" (hence there is still
"hope"), it also points to the dilemma of any revolutionary
attempt to drag men out of the present. All revolutionary
appeals (even those made explicitly to the past) require a
transference of affections—the substitution of one object
for another.[122] While capable of producing bursts of passion, attachment to any one object is made uncertain, "subject to alterations of strength and weakness; all powerful
today, almost imperceptible on the morrow." Under such
circumstances, the "radiance" of political action quickly
"fades away." "Acclamation" and "enthusiasm" are soon
followed by "silence and solitude." The "martyr" becomes
a "madman," the "great man" a "joke." In such times,
deeds are but "sudden claps," and men pass from enthu-

[120] *Democracy*, vol. 2, pp. 62, 336; Gargan [1], p. 19.

[121] *Democracy*, vol. 2, 310.

[122] Tocqueville's own appeal to a revolutionary past is ambivalent and
made necessary by the fact of Napoleon III. It is not a solution to the
French problem, only an attempt to establish the preconditions for any
solution. All solutions depend upon the reintroduction of local liberty; to
believe that local liberty is possible "while general liberties are sup-
pressed" is "pure dream" (*European Revolution*, p. 170).

siasm to exhaustion, and, lastly, to acrimony. Indeed, we need look no further than our own time for confirmation.[123]

"The new science" struggles with solutions. The problem of how to create and fortify true and lasting remembrance is resolved into multiplying the "opportunities for acting in concert" so as to recreate the framework for the "familiar" and the "dear." Tocqueville anxiously seizes upon one such "opportunity" after another, their tentativeness suggesting the difficulty. The "generous passions" and "real convictions" of "great parties," civil and political associations whose "art" is "the mother of action," municipal institutions, without which "a nation may establish a free government," but "cannot have the spirit of liberty," all these present the theorist with the potential for *histories* of affection.

"Transient passions, the interests of an hour, or the chance of circumstances" may create momentary wonders. But unless "the same occurrences suggest the same thoughts and impressions to [the] minds of a great number of men," the despotic tendency "which has been driven into the interior of the social system will sooner or later reappear on the surface." Sadly, Tocqueville also knew that democratic nations are inclined to follow the example of his own, to take "into account only what [is] under their eyes and forget what they [have] seen before."[124]

The deepest need of democratic times, the establishment of affections that are both shared and persistent ("true and lasting"), remains problematic and seems unlikely. Political theory is perhaps best measured not by the success of its enterprise, but by the depth of its vision. And yet, such criteria must always be unacceptable to the theorist. Hence

[123] A striking example is recounted by Tocqueville in the fall of the parliaments, those "relics" of the past conjured up during the first period of the Revolution, and the fate of their hero, D'Epremennil (*European Revolution*, pp. 64-65). See also "France Before the Revolution," p. 249; Nietzsche, p. 28; *Democracy*, vol. 1, p. 208.

[124] *Democracy*, vol. 1, pp. 68, 409; vol. 2, p. 110; *The Old Régime*, p. 209; *Journey to America*, p. 239.

it is not surprising that the theorist often has been an ironist also. But in the irony of "the new science" is also a new mood, one of tristesse, as the theorist doubts the power of his vision.

> Sometimes the legislator succeeds after a thousand efforts in exerting an indirect influence on the destiny of nations, in which case his genius is applauded; often on the other hand, a geographical position which he cannot affect, a social structure which was created without his help, manners and ideas of whose origin he is ignorant, all these push society irresistibly in a certain direction, a movement which controls him, but which he cannot control.

It is here that, as yet, we remain.[125]

[125] Quoted in Lively, p. 45.

F I V E

* * * *

THINKING ABOUT THE REPUBLIC:

A NOTE ON

EQUALITY AND AUTHORITY

We have lived to see a time when the heroic legend of
the Republic and the Citizen, which seemed to Jefferson
the eternal youth of the world, has begun to grow old in
its turn.—G. K. Chesterton

How tiresome these people be, soured and toothless and
old, that go on living for no end, it seemeth, but to keep
flinging in one's face the overrated marvels of an age that
is forgot and that none regret but they themselves. Old
age hath its charms, but this fashion is not of them. I had
told him so, indeed, if such language might become my
meager years and downy beard.
                                    —Mark Twain's Methuselah

These essays have been concerned primarily with the nature of political action and its relation to the past. Remembrance is the faculty and the metaphor of this relation.
In these inquiries, my particular focus has been the republic
as a form of government. It remains for me to assess the
place of remembrance within a more comprehensive teaching of the republic. I believe it to lie in the difficult nexus
between equality and authority. In these concluding pages,

251

I will attempt to provide a provisional account of this connection.

✳ ✳ ✳

Reflecting on what he saw in America, G. K. Chesterton imagined himself "the last republican," poking about amid the ruins of an idea. For those who have come after, these ruins have become, if anything, more overgrown. The precariousness of public life (the sense of which has always haunted the minds of republicans) could hardly find more forceful testimony than the experience of our own time. There is no small irony in this, for, while this century has seen the proliferation of "republics," few other periods have been less hospitable to civic life. The idea of the republic generally has signified "no king." But it also has meant a form of government in which every citizen could be, in Jefferson's phrase, "a participator in the government of affairs." Most would agree that, in these terms, our time has witnessed less the growth than the decline of republican institutions.[1]

Several decades ago, Walter Lippmann warned that the traditions of civility, in which were embedded the ideas and ideals of public life, were losing their force. This "forgetting" more recently has come to be seen as only a part of a larger crisis of modernity—a crisis of authority. While this crisis is real, its formulation raises difficulties both practical and conceptual. The very comprehensiveness of such a diagnosis pits understanding against practice. The magnitude of the problem so conceived cannot fail to bring all attempts at recovery to despair at the very outset.

Even as diagnosis, the formulation is not free of difficulty. The idea of "a crisis of authority" conceals as much as it reveals about the nature of authority; indeed, it may obscure precisely that knowledge which would be the most

---

[1] Chesterton, *What I Saw in America*, p. 197; Jefferson, Letter to Joseph C. Colwell, February 2, 1816, in *The Political Writings of Thomas Jefferson*, p. 99.

practical—namely, an understanding of the distinctiveness of *political* authority. To emphasize such distinctiveness is not simply expedient, but rooted in experience. While religious sentiments, says Hegel, are "in themselves complete—constantly present and satisfying," the "outward existence of a political constitution . . . is an imperfect Present and cannot be thoroughly understood without a knowledge of the past." We shall return later to the nature of this imperfection and political authority's attempt to repair it through remembrance. Here, it is sufficient to observe that political authority, unlike religious or parental authority, has, in some sense, always been in crisis. This is not to minimize the seriousness of our present predicament, but only to suggest that in political matters, at least, we are not confronted with a spectre wholly novel, where earlier experience is useless. Such knowledge may assist us in finding our location and may reveal vantage points from which new directions, if not final destinations, might suggest themselves.[2]

Unfortunately, our understanding of political authority has become impoverished in proportion to its decay. Inexperienced, we risk mistaking one thing for another. Commonly, relations of authority are seen as being in conflict with relations of equality. Authority seems to presuppose inequality. It is an attribute of which some are possessed and to which others are subject. The exercise of authority, we say, is always *over* something. In politics, both the Right and the Left have understood the history of the past few centuries as a struggle between the principle of authority and that of equality. In this history, the triumph of the latter increasingly has spelled defeat for the former. Authority, in this view, is most at home in a society characterized by hierarchical structures and generally stable relations among its several strata. So understood, it is hardly

---

[2] Hegel, p. 62. For a discussion of the interconnectedness of tradition, religion, and authority, see Arendt, *Between Past and Future*, p. 93.

surprising that a growing equality of condition should have
proved the undoing of traditional authority. That this is
the history of "the old regime" is well known, but this
history throws little light on the place of authority in the
republic.[3]

✳ ✳ ✳

Recovery, says Arendt, consists to a certain extent in attempting to think about "combining meaningfully what
our present vocabulary presents to us in terms of opposition and contradiction." The dilemma of the republic has
at its center the reconciliation of authority and equality.
The difficulty of such a reconciliation is suggested by the
role analogy has always played in it. Political authority
generally has called upon analogies drawn from the domain of natural authority. Founders are the "fathers" of
their republics and often, too, "the beloved of God." But
unlike the relations of parents and children, or those of
gods and men, the first principle of civic relations is equality. Aristotle said it best: "The state is an association of
equals, and *only* of equals" (italics mine). Rousseau posed
the difficulty as a logical paradox: "Putting law over men
is a problem in politics that I like to compare to that of
squaring the circle in geometry." In practice, however, as
Rousseau knew, the problem is less logical than psychological. The face of egalitarian psychology is protean, its
inclinations manifold. Indeed, deep knowledge of its dynamics is perhaps the core of what we call statecraft. "Who
knows the reasons for obedience," says De Jouvenel, "knows
the inner nature of Power."[4]

It is the power of republics that has recommended them
to many. This was certainly true of Machiavelli. But even
more cautious admirers such as Montesquieu and Tocque-

---

[3] See, for instance, Nisbet, *Twilight of Authority*, and Sennet, *Authority*.

[4] Arendt, *On Revolution*, p. 224; Plutarch, p. 52; Aristotle, p. 298; Rousseau, *The Government of Poland*, p. 3; De Jouvenel, *On Power: Its Nature
and the History of Its Growth*, p. 17.

ville, who were careful not to overlook the excesses and dangers to which such power is prone, were nonetheless enamored of republican energy. The source of this vitality is to be found in the nature of civic relations. Equality "alone," insists Montesquieu, produces "a powerful people." Power is more than the bringing together of the strengths of individuals. Power is always greater than the sum of its parts. "Power comes into being," says Arendt, "only if and when men join themselves together for action, and it will disappear when, for whatever reason, they disperse and desert one another." Political equality, or the sense that "we" possess (and are "possessed" by) a thing shared in common and equally—"the public's thing"—is the wellspring of republican power.[5]

Necker once characterized power as "magical." This is true in at least two senses. The appearance of power in the world is wondrous and often shocks and astonishes many, including the possessors of power (the participants) no less than the spectators to it. But equally magical is power's disappearance. Sometimes, power is destroyed by even greater power, after the manner of Rome which laid low the ancient republics of Italy. At other times, power is extinguished by tyrannical violence. Such was the fate of the Soviets at the hands of the Bolsheviks. But most often, power disintegrates from within. We often speak of the "decay" of civic life. Republics resemble the natural order in that they come into existence and then pass away. Yet here the analogy falters; it portrays public life as gradually eroding, similar to the way life in nature seems simply to slip into death. To be sure, a way of life conducive to liberty

---

[5] Montesquieu, *Considerations on the Causes of the Greatness of the Romans and Their Decline*, p. 39; De Jouvenel, *Sovereignty: An Inquiry into the Political Good*, p. 21; Arendt, *On Revolution*, p. 175; De Jouvenel, *On Power*, p. 90. De Jouvenel's suggestion, that in monarchies subjects are "possessed in common" whereas, in republics, citizens are "associated in common," is not without its truth, but it obscures a certain dimension of the republican psyche. For in another sense, one can hardly think of a people more "possessed" than those Romans who left their fields to conquer the world.

can gradually lose its hold on a people. But that which it augments—power—seems frequently to meet an untimely end, destroying itself in a fireball or evaporating, as it were, overnight. The disappearance of public spaces, particularly in our own time, has resembled less "death from natural causes" than "suicide."[6]

Historically, despite its wonders and the great affection all human beings have shown for liberty once they have acquired a taste for it, the republic, as a form of government, has been comparatively short-lived. Of those bodies which Machiavelli called "composite," the republic, or the condition of public liberty, has been the most difficult to sustain. The republic's intermittent and uncertain appearance in the world is troubling and points to certain difficulties deep in the egalitarian psyche.[7]

Power, the result of people joined together, vanishes when they "disperse and desert one another." Paradoxically, both the creation of power and its disintegration are fostered by the condition of equality.

The passion for equality which thinkers such as Montesquieu, Rousseau, and Tocqueville map is complex and contradictory. Sometimes a "manly and lawful" sentiment, the love of equality also can become "a depraved taste." In republics, equality rests on a conception of civic relations as the *having* and *holding* of certain things in common. Fellow-citizens are therefore, in some sense, alike. It is this "likeness" that underlies the egalitarian dynamic. Yet, as Rousseau knew, the discovery of likeness is the father of comparison—the recognition of comparability. And comparison often must uncover unlikeness: greater and lesser men. This discovery, of course, need not corrupt public life. Indeed, it is often the source of great public spirit. Great individuals are the jewels of a healthy republic. At the height of Rome's virtue, her senate was said to resemble

[6] Necker, quoted in De Jouvenel, *On Power*, p. 22.
[7] Machiavelli, *Discourses*, III-1, p. 459.

an assembly of kings. Yet the movement from likeness to unlikeness inherent in the faculty of comparison suggests the direction of decay. In virtue, citizens examine their fellows for marks of a common devotion. Each is judged by his willingness to serve with equal alacrity. But in the agitation of public life, praise is bestowed unevenly, and some come to see that others have what they lack. Thus arise those great jealousies that frequently have plagued republics.[8]

It is in public life that human beings are most completely "outside themselves." The political world is a world of projections. In this domain of appearances, we seek to become the object of the attention of others, to be the speakers of words and the doers of deeds. Political equality in its most primitive form probably meant simply the right to be seen and heard. This right is adequately symbolized in the staff of council which passed from one to another that each might speak. The "ardor to be talked about," which Rousseau discovered in the crib of civilization, finds its completion in the publicity of the republic. The ancient equation of the republic with the idea of "no king" is more than an institutional description. It is also the rejection of monarchical presumption—that the space of appearances belongs to one alone. The injunction, "Thou shall not presume to be a Master," which D. H. Lawrence saw inscribed on the portals of America is, in truth, the first law of all republics. That republics often seem to leap into existence, like Athene from the forehead of Zeus, full-bodied and armored, is, in part, a consequence of the sudden discovery of public space and the ambition it unleashes. At its first appearance, this public space is as startling as it is pleasing.

[8] See, for example, Montesquieu, *Considerations*, especially chapters 9-13. The extent to which these two aspects of the passion for equality can be distinguished and separated out is not clear. I am inclined to see them as inextricably bound up together. For a somewhat different account, to which I owe much, see McWilliams, "On Equality as the Moral Foundation for Community," pp. 184-85.

But the value of public esteem quickly brings forth lush and vigorous fruit.[9]

It is not surprising that the two vices to which public life is prone are vanity and envy. Lycurgus cautioned the citizens of Sparta to avoid especially "coveting each man to be greater than his fellow." Yet it is probably true that a portion of the spirit of Ahab—of whom Starbuck said, "Aye, he would be a democrat to all above, look how he lords it over all below"—makes its abode in every egalitarian soul. It is also probably true, at least for some, that the love of glory knows no natural limit. Machiavelli suggested as much in finding the practical solution to the problem of the great man in the presence of many great men. The problem of envy is more endemic. A prince, says Montesquieu, is so "distant" that he is almost "unseen." But in a republic, the great are "visible to all, and are not so elevated that odious comparisons are not constantly made." To this, Montesquieu adds, almost parenthetically, "Therefore it has at all times been seen, and is still seen, that the people detest senators." If perhaps not as compelling as the desire for glory, envy is more often associated with the many, and enjoys, so to speak, the majority's advantage. The condition of equality is notable, then, as a way of life that is at once loved and hated.[10]

These dynamics are always to be found in public life. They necessarily figure in the republican experiment. They also are frequently its undoing.

Rousseau, who plumbed the depths of these matters, linked vanity with contempt and envy with shame. However contempt and shame may differ, they share this: both break the bonds among men, causing them to leave and

[9] Rousseau, "Discourse on the Origin and Foundations of Inequality Among Men," pp. 171-75 (see also pp. 148-49); Lawrence, *Studies in Classic American Literature*, p. 5.

[10] Plutarch, p. 65; Montesquieu, *Considerations*, p. 84; Melville, *Moby Dick*, p. 244. Compare Starbuck's characterization of Ahab with Rousseau's speculations on the "secret pretensions of the heart of every civilized man," in "Discourse on Inequality," p. 195.

depart the company of others. Two political consequences result from the entry of contempt and shame into public space: the quest for domination and the flight from public life. To these vices correspond the polar illusions to which civic relations are susceptible—omnipotence and impotence. Both are surely illusions, yet public life no sooner casts them down than it restores them again. For many of us, our condescension toward political things masks a deeper sense of powerlessness. Detachment is the bastard child of weakness.[11]

Put somewhat differently, res publica is threatened when citizens either flee the realm of appearances or seek to have it all to themselves. Indeed, these two phenomena are not the opposites they appear. For when most "disperse" or "desert" the republic, the few are made more confident of their opportunity. Likewise, when one or few dominate public space, the others—denied the mutuality of seeing and being seen, hearing and being heard—despair of public joy and go in search of private pleasures.

Against the twin tendencies of dominion and dissolution public life has always stood in need of authority.

＊　＊　＊

The status of political authority is uncertain. Lycurgus, in whom, says Plutarch, "the true foundation of sovereignty [was] to be seen," nonetheless lost an eye to the envious. The ancient analogies in which political authority has always clothed itself explain less the nature of political authority than political authority's predicament. The task of natural authority is ordering. Hierarchy is appropriate to it, for each thing must be put in its place. Such authority is often and adequately depicted as a pyramid. In republics, however, order is "a very equivocal thing." If the acropolis lay at the center of the polis and retained its association with *archai*, "beginnings," "res publica" had modified the

---

[11] Schaar, *Legitimacy in the Modern State*, p. 321.

presumption of first principles. To take a singular example, the Roman people were not unwilling to establish themselves on their own mountain.[12]

If one were to insist on a geometric equivalent for political authority, the circumference of a circle would suggest itself. It was less the acropolis than the walls which gave shape and definition to the ancient republic. Walls, like the circle on which they were patterned, distinguished inside and outside, marking off a determinate space in which men were associated not only by proximity, but by sentiments, interests, and acquaintance as well. It is the ring, Peter Euben rightly suggests, that best symbolizes a people united in a common endeavor.[13]

The idea of the circle also hints at the nature of authority's enterprise. Political authority specifically has to do with the problems of action. Authority is the cause of that which De Jouvenel calls "the political achievement." It is an active principle that "builds, consolidates, and *keeps in being* aggregates of men" (italics mine). Such a definition is attractive for it places emphasis on the central problem of the political project—"its essential durability." This definition also permits us to see that while political authority often keeps power *in check*, this task is subordinate to (and but a part of) the primary task of authority: keeping power *intact*. While power can be terrifying in its aspect and tyrannical in its extent, *power structures* are among the most fragile of human institutions. Authority is justified first by the frailty of public things.[14]

The tasks of political authority correspond to the prodigalities of political life. These have a pendular quality. Montesquieu expresses this idea perfectly: "Sometimes with

[12] Plutarch, pp. 52, 57; Montesquieu, *Considerations*, pp. 84-85, 93; de Grazia.

[13] Euben, "Creatures of a Day: Thought and Action in Thucydides," pp. 30-31.

[14] De Jouvenel, *Sovereignty*, pp. 20-21. Consider also Schaar's reflections on the subject (p. 318).

a hundred thousand arms [the people] overturn all before them; and sometimes with a hundred thousand feet they creep like insects." Effective authority must stir as well as calm. It must be, as De Jouvenel puts it, the "source of heat" as well as "cold." It must contain within it "the principle of order" *and* "the principle of movement."[15]

The word *authority* derives from the Latin word *auctor*, "a source, an instigator, an architect." Significantly, *auctor* connotes "that which causes increase." In action, that which causes increase is that which maintains and augments expectations. Tocqueville is our great teacher here. His work points to the consequences of the dislocation of expectations—the wild vacillations of hope and despair and the reduction of public life to the unleavened categories of war: conquest or defeat. These difficulties are in the nature of action. The unique quality of action (in contrast to other forms of human endeavor) is the sense of its utter unpredictability. Whether this is illusion is less important than the fact of its *felt truth* among those preparing for action. While insubstantial—the sense of "something in the air"— it is the character of this uncertainty which those who excel in action attempt to divine. It is probably for such reasons that the Romans inaugurated all action—the making of laws no less than the making of war—with the taking of the auspices, and why they would proceed only if these were good. Authority does not insure victory or even safety, but it placates the terror which is the natural response to a future gone opaque, and thus it instills confidence. Authority, says Schaar, justifies action and assures those who are about to engage in it that they will be "enlarged" and not depleted by their deeds. Authority testifies to the propriety of the end to which each is coming. Through it, we are confirmed in our destiny.[16]

[15] Montesquieu, *The Spirit of Laws*, p. 109; De Jouvenel, *Sovereignty*, p. 40.

[16] De Jouvenel, *Sovereignty*, p. 21; Rousseau, *On the Social Contract*, Book IV, chapter 4; Schaar, p. 278.

In action, authority is experienced as the satisfaction of a *need*. The sometimes sudden realization that almost anything has become possible—the cause of both the exultation and the terror which often accompany action—gives political authority its "opportunity."[17] In practical matters, especially, human beings think "by pictures." In public life, where many citizens act simultaneously, the necessity of common or shared images has long been acknowledged. The creation and maintenance of this common world is surely one of authority's principal tasks. But the task of unification goes deeper. In action, different persons may *see* different things. Yet this is also true of each person. For an individual's imaginings—the apparitions which haunt practice—often change their shape as there is cause to hope or fear. To unite human beings in action, authority must take hold of what Rousseau called the "unruly imagination," for the constancy of each is the condition for the unity of all. It is this new-found constancy that gives authority its quality of immanence and the aspect of a divine gift.[18]

The most reliable principle of authority in public life has been the idea of foundations. It is this idea that has given to political authority its distinctive character. A full account of this principle would consider the transformation of authority incarnate into authority recollected. In republics, the founding—its status as an event—provides a focus for remembrance. For in the founding are lodged common symbols, images, and memories that, when taken together, constitute the identity of a people and give them an ori-

---

[17] Among other things, this fact helps explain the extreme attachment of revolutionists to doctrine and the ferocity with which doctrinal disputes are carried on among them. Contemplating the destruction of all existing order, revolutionists, above all others, seek a ground for action. Because they find it only in doctrine, all challenges to doctrinal integrity (no matter how small) threaten to cut loose the Archimedian point on which they stand.

[18] De Jouvenel, *Sovereignty*, pp. 36-37; Poulet, *Studies in Human Time*, p. 163.

entation in time and space. Such recollections are a kind of refuge, a place to which a people may repair for warmth and inspiration. Accessible to everyone, the special gift and burden of each, the beginning offers itself to all who, in Plato's phrase, will show it "proper honor." Thus, to remember is to testify to the mystical truth of civic equality. It is no accident that, in republics, the people have always been the repository of the Word.[19]

The utility of the founding principle lies in its ability to shield political life from the disintegrative tendencies so natural to public spaces. Ambition is humbled and envy allayed in the wonder of an authority heavy with the weight of time. This wonder originates in the astonishment of the young—a consequence of the realization that others antedate them and have experienced things of which they are not a part. To be so astonished is to come to have knowledge of the existence of a patrimony. In republics, such knowledge is essential, for, as the great founders knew, only with the vision of the first and last things before their eyes can citizens be made to truly love equality. Thus, it may be that the cultivation of astonishment is the cardinal task of civic education. Such an education would be a pedagogy of the heart. Yet such knowledge is preserved with difficulty.[20]

Republics often have drawn great strength from man's natural conservatism. We are inclined to love and place all value in those things which are palpable, within the compass of the senses—that which we may call our own. Custom and the affection for the familiar have been bulwarks of virtue in many republics, but public liberty has always stood in need of more than these. For that condition which

---

[19] Arendt, *Between Past and Future*, p. 125; Schaar, p. 26; Plato, *The Laws of Plato*, §775; Machiavelli, *Discourses*, I-16.

[20] For one account of youthful astonishment, see Faulkner, *Go Down, Moses*, p. 115. For Faulkner, this realization partook of both grief and rage, and his work often illuminates the complex interrelations between these emotions and the sentiment of reverence. For a brilliant discussion of authority and the heart, see Rousseau's *Poland*, especially chapter 2.

is the sine qua non of public liberty—equality—is never unambiguously loved. For this reason, republican thinkers have always placed great importance on the experience of public life. The affection for equality is peculiar in at least one respect: it partakes of the fleeting and intermittent quality of collective action (which is its parent). Such affection originates in the experience of ruling and being ruled, of possessing and being possessed in common by a public thing. Yet the truth of such experiences is always in danger of being denied or obliterated by the other truths to which equality attests daily—those encompassed in the Tocquevillian epithet: "individualism." One of the enduring difficulties of the republic—a difficulty made radical in our own time—has been the maintenance of a truth so deeply experiential. Public life is forever in need of testimony. In earlier times, it often found such a testament in the memories of men, in the recollections of what Machiavelli called an "ancient liberty."[21]

Such recollections, Machiavelli knew, are compelling. Indeed, this is a part of their genius, forcing citizens to master the darker portions of their egalitarian souls. In memory, citizens discover images that drive them to take up the burdens of public liberty. In this, Rousseau only echoed an old teaching: in republics, men are forced to be free. Without the compelling bonds of recollection, the people must become "chimerical things," and in place of the people will stand but a multitude. In such times, said Tocqueville and Hobbes, "the master is near."[22]

✳ ✳ ✳

The disintegrative dynamics of public life are endemic. Historically, republics have sought solutions to these difficulties in the legend of foundation. In our time, however, this principle has lost much of its vitality. While the acids of modernity have attacked this as well as other legends, the

---

[21] Tocqueville, *The Old Régime*, p. 96; Machiavelli, *The Prince*, chapter 5.
[22] Montesquieu, *Considerations*, p. 93; Tocqueville, *European Revolution*, p. 139.

teaching of foundations has suffered also from causes more specifically political. I have two in mind. The first is a consequence of democratic confidence, the second of democratic failure. These difficulties have doctrinal roots, but they are as much humors as ideas. And while each arose under particular historical circumstances, these humors also can be seen as coexisting, sometimes alternating, and common enough in democratic movements to be considered inclinations.

The origins of democratic confidence are multiple. Certain aspects of social contract theory, the awe inspired by the great democratic revolutions themselves, the apparent congeniality of fraternity and the principle of equality, all have contributed to a conception of foundation in which the problem of public life is reduced to the problem of setting it in motion. One need only create public space and human beings will become citizens. Manifestations of this view range from the mechanical institutional recommendations of some participatory democrats to the more profound reflections of Hannah Arendt. In general, contemporary democratic theory has treated the political deed with an easy integrity that obscures the problem of the maintenance of public life. Significantly, Arendt has revived the idea of the covenant as an adequate foundation for political action. Deeply rooted in the American experience, this idea retains great potency as a means to the opening up of public spaces; for this reason, it must be cherished. But the solemn pledge unaided, even among friends, must prove insufficient to the task of initiating things that last.[23]

In practice, the failure of the American Left to build enduring democratic institutions has been far-reaching. If the Old Left created institutions in which the affection for democracy quickly waned (the industrial union being the most tragic example), the New Left sought to avoid these problems through democracy without institutions. The brief history of this experiment speaks plainly. Since Machia-

[23] Arendt, *On Revolution*, pp. 167-71, 175-76.

velli, the problem of political creation has, of necessity, become prominent. In circumstances such as ours, in which to the naturally disintegrative dynamics of public life are added a thousand new difficulties originating in problems as deep-rooted as the revolutionary character of capitalist production, ever larger concentrations of private power, and the centralization of decision-making structures, emergent publics will always be in jeopardy, and their creation and recreation must remain for us an inescapable and perennial task.

But the failure to create what Tocqueville called "true and lasting passions," as well as institutions capable of providing a home for such passions, deserves the most serious consideration. This failure is, in part, a theoretical one. While the doctrine of foundations still retains a measure of its deserved honor, democratic theory has depleted its substance. We remain fascinated with laying foundations, but our interest too often is reduced to the problem of mobilization. The more ancient question, "How is public life to be preserved?" is infrequently asked, suggesting not only that we have forgotten that public things must be cared for if they are to remain healthy, but also that we suffer from certain misapprehensions about the nature of the founder's art itself. While creating public life logically precedes maintaining it, there has always been something inscrutable in this first problem. In this, all republics have resembled America which was, said Tocqueville, "wafted by Providence to a pre-destined shore." In practice, founders often find the potential for public life just lying around— the gift of Fortune. It is not the creation of momentary wonders, however, but the planting of a public life which endures that finally measures a founder's worth. Even Machiavelli thought Numa more deserving of praise than Romulus, for, while Romulus made Romans of shepherds and outcasts, Numa made citizens of Romans.[24]

[24] Tocqueville, *Democracy*, vol. 1, p. 34; Machiavelli, *Discourses*, I-11.

Any serious consideration of foundations in public life must come (not first, but finally) to the question of institutions. The impoverishing of the doctrine of foundations has been conspicuous in the confusion and uncertainty regarding the purpose or even the desirability of institutions in the recovery of a more participatory politics. To be sure, all institutions, because of their regularity and inertia, distort democratic practice, but the precariousness of public space makes institutions especially necessary in sustaining such a practice.

One of the principal tasks of republican institutions is to provide an enduring setting for the narration of political life. Walter Lippman's reflections, which found a place at the beginning of these inquiries, come again to mind. Lippmann knew that the public world was a world structured by traditions, and that such a world could come into and remain in existence only if there was a "continuum of public and private memories [which] transcend all persons in their immediate and natural lives and . . . tie them all together." He also knew, however, that the old traditions, symbols, and images were losing their hold on the political imagination—that modern men had a limited capacity for memory and that new forms of order and action would be necessary if we were not to lose our heritage of public life. These new forms would have to contend with the fragile dignity of democrats, their insistence on seeing things for themselves, and their inclination to shun public burdens in the pursuit of private pleasures. Lippmann sought to make "participants" of democrats by making them protagonists in what he called an "unfinished story." For Lippmann knew that democrats must find themselves in their deeds if they are to sustain "high purposes."[25]

Nothing is more necessary, politically speaking, than for democrats to make "high purposes" their own purposes. As Alasdair MacIntyre has argued recently, narratives pro-

[25] Lippmann, p. 105; Schaar, pp. 26, 35.

vide a ground for judgment, a setting in which it becomes both possible and necessary to give "a certain kind of account of oneself." Narratives remind us that our identities have histories. These histories almost always turn out to be the histories of relations. (Aristotle called the few exceptions either beasts or gods.) Such recollections help combat the solitude of heart and mind that Tocqueville saw as the secret fantasy of the democratic psyche.[26]

Without such stories, democratic leadership must atrophy. For when "high purposes" are forgotten, those who would lead a people into the future are replaced by those who claim only to manage the present, as the people come to have few expectations. Under such circumstances, accountability must disappear from the political relation while the people, unable to judge and unwilling to be judged, ask only to be taken care of or left alone.[27]

We need to build and rebuild institutions capable of preserving and enlarging historical self-conceptions in which citizens can come to see themselves as carrying the burdens and possessing the possibilities of the stories of which they are a part. Among other things, such an account would help rehabilitate the status of form in democratic theory. This is especially the focus of my lover's quarrel with the American Left, which has been painfully unsuccessful in creating institutions that might sustain narrative self-understandings. It is in specific, determinate spaces that histories understood as narratives thrive. The creation and maintenance of a fabric of stories depends, in large measure, on the proximity of actors and the frequency of interaction. Only where citizens can speak and act with some promise that their fellows will see and hear—and remember—will those passions grow which are "true and lasting." From a new angle, we have arrived at familiar conclusions. Unless we can recreate or restore what Tocqueville

[26] MacIntyre, *After Virtue*, p. 202; Tocqueville, *Democracy*, vol. 2, p. 106.
[27] Barber, "Command Performance," pp. 51-56.

called "little republics" within the frame of the Republic, both within those institutions such as political parties and trade unions that can aggregate public opinion and sustain public discourse, as well as in local communities and elsewhere, our political objects must remain indefinite and political action short-lived.

These reflections might have ended here if the idea of foundations suffered simply from an impoverished content. But we also have seen the decline of the status of this doctrine as a principle for political action. Originating in the mood of the Enlightenment, this decline was given lasting theoretical significance by Marx. Like the impoverishment of the doctrine of foundations, the decline of its status as a principle has a history. At its center is the reformulation of the content of political action.

While rooted in the Enlightenment's prejudice in favor of the future, this reformulation was nurtured in the democratic failures of 1789 and those which followed. The Enlightenment (for rather particular historical reasons) inverted the primordial political equation of the ancient with the good. Tocqueville remarked that for the generation who preceded the Revolution it was enough for something to be old for it to be bad. Originally the posture of the enemies of the ancient regime, the equation of the old with the bad was enlisted after 1789 in the effort to explain the failure of democracy, thereby acquiring greater theoretical importance. Although it was the complement of the doctrine of progress, or the equation of the new with the good, the equation of the old with the bad led to conclusions independent of the teaching of progress. To the extent that the equation of the old with the bad infected the understanding of practice, political action came to be seen not as an activity of conservation, or recovery, or even reformation, but rather as an activity in which the past was to be continuously and self-consciously overcome.

Marx had hoped that revolutionary action would be able to "let the dead bury their dead." But the disquieting suggestion of *The Eighteenth Brumaire*—that "self-deceptions" remain and that the new public men must "deride with unmerciful thoroughness, the inadequacies, weaknesses and paltriness of their first attempts"—has come back to haunt the practice of the Left too often not to be seen as a difficulty with deep theoretical roots. Lukács was perhaps the first to discern the fundamental difficulty in achieving a revolutionary standpoint—that it entailed the dissolution of the predominance of seeing over doing. He might have guessed that the motto of this standpoint—*Hic Rhodus, hic salta! Hier ist Die Rose, hier tanze!*—was at war with the very nature of political action.[28]

Despite its radical pretensions, the revolutionizing of the idea of action owed much to the capitalist conception of production. The theory of praxis sought to accomplish in the public realm what capitalism had accomplished in the social realm, namely, the destruction of all fixed points of reference. Only then, it was thought, would it be possible to free public life of "the muck of ages." Such were the requirements of proletarian sobriety. In this, praxis furthered and completed the pedagogy of capitalism which taught, above all, that "all that is solid melts into air."[29] Henceforth, all images (the very stuff of public life) became illusions which had to be unmasked as impediments to the perfection of praxis. Dialectics itself, with its annoying habit of preserving the past in inverted forms, was unequal to the task. While once it had been sufficient that old gods should become demons, it was now thought necessary to destroy the spirit world in its entirety.

As long as the doctrine of progress remained vital and alive, the deep self-hatred of this new view of action—the impotent center of the technological illusion—lay hidden. While still showing the pertinacity of all-powerful ideas, the Enlightenment's teaching has eroded steadily through-

---

[28] Marx, *Eighteenth Brumaire*, pp. 439-40; Lukács, pp. 257-78.
[29] Marx, *The Manifesto of the Communist Party*, in *The Marx-Engels Reader*, p. 338.

out this century, so that many now see what Chesterton prophesied—that the idea of progress is the death of nations. The emergence of the political nihilist, who would destroy the present even while believing that the future too is lost to him, signals the advanced decay of the eighteenth century's faith.[30]

Short of the destruction of public life itself, the attempt to destroy the imagery of the past within public life must fail. Still, Marx's lament, that "the tradition of all the dead generations weighs like a nightmare upon the brain of the living," has penetrated the very structure of political action and left its mark on the theory of practice. With the radical assault on political illusion, those enduring images, which structure the space of appearances by the gravity of their example, are destroyed and action is loosed from its mooring. In the kaleidoscopic madness of such a world, where every good thing changes its form, all things become possible and nothing is unthinkable. Stripped of the solace that is the promise of res publica, most men flee to the safety and sanity of private life. Those who remain seek the only good left—mastery. If this is a stark portrait, it is not an unrecognizable one. It describes the history of some of the more promising democratic movements of our time.[31]

Still, ours has not been a time without public life. In truth, we have made many beginnings. Our difficulty lies not there, but rather in our inability to lay new foundations or repair old ones—to build lasting things. As a people, I believe that we retain a portion of those political sentiments Tocqueville once praised. But the most recent outpourings of such sentiments have had an episodic character. They have appeared as moments—almost accidents—in the flow of time, hardly connected with their predecessors and holding little promise of bequeathing legacies. We have come to be a people of small political experience, and with the

[30] Chesterton, p. 56.
[31] Marx, *Eighteenth Brumaire*, p. 437.

vulnerabilities which always attend that condition. We have forgotten what we once saw, and can imagine only that which is now before our eyes. Once a fabric of stories, America increasingly finds itself simply a place. It is the capacity to remember that we must try to recover.

In my account of the political affections, I have emphasized the temporal texture of public life. I have argued that it is in the memories of men that these affections find their ground. If there is a teaching in these several considerations of political memory, it is not that we should restore the past, but that we must have one.

BIBLIOGRAPHY

*

In the footnotes, an item listed here is, at its first mention, referred to by the author's last name, full title, and relevant volume and/ or page number(s). Thereafter, unless otherwise noted, the item is referred to only by the author's last name and page number(s), or, in the case of those authors represented by more than one work, by the author's last name, a shortened title (when appropriate), and page number(s).

Arendt, Hannah. *Between Past and Future*. New York: The Viking Press, 1968.

———. *The Human Condition*. Chicago: University of Chicago Press, 1974.

———. *On Revolution*. New York: Penguin Books, 1981.

Aristotle. *The Politics of Aristotle*. Edited and translated by Ernest Barker. New York: Oxford University Press, 1979.

Barber, Benjamin R. "Command Performance." *Harper's Magazine* (April 1975): 51-56.

Burke, Edmund. *The Works of the Right Honorable Edmund Burke*. Boston: Little, Brown & Co., 1894.

———. *On the Sublime and Beautiful*. In *Orations and Essays*. Edited by Aldine. New York: D. Appleton & Co., 1900.

———. *Reflections on the Revolution in France*. New York: The Bobbs-Merrill Co., 1955.

———. "On Conciliation with America." In *Speeches on the War*. Boston: Gregg Press, 1972.

Chesterton, Gilbert K. "Place de la Bastille." In *Tremendous Trifles*. New York: Dodd, Mead & Co., 1917.

———. *What I Saw in America*. New York: Dodd, Mead & Co., 1922.

Collingwood, R. G. *The Idea of History*. New York: Oxford University Press, 1975.

Copeland, Thomas W. *Our Eminent Friend Edmund Burke*. Westport, Conn.: Greenwood Press, 1970.

de Grazia, Sebastian. "Senses of Republic: Machiavelli and Bodin." In *Symposium Internacional: Juan Bodino*. Mexico: Universidad Nacional Autonoma de Mexico, 1979.

De Jouvenel, Bertrand. *On Power: Its Nature and the History of Its Growth*. New York: The Viking Press, 1949.

————. *Sovereignty: An Inquiry into the Political Good*. Chicago: University of Chicago Press, 1957.

Dickens, Charles. *A Child's History of England*. In *Dickens Works*, vol. 30. Boston: Estes & Lauriat, 1895.

Drescher, Seymour. *Tocqueville and England*. Cambridge, Mass.: Harvard University Press, 1964.

Eliade, Mircea. *The Myth of the Eternal Return or Cosmos and History*. Translated by William R. Trask. Princeton: Princeton University Press, 1974.

Erikson, Erik H. *Young Man Luther*. New York: W. W. Norton & Co., 1962.

Euben, J. Peter. "Creatures of a Day: Thought and Action in Thucydides." In *Political Theory and Praxis*, edited by Terence Ball. Minneapolis: University of Minnesota Press, 1977.

Faulkner, William. *Go Down, Moses*. New York: Vintage Books, 1970.

Fleisher, Martin, ed. *Machiavelli and the Nature of Political Thought*. New York: Antheneum, 1972.

Franklin, Benjamin. *Autobiography*. N.p.: The Spencer Press, 1936.

Freud, Sigmund. *Totem and Taboo*. Edited and translated by James Strachey. New York: W. W. Norton & Co., 1950.

————. *Civilization and Its Discontents*. Edited and translated by James Strachey. New York: W. W. Norton & Co., 1961.

Gargan, Edward T. *Alexis de Tocqueville: The Critical Years 1848-1851*. Washington, D.C.: The Catholic University of America Press, 1955.

————. *De Tocqueville*. New York: Hilary House Publishers, Ltd., 1965.

Grene, David. *Greek Political Theory*. Chicago: University of Chicago Press, 1967.

Gunnell, John G. *Political Philosophy and Time.* Middletown, Conn.: Wesleyan University Press, 1968.

Hamilton, Alexander et al. *The Federalist.* New York: E. P. Dutton & Co., 1937.

Havelock, Eric A. *Preface to Plato.* New York: Grosset & Dunlap, 1971.

Hegel, G.W.F. *The Philosophy of History.* Translated by J. Sibree. New York: Dover Publications, 1956.

Herr, Richard. *Tocqueville and the Old Regime.* Princeton, N.J.: Princeton University Press, 1962.

Jacobson, Norman. *Pride and Solace.* Berkeley, Calif.: University of California Press, 1978.

Jefferson, Thomas. *The Political Writings of Thomas Jefferson.* Edited by Edward Dumbauld. Indianapolis: The Bobbs-Merrill Co., 1981.

Kramnick, Isaac, ed. *Edmund Burke.* Englewood Cliffs, N.J.: Prentice-Hall, 1974.

———. *The Rage of Edmund Burke.* New York: Basic Books, 1977.

Lawrence, D. H. *Studies in Classic American Literature.* New York: The Viking Press, 1969.

Lerner, Max. *Tocqueville and American Civilization.* New York: Harper & Row Publishers, 1966.

Lippmann, Walter. *The Public Philosophy.* New York: The New American Library, 1955.

Lively, Jack. *The Social and Political Thought of Alexis de Tocqueville.* Oxford: Clarendon Press, 1962.

Livius, Titus. *Roman History.* Translated by John Henry Freese, Alfred John Church, and William Jackson Brodribb. New York: D. Appleton & Co., 1904.

Locke, John. *Some Thoughts Concerning Education.* Edited by Peter Gay. Richmond, Va.: William Byrd Press, 1964.

Lukács, Georg. *History and Class Consciousness.* Translated by Rodney Livingstone. Cambridge, Mass.: The M.I.T. Press, 1972.

MacCunn, John. *The Political Philosophy of Burke.* London: Longmans, Green & Co., 1913.

Machiavelli, Niccolò. *The Chief Works and Others.* Translated by Allan Gilbert. Durham, N.C.: Duke University Press, 1965.

———. *The Discourses of Niccolò Machiavelli.* Translated by Leslie J. Walker, S. J. London: Routledge & Kegan Paul, 1975.

Machiavelli, Niccolò. *Mandragola*. Translated by Mera J. Flau-menhaft. Prospect Heights, Ill.: Waveland Press, 1981.

MacIntyre, Alasdair. *After Virtue*. Notre Dame, Ind.: University of Notre Dame Press, 1981.

McWilliams, Wilson Carey. *The Idea of Fraternity in America*. Berke-ley: University of California Press, 1974.

———. "On Equality as the Moral Foundation for Community." In *The Moral Foundations of the American Republic*, edited by Robert H. Horwitz. Charlottesville, Va.: University Press of Virginia, 1978.

Mansfield, Harvey, Jr. *Statesmanship and Party Government*. Chi-cago: University of Chicago Press, 1965.

Marx, Karl. *The Marx-Engels Reader*. Edited by Robert C. Tucker. New York: W. W. Norton & Co., 1972.

Mayer, J. P. *Alexis de Tocqueville, A Biographical Study*. Gloucester, Mass.: Peter Smith, 1966.

Melville, Herman. *Moby Dick*. New York: The Modern Library, n.d.

Merleau-Ponty, Maurice. *Signs*. Translated by Richard C. Mc-Cleary. N.p.: Northwestern University Press, 1964.

Montesquieu. *Considerations on the Causes of the Greatness of the Romans and Their Decline*. Translated by David Lowenthal. Ithaca, N.Y.: Cornell University Press, 1968.

———. *The Spirit of Laws*. Edited by David W. Carrithers. Berke-ley: University of California Press, 1977.

Nietzsche, Friedrich. *On the Advantage and Disadvantage of History for Life*. Translated by Peter Preuss. Indianapolis: Hackett Publishing Company, 1980.

Nisbet, Robert. *Twilight of Authority*. New York: Oxford University Press, 1975.

Oakeshott, Michael. *Rationalism in Politics*. London: Metheun & Co., Ltd., 1962.

O'Connor, Edwin. *The Last Hurrah*. Toronto: Bantam Books, 1980.

Parel, Anthony, ed. *The Political Calculus*. Toronto: University of Toronto Press, 1972.

Pierson, George Wilson. *Tocqueville and Beaumont in America*. New York: Oxford University Press, 1938.

Plato. *Collected Dialogues*. Edited by Hamilton and Cairns. New York: Pantheon Books, 1961.

———. *The Laws of Plato*. Translated by Thomas L. Pangle. New York: Basic Books, 1980.

Plutarch. "Lycurgus." In *The Lives of the Noble Grecians and Romans*. Translated by John Dryden. New York: The Modern Library, n.d.

Pocock, J.G.A. *The Ancient Constitution and the Feudal Law*. New York: W. W. Norton & Co., 1967.

———. *Politics, Language and Time*. New York: Antheneum, 1973.

———. *The Machiavellian Moment*. Princeton, N.J.: Princeton University Press, 1975.

Poulet, Georges. *Studies in Human Time*. Translated by Elliot Coleman. Baltimore: The Johns Hopkins Press, 1956.

Rousseau, Jean-Jacques. *The First and Second Discourses*. Edited by Roger D. Masters. New York: St. Martin's Press, 1964.

———. *The Government of Poland*. Translated by Willmoore Kendall. New York: The Bobbs-Merrill Co., 1972.

———. *On the Social Contract*. Edited by Roger D. Masters. New York: St. Martin's Press, 1978.

———. *Emile*. Translated by Allan Bloom. New York: Basic Books, 1979.

———. *The Reveries of the Solitary Walker*. Translated by Charles E. Butterworth. New York: Harper Colophon Books, 1982.

Schaar, John H. *Legitimacy in the Modern State*. New Brunswick: Transaction Books, 1981.

Senior, Naussau William. *Correspondence and Conversations of Alexis de Tocqueville with Naussau William Senior, 1834-1859*. Edited by M.C.M. Simpson. 2 vols. New York: Augustus M. Kelley, 1968.

Sennet, Richard. *Authority*. New York: Alfred A. Knopf, 1980.

Shumer, S. M. "Machiavelli-Republican Politics and Its Corruption." *Political Theory* 7 (February 1979): 5-34.

Strauss, Leo. *Thoughts on Machiavelli*. Seattle: University of Washington Press, 1969.

———. *Natural Right and History*. Chicago: University of Chicago Press, 1971.

Thucydides. *Hobbes' Thucydides*. Edited by Richard Schlatter. New Brunswick, N.J.: Rutgers University Press, 1975.

de Tocqueville, Alexis. *Memoir, Letters and Remains*. 2 vols. Boston: Ticknor & Fields, 1862.

de Tocqueville, Alexis. *Democracy in America*. Translated by Henry Reeve. 2 vols. New York: Vintage Books, 1945.

———. *The Old Régime and the French Revolution*. Translated by Stuart Gilbert. Garden City, N.Y.: Doubleday & Co., 1955.

———. *Journeys to England and Ireland*. Translated by George Lawrence. Edited by J. P. Mayer. New Haven: Yale University Press, 1958.

———. *Journey to America*. Translated by George Lawrence. Edited by J. P. Mayer. New Haven: Yale University Press, 1960.

———. *The European Revolution and Correspondence with Gobineau*. Edited and translated by John Lukacs. Gloucester, Mass.: Peter Smith, 1968.

———. *Recollections*. Edited by J. P. Mayer and A. P. Kerr. Garden City, N.Y.: Doubleday & Co., 1970.

Twain, Mark. *Letters from the Earth*. Edited by Bernard De Voto. New York: Harper & Row, 1962.

Whitfield, J. H. *Machiavelli*. Oxford: Basil Blackwell, 1947.

INDEX

✻

Achilles, 49, 72
action, 3, 5, 13, 14, 18, 22, 23, 38,
    40-47, 49, 53, 57, 58n, 79n, 96,
    99n, 118, 121, 124, 128-32, 135,
    145, 147, 163n, 201, 204, 205,
    208n, 222, 225, 226, 228, 234,
    239-40n, 243-45, 247-49, 251,
    255, 260-71
Acton, Lord, 111, 112n
Aeneas, 55, 63n
affection(s), 4, 15, 18, 64, 85-87,
    98n, 118, 122, 124, 134, 138n,
    141, 154, 157-67, 171, 174-80,
    256, 263, 264, 272; origin of
    American, 174-77; aristocratic,
    189, 192, 197, 198; democratic,
    197, 199. *See also* love; patriot-
    ism; sentiments
Alexander the Great, 215
allegiance, 198-200
ambition, 49, 50, 66, 93, 101, 107,
    139-51, 152n, 209, 242, 257, 263
America, 111n, 137n, 154, 156,
    162, 163n, 168-80, 194-99, 224n,
    233, 240, 244, 252, 257, 265,
    266, 268, 272
American Revolution, 137n, 224n
anxiety, 5, 185, 189n
appearances, 43, 94, 96, 97, 112,
    137, 140, 257, 259, 271
Arendt, Hannah, 4, 6n, 19, 21,
    27, 28, 41n, 43n, 49, 58n, 128,
    133n, 135, 240, 254, 265

aristocracy, 56, 86, 90n, 94, 105,
    110n, 131, 132n, 140n, 143,
    165n, 172, 182, 183, 187, 192,
    195, 197, 223, 232, 244, 245; of
    France, 182, 183, 186-91, 197,
    220
Aristotle, 6, 9, 18, 19, 56, 100, 254
Athens, 49, 58n, 110n
Augustine, 26, 29, 34
authority, 15, 26, 28, 32, 66-70,
    72, 90, 91n, 98n, 115, 119, 122,
    123, 125, 135-38, 140, 142-43n,
    144, 146-47, 153, 154, 160n, 222,
    237, 241, 251-54, 259-63; of cus-
    tom, 15, 45, 119, 122, 123, 125,
    136, 137, 154, 237; of ancients,
    33; relation of paternal and po-
    litical, 66, 69, 70, 90, 135, 138,
    144-47, 153, 160; of the great
    man, 72; Locke's theory of, 143;
    and equality, 241, 251-54, 259-
    63

Bastille, the, 106n, 107
Beaumont, Gustave de, 156n, 166,
    189, 195, 206, 207, 213, 216,
    217, 236, 240n
belief, 46, 83, 231
Blackstone, William, 114, 115n
blood, 9, 88-91, 122, 124, 131,
    132n, 143, 187
Bolingbroke, 129n
Bolshevism, 255

Bonaparte, Napoleon, 213-19, 221, 222, 226, 238
Borgia, Cesare, 62n
Boswell, James, 107n, 138n
Bradford, William, 174-76, 179
Brutus, 47n, 60, 62, 64n, 66, 68, 88, 89, 99
Bryce, James, 169n
Burke, Edmund, 3n, 7, 8, 14-16, 18, 102-54, 156

Caesar, Julius, 51-53
Camerthen, Lord, 137n
Carneades, 28n
Castricani, Castruccio, 89n, 96
Cataline, 51
Cato, 25, 28n, 71
centralization, 153n, 161, 163, 198, 216-18, 222, 234, 235, 237, 240n, 266
chance, 43, 69, 71, 93, 94n, 117, 179, 180, 247, 249, 266
change, 33, 34, 116, 117, 123, 167, 168; in democracies, 178, 193, 194, 243
character, 11, 57, 96
Charles I, 108, 109
Chesterton, G. K., 3, 252, 271
Chiron, 72, 93
Christianity, 34, 40n, 43-46, 48, 75, 113
Cicero, 6, 41, 49
citizen and citizenship: idea of, 6, 10, 18, 24, 27, 56, 57n, 69n, 85, 89, 90, 118, 130, 132, 144n, 162, 251, 255-59, 262-65; Roman, 27, 29, 48, 69, 88, 266; and Christianity, 45; and remembrance, 52, 268; Florentine, 54n, 81n, 85n; American, 196; French, 223; Spartan, 258
civil society, 155, 239-40n, 253
civil war, 66, 73n, 86, 92, 105, 106, 109, 110, 117, 128, 145-47, 225, 235, 261
class, social, 56, 90n, 132, 188-90, 198, 200, 210, 220, 221n, 222-24
Coke, Edward, 114, 115n
Collingwood, R. G., 27, 28
common law, 103, 104, 114, 115, 125, 126, 177
community, 23, 81, 90, 110, 111, 145, 162, 196, 233, 247, 269; political, 9, 41, 45, 48, 88-90, 162, 207; aristocratic, 189; of nature, 241; democratic, 242
compassion, 152n
conquest. See imperialism
conservatism, 102, 112, 114, 116, 117, 124, 129n, 146, 148, 149, 151, 153, 154
contemplation, 44
corruption, 4, 7, 11, 58-59n, 61n, 71, 84-87, 91, 92, 129n, 130, 247, 255, 257, 271
covenanting, 265
Critolaus, 28
Cromwell, Oliver, 105, 109n, 132n, 140, 143, 147, 170n
custom, 6, 12-17, 21, 23, 76, 78, 79, 102, 111n, 113-17, 119-23, 131n, 132, 136, 137, 138n, 140, 151, 155, 156, 159, 162, 163, 173n, 178, 185, 194, 195, 210, 220, 263
customary societies, 9, 14-16, 19, 23, 24, 113, 117, 140, 185
Cyrus, 61, 96, 98

death, 40, 44, 46, 62, 65, 73n, 121, 122, 245
decay. See corruption
de Grazia, Sebastian, 25
De Jouvenel, Bertrand, 254, 255n, 260, 261
democracy, 106, 110n, 140, 144, 146, 156, 161, 162n, 168, 172,

173n, 182, 183, 187, 189-91, 193, 195, 197-99, 205, 206, 208, 209, 220, 221, 233-35, 239, 242-49, 265-71; in America, 177, 178. *See also* egalitarian: societies
Descartes, 37
desire, 65, 146n, 193
despotism, 240n, 244, 249; in France, 181, 200, 208, 209, 212, 213, 223, 225, 226, 235, 236
devotion, 196, 230, 257, 267, 268
dignity, 267. *See also* honor
Diogenes, 28n
dominion, 9, 144, 259

egalitarian: -ism, 90n, 140n, 143, 145, 241; psyche, 162n, 199, 239n, 241-43, 246-48, 254-59, 264, 268; societies, 210. *See also* equality; democracy
egotism, 57
Eliade, Mircea, 16n
Elizabeth I, 126, 128n
empiricism, 16
energy, 22, 57, 125, 130, 131n, 142, 159, 160n, 161, 163, 199n, 211, 225, 226, 227n, 230, 239-40n, 244, 248
English constitution, the, 103, 112, 124, 147n, 148n
Enlightenment, the, 130n, 140, 145, 146, 210, 267, 270
envy, 35, 48n, 65, 99, 258, 259, 263
equality, 146, 189, 190, 192, 193, 195, 196, 198, 241, 247, 251, 263, 265; of condition, 86, 93, 155, 199, 239-40n, 242, 243, 249, 254, 256, 257; love of, 156n, 256, 257n, 263, 264. *See also* egalitarian; democracy
Euben, Peter, 260
excellence, 23, 41, 61

faction, 86-92
Faguet, Emile, 156
faith, 159, 203, 204, 209, 229, 231, 246, 271
family, 88-92, 117, 118, 122, 128, 144n, 152n, 159, 164n, 167n, 196, 199, 200, 239n, 245; aristocratic, 192, 193, 197
fatherhood and fathers, 9, 26, 27, 49, 53, 54, 58-60, 62-72, 75, 81n, 82, 89-91, 122, 128, 134-40, 143-48, 151-53, 154n, 254. *See also* patriarchy; patricide; patrimony
Faulkner, William, 263n
fear, 35, 38, 69n, 99, 183, 186, 209, 212, 224; of death, 40, 44, 45; and foundations, 59, 63-65, 69; fearlessness, 67n; and conservatism, 123n, 128, 146n; of action, 130n; and obedience, 136; aristocratic, 193, 195; and public life, 229-31, 239-40n, 242, 262. *See also* terror
feudalism, 198, 199, 232, 233
Florence, 42n, 53, 54n, 81n, 84-93
fortune. *See* chance
foundations, 9, 27, 54n, 55, 59-61, 68-77, 90-93, 101n, 105, 106n, 119, 127, 135, 137, 138n, 159, 161, 167, 170-81, 209, 233, 259, 262-71; of Florence, 84-86; of America, 174, 176, 179
founder(s) and founding, 7, 9, 10, 24, 40n, 41, 42, 49-55, 59-65, 69-85, 93, 94n, 95-97, 100, 101n, 137, 254, 262, 266
Franklin, Benjamin, 4
fraternity, 70, 145-47, 242, 265
fratricide, 46n, 47n, 49, 50, 52, 54
freedom, 50, 55, 62, 80-82, 85, 152, 194, 201, 207, 208, 213, 226, 230, 234, 236, 240n, 264. *See also* liberty
French Revolution, the, 107, 140-

French Revolution (*cont.*)
42, 143n, 149, 150, 153, 154n,
165n, 190, 200n, 203, 209, 213-
24, 227-32, 234, 238, 269
Freud, Sigmund, 39, 44n, 64, 65,
83-84n, 143, 152n
friendship, 196, 265

Gargan, Edward, 207, 227, 245n,
248
generations, 10, 11, 65, 83, 87,
131, 143-45, 158, 192, 226, 230,
231, 242, 245, 247
Ghibelline, 87
Glorious Revolution, the, 105n,
107, 109, 112, 126
glory, 4, 40-45, 47-54, 57, 58, 83,
89, 91, 93, 98-100, 132, 134, 135,
139, 140, 143, 150, 151, 160,
161n, 192, 258
Gobineau, Arthur de, 203, 204,
227, 228
God, 40, 46n, 74-78, 179, 247, 254,
266; gods, 11, 25, 26, 27, 30, 63,
67
good, the, 26, 28, 58n, 71, 72, 86,
117, 227, 269
greatness, 24, 48, 86n, 100n, 121,
132, 134, 135, 138, 139, 142,
164, 176, 216, 221, 226, 227,
240n, 258
Grote, George, 215
Guelf, 87
Guicciardini, Francesco, 31
guilt, 65, 67n, 70, 154n
Guizot, François, 202

habit, 6, 15, 16, 23, 91, 106, 112-
21, 131n, 138n, 151, 159, 160,
164n, 171, 173n, 177-79, 215,
219, 237, 243
Hannibal, 39n, 62
Hastings, Warren, 130, 144
hatred: from fear or envy, 35; of

nobility, 56; from loss of liberty,
59; of authority, 65, 67; of
kings, 69; of fellow-citizens, 86-
88, 91, 92, 119, 215, 222, 223;
old hatred, 87, 88, 92, 166, 167,
186, 188, 209, 215; of equality,
180, 182, 184, 195, 258; of past,
180, 182, 184, 186, 188, 210,
211, 215, 218; nature of, 212; of
self, 270
Havelock, Eric, 19
Hawthorne, Nathaniel, 127
Hegel, G.W.F., 6n, 11n, 253
Henry II, 126, 143
Herodotus, 28
Herr, Richard, 201, 208n
historicism, 203
history, 23, 24n, 30, 33-38, 51, 52,
54n, 92, 95-97, 99, 106, 111,
113, 118, 122, 186n, 200-9, 215,
218, 231, 232, 238
Hobbes, 38, 104n, 110, 114, 117,
239-40n, 241, 242, 244
Holy Commonwealth, 104, 126
honor, 11, 33, 43-46, 53, 60, 88,
91, 99, 100n; in democracies,
189, 197, 198, 263
hope, 59, 76, 84, 201, 224, 226,
230, 246, 247n, 248, 261, 262
horror, 83, 111, 113, 136, 140, 141,
147, 149, 150n, 151

identity, 97, 180, 262, 268
ideology, 131, 143, 145, 154n
imagination, 3, 40, 142, 199, 213-
16, 221-27, 230, 237, 238, 262,
267
imitation, 29, 31-34, 50, 85n, 87,
88, 96-100, 106, 108, 118, 194,
228, 229, 231
imperialism, 49, 79, 80, 160, 161
impiety, 119, 144
impotence, 44, 48, 122, 135, 215,
222, 225-31, 239-42, 259

independence, 209, 239n, 241
individualism, 162-63n, 241, 264
inheritance, 122, 124, 125, 128,
132, 144n, 146n, 151, 215, 231,
271. *See also* patrimony
innovation, 31, 35, 36, 39, 58n,
71-73, 82, 83, 85, 98, 103, 111,
113, 116, 124, 128, 145, 167,
222; in egalitarian societies, 179,
193, 194, 210, 242
institutions, 6, 7, 61n, 79, 81, 100,
127, 146, 155, 156, 157, 161,
177, 178, 206, 207, 210, 232,
237, 240n, 246, 252, 260, 265-68;
Florentine, 86n; English, 104,
106n, 169n; American, 162n,
169n, 172; aristocratic, 193, 197-
99; democratic, 197; French,
223, 237
intellectuals, 110, 145
interest, 109, 110, 145, 162-63n,
181, 220, 249, 260
irreverence, 4, 53, 62-67, 70, 72

Jacobins, 130, 141n, 144, 150
Jacobson, Norman, 69, 98
Jefferson, Thomas, 251, 252
Jesus of Nazareth, 34, 45, 101
Johnson, Samuel, 107n, 138n,
153n
July Monarchy, the, 165, 205, 226
jurisprudence, 114, 123n

Kergorlay, Louis de, 168, 200
kingship. *See* monarchy
kinship, 88-91, 124
Kirk, Russell, 113n, 132
Kramnick, Isaac, 103, 107, 115n,
134, 144n, 149

Lamartine, Alphonse, 202, 231
language, 75, 76, 78, 79, 163n, 177
law, 61n, 76, 83, 100, 114n, 119,

157, 161, 167, 178, 181, 194,
207, 261
Lawrence, D. H., 257
leadership, 131, 268
Ledru-Rollin, Alexandre, 229
legitimacy, 79, 104
Lerner, Max, 192n, 201, 239n
lethargy. *See* impotence
liberalism, 23, 162-63n, 239n
liberty, 12, 13, 20, 43, 57, 58, 68n,
81, 85, 97n, 104, 105, 128, 129,
146, 234, 237, 248n, 249; public,
9, 12, 13, 18, 20, 43, 57, 58, 160,
162, 206, 239-40n, 255, 256, 263,
264; constitutional, 104, 105,
128
Lippmann, Walter, 4, 23, 251, 267
Lively, Jack, 245n
Livy, Titus, 29, 34-36, 54, 62-69,
96, 97n
locality, 109, 161-63, 170, 172, 223,
232-37, 240n, 248n, 249, 260,
269
Locke, John, 104n, 114, 117-20,
143-44n, 239n, 241
Louis Philippe, 200n, 227
love, 67n, 70, 86, 152n, 174, 186,
189n, 200, 212; of country, 45,
46, 85, 86, 88, 91, 101n, 141,
153n, 159, 160, 200, 222; Christian, 46; of the powerful, 65,
69, 136; old love, 87, 166; of
kin, 89n; maternal, 122, 135,
136; origin of, 133; of past, 180;
democratic, 194, 210, 211, 242-
46, 256, 257; aristocratic, 195; of
French Revolution, 213, 222; of
liberty, 237, 238; of peace, 240n;
of glory, 258. *See also* affection;
patriotism
loyalty, 69, 91, 145, 152n
Luther, Martin, 150
Lycurgus, 7, 10, 19, 27, 73n, 258,
259

MacCunn, John, 102
Machiavelli, Niccolò, 6-8, 12-15, 20, 24, 26-101, 115n, 117, 121, 128, 131, 147, 148, 160n, 180, 200, 222, 225, 240n, 255, 258, 264, 265, 266
McWilliams, Wilson Carey, 162n
Manlius Capitolinus, 65n, 88
Manlius Torquatus, 39n, 89n
manners, 149, 169, 197, 220, 250
many, the, 49, 54, 58n, 63, 94, 97, 110, 132, 195, 222, 258. *See also* the people
Marx, Karl, 5, 131n, 200, 229n, 269, 271
maternal principle, the: and the culture of glory, 121, 122, 140, 141; and the Sublime, 134-38
Mayer, J. P., 169n, 201, 208n, 247n
Medici, the, 42n, 92, 93; Giulio de', 98; Lorenzo de', 100
Melville, Herman, 3
Merleau-Ponty, Maurice, 31
modernity, 32, 34, 37-39, 43, 48, 49, 84, 94, 109, 110, 112, 116, 117, 125, 139-54, 155, 156, 161, 162n, 180, 235, 239, 240, 247, 248, 252, 264, 267
monarchy, 6, 9, 62, 67n, 70, 72, 85, 93, 109, 130n, 133, 135, 138, 140, 143n, 255n, 257; of France, 211, 217, 219, 223
Montesquieu, 24n, 181, 254, 255, 256, 258, 260
More, Thomas, 110
Morton, Nathaniel, 172n, 175n, 179
Moses, 7, 46, 64, 83, 84

Napoleon, Louis, 201, 213, 214, 224, 248n
nation, 81, 88-90, 140, 141, 147, 156, 157, 169, 196-200, 208, 223, 244. *See also* national character; peoplehood
national character, 120, 156, 157, 163n, 169, 170, 173, 177, 179, 244; English, 130; American, 156, 168, 173; French Canadian, 156, 172, 173, 177; French, 173, 180, 211. *See also* spirit; soul
nationalism, 161
natural right, 105
nature, 15, 39, 93, 104n, 116, 118, 120, 122, 131, 133, 134, 137-39, 140n, 145, 255; human, 55, 79, 90n, 96, 120, 137-39, 145, 148, 149, 157, 160n, 162, 163, 166, 185, 258, 261, 263; unnatural, 90, 149
necessity, 44n, 60-62, 64, 68, 69n, 73, 77, 78, 82-84, 91, 97n
Necker, Jacques, 255
New England, 167, 169, 170, 179
New World, the, 168, 169, 172, 174, 175, 233
Nietzsche, Friedrich, 3n, 41, 99n, 121, 132
nobility, 90n
Norman Conquest, the, 104, 105, 113, 126, 137, 164
Numa Pompilius, 38, 54, 64n, 100, 266

Oakeshott, Michael, 4, 15, 16, 21, 24n
obedience, 140, 143, 144n, 153, 159, 160n, 254
O'Connor, Edwin, 20
opinions, 149, 155, 156, 183, 207, 222, 223, 250; democratic, 156, 189; American, 169; aristocratic, 195, 198; of free people, 229
order, 114n, 129, 140, 152, 259, 261, 262n, 267

Pacuvius Calavius, 56

Paine, Thomas, 105, 140n
participation, 10, 56, 57, 161n, 252, 255, 265, 267
passion, 22, 30, 54, 98, 101, 119, 130, 133, 139-41, 148, 153-56, 164, 166, 167n, 171, 174, 185, 193, 198, 204, 213, 221n, 223-30, 232, 238, 239, 242-44, 246-49, 256, 257n, 266, 268. *See also* affection; desire; fear; hatred; love; sentiment; sympathy
paternity. *See* fatherhood
patriarchy, 66, 67, 145
patricide, 62, 63n, 65-70, 109, 138n, 144-49, 150n
patrimony, 71n, 102, 122, 125-28, 151, 152, 187, 188, 190, 191, 193, 228, 232, 233, 246, 263. *See also* inheritance
patriot, 10, 185, 199, 201, 230; nature of, 10, 57, 148, 160-62
patriotism, 223, 226, 227, 246; Roman, 27, 67n; Florentine, 81n, 86n; English, 153; American, 154n; rebirth of, 154n, 198-200, 207, 246; Tocqueville's view of, 158-62; French, 220, 223, 226, 227
people, the, 56, 62n, 70, 81, 89, 110, 131, 155, 218, 220, 236, 264, 268
peoplehood, 10, 21, 22, 55, 61, 74, 75, 82, 83, 97, 120, 124, 163n, 169n, 172, 173, 178, 180, 198, 244, 247, 255, 271
permanence, 38, 44n, 80, 157, 165, 168, 178, 193, 194, 202, 211, 236
Peters, Hugh, 108, 139
Philip of Macedon, 82
philosophes, the, 140, 145, 146, 149, 210
philosophy, 8, 28, 58n, 71, 94-97, 110, 130n, 145

Pierson, George, 164
piety, 4, 26, 129, 132, 135
Plato, 11, 49, 58n, 69, 71, 94, 100, 110, 140n, 263
pleasure, 196, 227, 237, 243, 259, 267
Plutarch, 10, 259
Pocock, J.G.A., 10, 13, 22, 78-79n, 113, 114, 115, 123n
Pompey, 52n
power, 71, 94n, 97, 100, 104, 146, 153, 154, 160n, 176, 187; and action, 48, 58n; founder's, 64, 65, 69n, 78n; Roman, 80; face of, 134-36, 138-40; affections turning towards, 163; loss of, 188; aristocratic, 192; centralized, 198; of imagination, 214; in democracies, 243; nature of, 254-56, 260; private, 266
powerlessness. *See* impotence
preservation, 60, 71-73, 76n, 78, 81n, 84n, 89, 90, 99n, 177, 193, 266, 268
Price, Richard, 105, 108, 126, 144
pride, 46, 148, 149, 152n, 163n, 199n, 239n; aristocratic, 189, 191, 193; democratic, 196, 197, 219
Priestley, Joseph, 105
principalities. *See* monarchy
progress, 269-71
property, 125, 127, 130, 143, 144n, 192, 193
Protestant Reformation, the, 110, 142-43n, 145
public life, 4, 9, 10, 18, 19, 67n, 163n, 206, 229, 243, 244, 252, 255-67, 270-72. *See also* freedom; liberty; space
Puritan Revolution, the, 103, 107, 147
Puritans, 174-76

rationalism, 156

reason, 36, 104n, 110, 120, 137, 140, 148, 159, 162n, 180, 185, 220, 221
rebellion, 66, 80, 82, 144, 145
Reeve, Henry, 183
regicide, 106, 108, 109, 111, 128, 146-49, 152n
religion, 24, 26, 43, 51, 54, 56n, 60, 64n, 75-78, 96, 100, 118, 119, 143, 157, 159, 163n, 199n, 246, 247, 253; in America, 169, 170n, 174, 178
Remus, 63n
republic, the; nature of, 6, 9, 11-13, 15, 17-25, 57, 78, 81, 86, 121, 129, 132, 251-63, 266, 271; Roman, 15, 52, 62, 68, 88; and glory, 42n, 47-49, 93, 95, 97, 100; and Christianity, 45; and history, 53; origin of, 54, 70-72; corruption of, 85, 91; Burke's view of, 130n, 135, 136, 147, 148n; Tocqueville's view of, 160, 161; in middle ages, 232, 233; American, 240
republican consciousness, 7, 9, 11, 20-23, 70, 148, 252, 255n
republican institutions, 6, 7, 45, 147, 202, 237, 252
republicanism, 43, 95, 129n, 147; in England, 106-9, 129; in America, 169, 170, 177; in France, 182n
republican tradition, 5, 7, 10, 25, 86, 160, 252
reverence, 4, 10, 18, 32, 57-71, 90, 100n, 102, 104, 118, 119, 129, 132, 135, 137, 139, 145, 148n, 159, 194, 263n
revolution, 4, 5, 68n, 73n, 92, 116, 128, 142, 144, 145, 146n, 149, 152, 165, 167, 179, 189-94, 204, 210, 213, 219, 223-26, 229, 230, 237, 239, 242, 248, 262n, 265, 269, 270

Revolution of 1848, 215, 225, 227-29
Richard III, 143
ritual, 16-18, 21, 24, 32
Rome, 15, 24n, 25-29, 47-50, 54-56, 58n, 60, 62, 63, 66, 67, 69, 71, 73n, 75, 78, 80, 84, 85, 88, 97, 98n, 100, 113, 117, 233, 255, 256, 260, 261, 266
Romulus, 27, 38, 47n, 50, 52-55, 62-65
Rousseau, Jean-Jacques, 12n, 57n, 73n, 145, 146, 254, 256, 257, 258, 262, 264
Royer-Collard, Pierre, 181, 232

Schaar, John, 261
Scipio, 51, 96, 98, 99
self, 4, 196, 199, 219, 229-31, 239n, 242, 268, 270
self-interest, 162n, 241, 243, 244
sentiments, 149, 155, 156, 159, 161-63, 185, 207-11, 222, 223, 229, 231, 232, 244, 246, 248, 256, 260, 271; aristocratic, 156n, 189, 195, 220; American, 170n; democratic, 197, 243
servitude, 55, 81n, 85, 163n, 201, 212, 213, 225, 234, 238, 244, 264
Severus, 62n
Shumer, Sarah, 53, 61n
Skinner, Quentin, 114n
slavery, 59, 64, 84, 163n. See also servitude
Smith, Adam, 152
social contract, 105n, 145, 265
Socrates, 27, 94n, 101
Socratic, 49, 56, 58n, 94
Solon, 19, 27, 217
Somers, Lord, 106n, 132
soul, 46, 101n, 156, 161, 163n, 175, 176, 201, 213, 227, 228, 231, 242, 243, 264
sovereignty, 103, 104n, 105n, 110, 147, 259

space, 6, 10, 246, 247, 260, 263, 268; public, 9, 135, 224, 256, 257, 259, 263, 265-67
Sparks, Jared, 169, 170, 174, 180
Sparta, 25, 73n, 110n, 233, 258
speech, 16, 18, 19, 21, 130n
spirit, 201, 213, 214, 232, 239n, 270; of public life, 23, 57, 106n, 256; free spirits, 85n, 92; of nations, 127, 172, 207, 230, 262; of freedom, 128, 129, 152, 209, 249; revolutionary, 194, 219; of democracy, 197, 233; of France, 207, 230. *See also* national character; soul
state of nature, 117
Strauss, Leo, 15, 38, 96, 111, 112n, 138n
sympathy, 196, 224, 231

Tarquins, the, 62, 63, 66-68, 73n
temporality, 9, 11, 12, 24
terror, 38-41, 46, 59-62, 64, 75, 121, 133-39, 142, 145, 148-50, 154, 231, 242, 261, 262. *See also* fear
theory and the theorist, 8, 29, 36, 54n, 84, 93-101, 105n, 109, 110, 113n, 114n, 123n, 143n, 179, 200-9, 221, 223, 249, 250, 266, 268, 269
Theseus, 27, 61, 90, 91n
Thiers, Adolphe, 202, 215
Thucydides, 12n, 24n
time, 6, 9-11, 13, 14, 18, 44, 73, 78, 81, 98, 123, 136, 194, 242, 246, 247, 263, 271, 272. *See also* temporality

Tocqueville, Alexis de, 7, 8, 14, 155-250, 254-55, 256, 264, 266
tradition, 6, 14, 15, 21-23, 28, 31, 80, 81, 110, 111, 123, 128, 132, 133n, 159, 162, 163, 164n, 169, 179, 189, 218, 222, 228, 229, 243, 267, 271; erosion of, 123n, 210, 241, 252
Tuscany, 47, 78, 93, 97
tyranny, 50, 51, 62, 68n, 81, 87, 95, 104, 105n, 128, 133n, 136, 137n, 146n, 152n, 163n, 164n, 177, 201, 206, 225, 239n, 244, 255, 260. *See also* despotism

uprootedness, 59, 75, 76, 82, 83

vanity, 139, 258
Vergil, 128n
violence, 46, 60, 61n, 88, 134, 137n, 138, 152n, 185, 190, 223, 228, 255
virtue, 11, 15, 29, 47, 48n, 60, 71, 78, 84, 85, 86n, 88, 94n, 95, 130, 171, 192, 193, 197, 209, 218, 219, 226, 230, 232, 236, 256, 257, 263

war, 39, 48n, 59, 74, 75, 160n, 161, 192, 261. *See also* civil war
weakness. *See* impotence
wealth, 29, 82, 90n, 157, 187, 241
Whig, 104, 105n, 125n
William the Conqueror, 137, 140, 164

Xenophon, 96, 98, 99

Library of Congress Cataloging in Publication Data

Smith, Bruce James, 1946-
  Politics & remembrance.

  (Studies in moral, political, and legal philosophy)
  Bibliography: p.
  Includes index.
  1. Republicanism. 2. Political participation.
3. Memory. 4. Machiavelli, Niccolò, 1469-1527—Political
science. 5. Burke, Edmund, 1729?-1797—Political science.
6. Tocqueville, Alexis de, 1805-1859—Political science.
I. Title. II. Title: Politics and remembrance.
III. Series.
JC421.S55 1985   323'.042   84-15946
ISBN 0-691-07681-2 (alk. paper)